BARRON'S

HOW TO PREPARE FOR THE
VIRGINIA
SOL

HIGH SCHOOL EXIT EXAM
IN ALGEBRA I

Craig A. Herring

and

Lois S. Cohen
McLean High School
McLean, Virginia

D1592886

BARRON'S

All inquiries should be addressed to:
Barron's Educational Series, Inc.
250 Wireless Boulevard
Hauppauge, NY 11788
www.barronseduc.com

International Standard Book No. 0-7641-2464-1

Library of Congress Catalog Card No. 2003052383

Library of Congress Cataloging-in-Publication Data
Herring, Craig.
How to prepare for the Virginia SOL high school exit exam in algebra I / Craig Herring, Lois Cohen.
p. cm.
Includes index.
ISBN 0-7641-2464-1
1. Algebra–Examinations, questions, etc. 2. Virginia Standards of Learning Tests–Study guides. I. Cohen, Lois, II. Title.
QA157.H47 2004
512′.0076–dc22

2003052383

Contents

Introduction

About This Review Guide and the Algebra I SOL Exam

The Algebra I SOL Exam is a 50-question, multiple-choice, untimed exam. Calculator use is encouraged. Four major categories of material are covered by the exam:

- Category I: Equations and Inequalities
- Category II: Expressions and Operations
- Category III: Relations and Functions
- Category IV: Statistics

Of the exam questions, 36% pertain to Category I, 24% to each of Categories II and III, and the remaining 16% to Category IV.

The exam reflects the "rule of four" in the design of the questions. This means that a problem may be presented in the form of a table or a graph, in symbols, or in words. Practical applications are emphasized.

Each chapter of this review guide covers one of the four major testing categories listed above. Because "Expressions and Operations" is necessary background material for "Equations and Inequalities," Chapter 1 of this guide covers Test Category II, while Chapter 2 covers Test Category I. Chapters III and IV cover Test Categories III and IV, respectively.

Each section of the book provides explanatory text followed by multiple-choice questions for self-checking and practice. Hopefully, the student will find the text engaging and easy to read. The problems in the practice sets are intended both to help the student review the major concepts in Algebra I and to simulate the types of questions encountered on the actual SOL exam.

At the end of this review guide, the student will find three practice tests that are presented in increasing order of difficulty. These tests are similar in format and design to SOL exams for Algebra I that have been administered in previous years and subsequently released for examination. Working through these practice tests will give the student a chance to experience what the actual SOL exam will be like.

The 18 Standards of Learning for Algebra I*

	What the Standard Involves (Major Concepts)	Test Category	Corresponding Section(s) in Review Guide
A.1	Solving linear equations and inequalities, including literal equations. Practical applications.	I	2.1, 2.3, 2.4, 2.5
A.2	Evaluating expressions. Translating words into symbols.	II	1.1, 1.2, 1.7
A.3	Identifying properties.	I	1.3, 2.2
A.4	Operating with matrices. Practical applications.	IV	4.2
A.5	Identifying patterns in data. Identifying functions, domain, and range.	III	3.1, 3.3, 3.5
A.6	Graphing linear functions and linear inequalities. Intercepts. Transformations. Practical applications.	I	2.7, 2.8, 2.9, 2.11
A.7	Finding and interpreting the slope of a line.	I	2.6
A.8	Writing an equation of a line.	I	2.10
A.9	Solving systems of two linear equations. Practical applications.	I	2.12
A.10	Using the laws of exponents. Scientific notation.	II	1.4, 1.8
A.11	Operating on polynomials.	II	1.5
A.12	Factoring.	II	1.6
A.13	Working with radicals. Square roots.	II	1.9
A.14	Solving quadratic equations. Interpreting quadratic functions.	II	2.13
A.15	Finding and interpreting function notation. Input/output and zeros.	III	3.1, 3.2, 3.4
A.16	Interpreting lines of best fit.	IV	4.5
A.17	Using statistical techniques. Measures of central tendency. Box-and-whisker plots.	IV	4.3, 4.4
A.18	Working with direct variations.	III	3.6

"The Mathematics Standards of Learning Curriculum Framework for Algebra I" details each of the 18 standards and can be found on the Virginia Department of Education website at www.pen.k12.va.us.

A Calculator Tutorial

A. Getting a Graph

You can graph an equation, say $y = 2x - 3$, in two easy steps. The top row of your TI-83 graphing calculator looks as shown below. You need only **Y =** and **ZOOM** to see the graph.

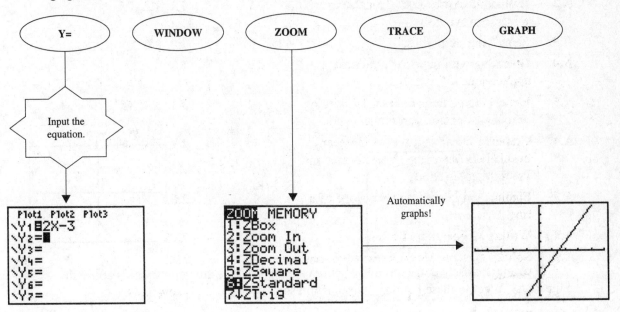

B. Using TRACE

If you want to see some points that lie on the line, such as the y-intercept, press the **TRACE** button. If you use the window **4:ZDECIMAL**, you will get "friendly" x-values when you trace.

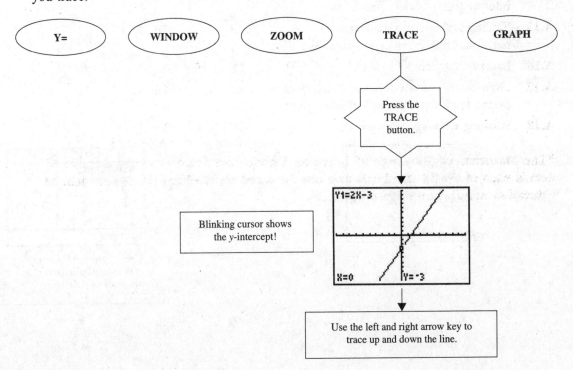

C. Changing the Viewing Window

If you don't like the **6:ZSTANDARD** graph, you can change it. After changing the viewing window, you will need to press **GRAPH** for the graph to display.

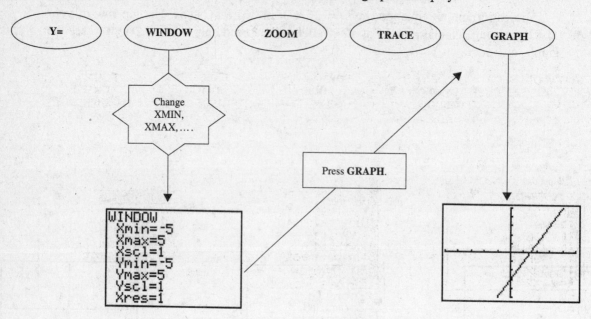

Look more closely at the top row of your calculator. There are yellow words above the blue keys. To get to these buttons, you must press the yellow $\boxed{\text{2nd}}$ key first.

D. Getting a Table

Your calculator can make a table of points that lie on your line.

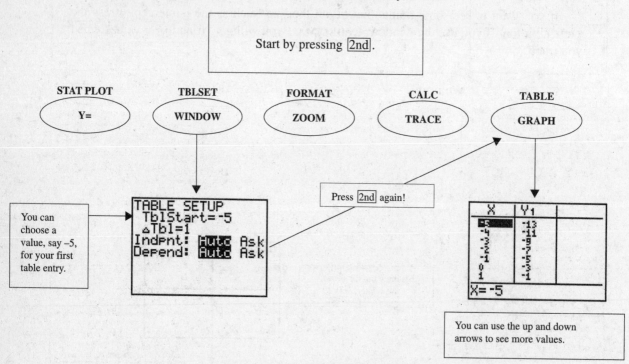

E. *Finding Values, Zeros, and Intersections*

Your calculator can locate exact points right on the graph itself.

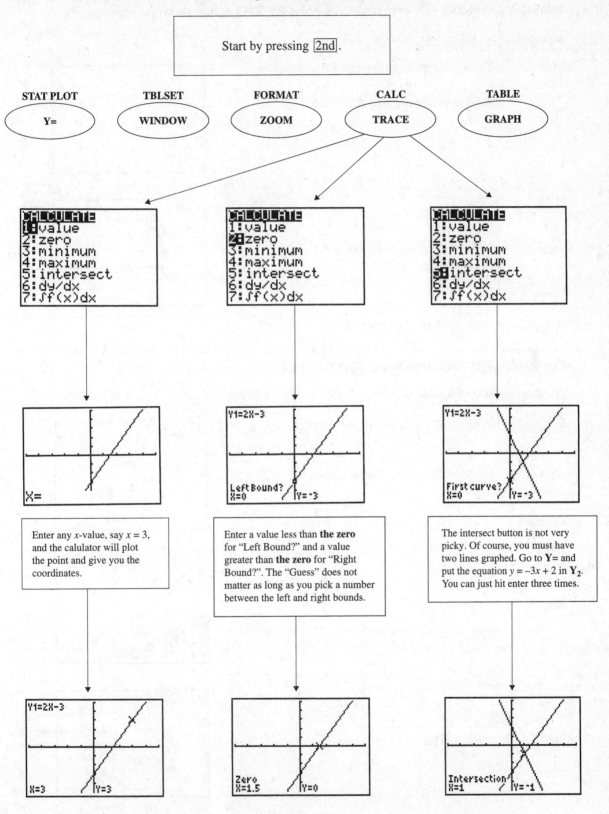

Start by pressing 2nd.

STAT PLOT   TBLSET   FORMAT   CALC   TABLE

Y=   WINDOW   ZOOM   TRACE   GRAPH

CALCULATE
1:value
2:zero
3:minimum
4:maximum
5:intersect
6:dy/dx
7:∫f(x)dx

X=

Enter any x-value, say $x = 3$, and the calulator will plot the point and give you the coordinates.

Y1=2X-3

Left Bound?
X=0   Y=-3

Enter a value less than **the zero** for "Left Bound?" and a value greater than **the zero** for "Right Bound?". The "Guess" does not matter as long as you pick a number between the left and right bounds.

Y1=2X-3

First curve?
X=0   Y=-3

The intersect button is not very picky. Of course, you must have two lines graphed. Go to **Y=** and put the equation $y = -3x + 2$ in Y_2. You can just hit enter three times.

Y1=2X-3

X=3   Y=3

Zero
X=1.5   Y=0

Intersection
X=1   Y=-1

F. The STO ▶ Key and the ALPHA Key

The **STO ▶** key stands for "store" and allows you to assign values to variables. It is located just above the **ON** key. When you press the **STO ▶** key, an arrow appears.

Example: Evaluate $5a - 6a^2$ if $a = 4$.

Step 1: Enter $4 \rightarrow A$ by following these keystrokes:

        4 **STO ▶ ALPHA MATH ENTER**

```
4→A
            4
```

Step 2: Now, type in the expression $5A - 6A^2$, and press **ENTER**.

```
4→A
            4
5A-6A²
          -76
```

When $a = 4$, the expression $5a - 6a^2$ is equal to -76.

G. Changing Decimals to Fractions

Another useful feature of your calculator is its ability to convert decimals to fractions.

Example: Write 0.625 as a fraction.

Step 1: Enter 0.625 on the home screen.

```
0.625
```

Step 2: Press the **MATH** key.

```
MATH NUM CPX PRB
1▶Frac
2:▶Dec
3:3
4:³√(
5:×√
6:fMin(
7↓fMax(
```

Step 3: Press **ENTER**.

```
0.625▶Frac
          5/8
■
```

Chapter 1

Expressions and Operations

1.1 What Is an Expression?

An **expression** is a combination of the following:

- Numbers.
- Variables (letters that stand for unknown quantities).
- Operations, such as $+$, $-$, $\cdot$, $\div$.

Expressions do NOT have equal signs ($=$). Here are some examples of expressions:

$3x + 2$	x	$3x^2 - 4x + 2$	$-5y^2 + xy - 3$
$2x - \pi$	$\dfrac{2x}{y} - 7$	36	$7 - 3xy$

Expressions consist of one or more *terms*. Terms are separated by $+$ or $-$ signs.

Expression	**Circle the +/− Signs.**	**Count the Terms.**
$3x + 4$	$3x \oplus 4$	2
$x^2 - 4x + 3$	$x^2 \ominus 4x \oplus 3$	3
$3xy - 7x + 5y - 6$	$3xy \ominus 7x \oplus 5y \ominus 6$	4
$3x$	$3x$	1

Helpful hint: To find the number of terms, count the +/− signs and add 1.

Almost all the expressions you study in Algebra I are *polynomial* expressions. These are named by the number of terms they contain.

Number of Terms	Name of Polynomial	Examples
1	**mono**mial	$3x$, $-2xy$, 5, and $3x^2$
2	**bi**nomial	$3x + 2$, $1 - 3x^2$, and $7 - y$
3	**tri**nomial	$x^2 + 3x + 2$ and $1 - 3a^3 + 2a$
4 or more	☹ No special name	$x^5 - 3x^3 + x - 10$

Helpful hint: Look at the prefix: "mono" means 1; "bi" means 2; "tri" means 3.

Some terms are called *like terms*. Like terms contain exactly the same variables, each raised to exactly the same power (exponent).

Like Terms	Not Like Terms	
x, $2x$, and $-3x$	3 and $5x$	(one term is constant; the other is not)
5, -3, 0, and π	$5x$ and $7x^2$	(different powers)
$-3y^2$, $4y^2$, and y^2	$5x$ and $7y$	(different variables)
$2xy$, xy, and $-8xy$	$6xy$ and $6x^2$	(different variables and powers)

Knowing which terms are like and which ones are not is important because only like terms can be added together.

Example 1: Simplify: $2x + 3x$.

$2x$ and $3x$ can be added together because they are like terms: $\qquad 2x + 3x = \boxed{5x}$

Example 2: Simplify: $2x + 3y$.

$2x$ and $3y$ are not like terms and CANNOT be combined. This expression is already in its *simplest form*.

There are three things that you can do with expressions:

- Evaluate them (find their *values*, some numbers).
- Simplify them (rewrite them in simpler form).
- Operate on them (add them, factor them, etc. . . .).

> NOTE: An expression can't be "solved." *Equations* are solved, NOT expressions.

Evaluating, simplifying, and operating on expressions are discussed in the following sections of this chapter.

Practice

1. Which of the following is *not* an expression?

   A. $3x^2 - 10$ **B.** 6 **C.** $3xy - 7x$ **D.** $3x - 7 = x + 2$

2. How many terms does the polynomial $x^2 - 3x + 5$ contain?

   A. 0 **B.** 1 **C.** 2 **D.** 3

3. Which expression is a binomial?

   A. $x + 3$ **B.** xy **C.** $x^2 + 2x - 5$ **D.** 5

4. Which pair of expressions represent like terms?

   A. 5 and $5x$
   B. $4x$ and $-5x$
   C. $4x$ and $4x^2$
   D. $3xy$ and $2yz$

Answers

1. **D** 2. **D** 3. **A** 4. **B**

Answer Explanations

1. **D** Since choice D contains an equal sign (=), it is an equation, not an expression.

2. **D** The polynomial $x^2 - 3x + 5$ contains three terms: x^2, $-3x$, and 5.

3. **A** A binomial is an expression with two terms. The expression $x + 3$ has two terms, x and 3.

4. **B** Like terms contain the same variable and same power. Both $4x$ and $-5x$ contain x with a power of 1.

1.2 Evaluating Expressions

Variables are letters that stand for unknown quantities. Most expressions contain variables. When you are given values for the variables, you can find the value of the expression by substituting. This is called *evaluating the expression*.

Example 1: What is the value of $2x + 3$ if $x = 4$?

$x = 4$

$2x + 3$ Given expression.

$2(4) + 3$ Substitute 4 for x.

$8 + 3$ Simplify.

$\boxed{11}$

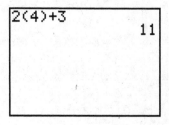

Example 2: Evaluate $x(4 + y)$ for $x = 3$ and $y = 4$.

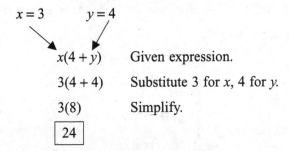

$x = 3$ $y = 4$

$x(4 + y)$ Given expression.

$3(4 + 4)$ Substitute 3 for x, 4 for y.

$3(8)$ Simplify.

$\boxed{24}$

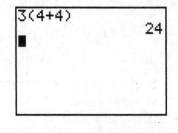

When the expressions are more complicated, you have to apply the rules for order of operations. You may have learned the mnemonic PEMDAS or **P**lease **E**xcuse **M**y **D**ear **A**unt **S**ally. This is what PEMDAS means:

Letter	What It Stands For	What It Tells You to Do
P	**P**arentheses	First, do all operations inside parentheses.
E	**E**xponents	Next, take care of the exponents.
M/D	**M**ultiply/**D**ivide	Then, do all multiplications and divisions *in order* from left to right.
A/S	**A**dd/**S**ubtract	Finally, do all additions and subtractions *in order* from left to right.

Example 3: What is the value of $3a^2 - ab + 4b$ if $a = -2$ and $b = 4$?

> *Helpful hint:*
> Always put
> parentheses
> around
> *negative* numbers
> when you
> substitute.

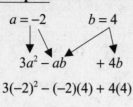

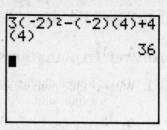

$3a^2 - ab \quad + 4b$	Given expression.
$3(-2)^2 - (-2)(4) + 4(4)$	Substitute -2 for both a's and 4 for both b's.
$3(4) - (-8) \quad + 16$	Simplify.
$12 + 8 \qquad + 16$	
$\boxed{36}$	

Example 4: What is the value of $a + b(a + b)^2$ if $a = 5$ and $b = -2$?

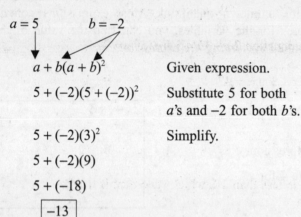

> *Helpful hint:*
> Count your
> parentheses!
> If three are
> "open," (((,
> then three
> must be
> "closed,"))) .

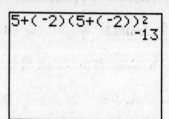

$a + b(a + b)^2$	Given expression.
$5 + (-2)(5 + (-2))^2$	Substitute 5 for both a's and -2 for both b's.
$5 + (-2)(3)^2$	Simplify.
$5 + (-2)(9)$	
$5 + (-18)$	
$\boxed{-13}$	

Alternative solution for Example 4:

Use the **STO** key on your calculator. Refer to A Calculator Tutorial, page 3, for a more detailed explanation.

Step 1   Step 2

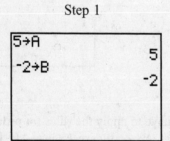

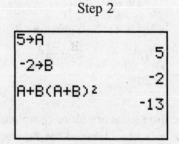

Practice

1. What is the value of $4 - 5x$ if $x = -3$?

   A. -11 **B.** -3 **C.** 3   **D.** 19

2. What is the value of $3x(x - y)$ if $x = 5$ and $y = 2$?

   A. 45   **B.** 9   **C.** 73   **D.** 18

3. What is the value of $a - b(5 + a)$ if $a = 2$ and $b = 1$?

   A. 7   **B.** 2   **C.** -5 **D.** -11

4. Which values can be substituted for x and y if $4x - 3y$ is equal to 42?

   A. $x = 12, y = -2$ **B.** $x = 9, y = -2$
   C. $x = 9, y = 2$ **D.** $x = 10, y = -1$

5. What value of b will make the equation $2a - 3b = 5$ true if $a = 7$?

   A. 13   **B.** 7   **C.** 5   **D.** 3

6. What is the value of $6x - y(2 + x)$ if $x = 2$ and $y = x + 1$?

   A. 0   **B.** 8   **C.** 4   **D.** 12

7. If $y = 1$, and $2(x + y)$ has a value less than 10, which statement is true?

   A. x must be greater than 10.
   B. x must be less than 4.
   C. x must equal 6.
   D. x must be negative.

8. Evaluate $\dfrac{2a + b^2}{b - 4}$ for $a = 10$ and $b = -5$.

   A. -5 **B.** -13 **C.** -3 **D.** $\dfrac{5}{9}$

Answers

1. **D**	3. **C**	5. **D**	7. **B**
2. **A**	4. **B**	6. **A**	8. **A**

Answer Explanations

1. **D**   Replace x with -3 in the expression $4 - 5x$. Then:

$$4 - 5(-3) = 4 - (-15) = 4 + 15 = 19$$

2. **A**   Replace x and y in the expression $3x(x - y)$ with the values $x = 5$ and $y = 2$. Then:

$$3(5)(5 - 2) = 15(3) = 45$$

3. **C**   Replace a and b in the expression $a - b(5 + a)$ with $a = 2$ and $b = 1$. Be careful with the order of operations. Make sure you save the subtraction for last.

$$2 - 1(5 + 2) = 2 - 1(7) = 2 - 7 = -5$$

4. **B**   If you replace x and y in the expression $4x - 3y$ with $x = 9$ and $y = -2$, you will get 42:

$$4(9) - 3(-2) = 36 - (-6) = 36 + 6 = 42$$

5. **D**   Replace a in the expression $2a - 3b = 5$ with 7 and then solve the equation for b:

$$2(7) - 3b = 5$$
$$14 - 3b = 5$$
$$-3b = -9$$
$$b = 3$$

6. **A**   Since $x = 2$ and $y = x + 1$, you can determine the value of y by substituting 2 for x:

$$y = 2 + 1 = 3$$

Now you know $x = 2$ and $y = 3$. Evaluate the expression $6x - y(2 + x)$ by replacing both x's with 2 and y with 3:

$$6(2) - 3(2 + 2) = 12 - 3(4) = 12 - 12 = 0$$

7. **B**   It is given that $y = 1$. Substitute 1 for y in the expression $2(x + y)$. The expression becomes $2(x + 1)$. It is also given that this expression is less than 10. Then:

$$2(x + 1) < 10$$
$$2x + 2 < 10$$
$$2x < 8$$
$$x < 4$$

Therefore, the answer is choice B: x must be less than 4.

8. **A**   Replace the variable a with 10 and both b's with -5 in the expression $\dfrac{2a+b^2}{b-4}$:

$$\frac{2(10)+(-5)^2}{(-5)-4}$$

$$\frac{20+25}{-9}$$

$$\frac{45}{-9}$$

$$-5$$

```
10→A
                    10
-5→B
                    -5
(2A+B²)/(B-4)
                    -5
■
```

1.3 Simplifying Expressions

Sometimes you can write an expression in a simpler form by applying certain properties and combining like terms. Three important properties are illustrated in the table below. These properties hold true for *all* real values of a, b, and c.

Name of Property	What It Says	Examples	What It Means
Commutative • For addition	$(a+b)$ and $(b+a)$ are equal.	$3+4=4+3$ $7=7$✔	You can add numbers (or variables) in any order.
• For multiplication	$(a \cdot b)$ and $(b \cdot a)$ are equal.	$2 \cdot 5 = 5 \cdot 2$ $10 = 10$✔	You can multiply numbers (or variables) in any order.
Associative • For addition	$(a+b)+c$ and $a+(b+c)$ are equal.	$(2+3)+4=2+(3+4)$ $5+4=2+7$ $9=9$✔	Changing the grouping by rearranging parentheses will not affect the value of an expression.
• For multiplication	$(a \cdot b) \cdot c$ and $a \cdot (b \cdot c)$ are equal.	$(5 \cdot 2) \cdot 3 = 5 \cdot (2 \cdot 3)$ $10 \cdot 3 = 5 \cdot 6$ $30 = 30$✔	
Distributive • For multiplication over addition	$a \cdot (b+c) = a \cdot b + a \cdot c$	$2 \cdot (3+4) = 2 \cdot 3 + 2 \cdot 4$ $2 \cdot 7 = 6 + 8$ $14 = 14$✔	The number outside the parentheses should be multiplied through to every term inside the parentheses.
• For multiplication over subtraction	$a \cdot (b-c) = a \cdot b - a \cdot c$	$5 \cdot (2 + x - 3y) = 10 + 5x - 15y$	

NOTE: The commutative and associative properties do *not* hold true for subtraction or division.

Example 1: Identify each statement as an illustration of the commutative property (C), the associative property (A), or the distributive property (D).

Given Statement		**Answer/Explanation**
$5 + (4 + 3) = 5 + (3 + 4)$	C	3 and 4 switched places.
$2x + (3x + 5) = (2x + 3x) + 5$	A	The grouping changed, not the order.
$(3x + 5) + 2x = 2x + (3x + 5)$	C	$2x$ and $(3x + 5)$ switched places.
$5(2x + 4) = 10x + 20$	D	Both $2x$ and 4 are multiplied by 5.
$(2x - 7)x = x(2x - 7)$	C	x and $(2x - 7)$ switched places.
$y(2x - 7) = y \cdot 2x - y \cdot 7$	D	Both $2x$ and 7 are multiplied by y.
$(5 + 3x^2) - 2x^2 = 5 + (3x^2 - 2x^2)$	A	The grouping changed, not the order.
$2 \cdot (3 \cdot x) = (2 \cdot 3) \cdot x$	A	The grouping changed, not the order.

To simplify an expression, apply the commutative, associative, and/or distributive properties; then, combine the like terms.

Example 2: Simplify each expression completely.

Expression		**Apply Properties**		**Simplest Form**
$7 - 2x + 4$	$\longrightarrow$	$(7 + 4) - 2x$	$\longrightarrow$	$11 - 2x$
$6xy + 3 - 2xy$	$\longrightarrow$	$(6xy - 2xy) + 3$	$\longrightarrow$	$4xy + 3$
$3x^2 - 2x + 5x^2 - 3x$	$\longrightarrow$	$(3x^2 + 5x^2) + (-2x - 3x)$	$\longrightarrow$	$8x^2 - 5x$
$6y - 3x + 4xy - x^2$	$\longrightarrow$	No like terms	$\longrightarrow$	Already in simplest form
$2(3 - 4x) + 5x$	$\longrightarrow$	$6 - 8x + 5x$		$6 - 3x$

Helpful hint: Terms retain their signs (+/−) when rearranged.

A polynomial expression should be written in *standard form* when simplified. This means that the terms should be written *in order* by power, typically from highest power to lowest. The constant term comes last.

Example 3: Change $x^2 - 5 + 7x^3 - 3x$ to standard form.

Standard form: $\qquad 7x^3 + x^2 - 3x - 5$

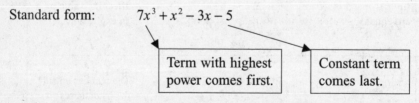

Term with highest power comes first.

Constant term comes last.

Example 4: Write $4x - x^2 + 3x + 10 + 5x^2$ in simplest form.

$4x - x^2 + 3x + 10 + 5x^2$	Given expression.
$(4x + 3x) + (-x^2 + 5x^2) + 10$	Rearrange terms using properties.
$7x + 4x^2 + 10$	Combine like terms.
$4x^2 + 7x + 10$	Write in standard form.

Polynomial expressions can be represented pictorially. Consider the following models:

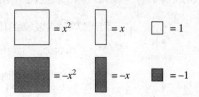

NOTE: Shaded blocks denote *negative* quantities.

Example 5: What polynomial is represented by the diagram?

Each of the two large squares □ represents x^2. ⟶ $2x^2$

Each of shaded rectangles ▮ represents $-x$. ⟶ $-4x$

Each of the white boxes □ represents 1. ⟶ 4

Each of the shaded boxes ▪ represents -1. ⟶ -2

Adding like terms gives the final answer, $2x^2 - 4x + 2$.

Practice

1. Which polynomial is in standard form?

   A. $x^3 + 5x$ **B.** $x + x^2 + 1$ **C.** $5 - x - 3x$ **D.** $(x+1) - (1-x)$

2. Which statement is an example of the distributive property?

   A. $3 + (4+5) = (3+4) + 5$
   B. $3 + (4+5) = 3 + (5+4)$
   C. $3 + (4 \cdot 5) = 3 + 20$
   D. $3 \cdot (4+5) = 3 \cdot 4 + 3 \cdot 5$

3. Which statement illustrates the commutative property?

   A. $5x + (4x + 3) = (5x + 4x) + 3$
   B. $5(4x + 3) = 20x + 15$
   C. $5 + (4x + 3) = 5 + (3 + 4x)$
   D. $5 + 3 + 4 = 5 + 7$

For questions 4–7, simplify each expression completely.

4. $6y - 3(y - 1) =$

   A. $3y + 3$ **B.** $3y - 3$ **C.** $3y - 1$ **D.** $3y^2 - 3$

5. $3 + 5(x + 4) - 2x =$

   A. $6x + 32$ **B.** $6x + 8$ **C.** $3x + 23$ **D.** $3x + 32$

6. $3(z-2)+(z+1)\cdot 4 =$

    A. $4z-2$ **B.** $7z-2$ **C.** $7z-5$ **D.** $14z-7$

7. $2x-3x^2+7+(x-3) =$

    A. $-3x^2+3x+4$ **B.** $-x^2-21$ **C.** $-3x^2+9x-21$ **D.** $-x^2+x+4$

---

8. Which statement is an application of the associative property?

    A. $2(x+y)=2x+2y$
    B. $(x+y)+z=z+(x+y)$
    C. $x+(y+z)=(x+y)+z$
    D. $2(x+y)=(y+x)\cdot 2$

Use the following representations for questions 9 and 10:

9. What polynomial is represented by this diagram?

    A. $3x^2+3x-3$ **B.** $4x^2-3x-3$ **C.** $3x^2+2x-3$ **D.** $4x^2+x+3$

10. What polynomial is represented by this diagram?

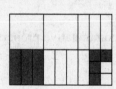

    A. $3x^2+10x+6$ **B.** $3x^2+4x-6$ **C.** $2x^2+7x+2$ **D.** $2x^2+4x-2$

Answers

1. **A**	3. **C**	5. **C**	7. **A**	9. **C**
2. **D**	4. **A**	6. **B**	8. **C**	10. **D**

Answer Explanations

1. **A**   Standard form lists each term in order from highest power to lowest with the constant last. Choice A, $x^3 + 5x$ fits this definition.

2. **D**   The distributive property states that $a \cdot (b + c) = a \cdot b + a \cdot c$. Choice D, $3 \cdot (4 + 5) = 3 \cdot 4 + 3 \cdot 5$, is arranged in this way.

3. **C**   The commutative property states that $(a + b)$ and $(b + a)$ are equal. Notice that, in choice C, $5 + (4x + 3) = 5 + (3 + 4x)$, $4x$ and 3 have switched places.

4. **A**
$6y - 3(y - 1)$	Given expression.
$6y - 3y + 3$	Distributive property.
$3y + 3$	Combine like terms.

5. **C**
$3 + 5(x + 4) - 2x$	Given expression.
$3 + 5x + 20 - 2x$	Distributive property.
$3x + 23$	Combine like terms.

6. **B**
$3(z - 2) + (z + 1) \cdot 4$	Given expression.
$3z - 6 + 4z + 4$	Distributive property applied twice.
$7z - 2$	Combine like terms.

7. **A**
$2x - 3x^2 + 7 + (x - 3)$	Given expression.
$-3x^2 + (2x + x) + (7 - 3)$	Commutative and associative properties.
$-3x^2 + 3x + 4$	Combine like terms.

8. **C**   The associative property states that $(a + b) + c = a + (b + c)$. Choice C, $x + (y + z) = (x + y) + z$, changes the grouping of the terms, *not* the order.

9. **C**   There are three large squares → $3x^2$, three white rectangles → $3x$, one shaded rectangle → $-x$, and three shaded small boxes → -3. Combining like terms yields $3x^2 + 2x - 3$.

10. **D**   There are two large squares → $2x^2$, seven white rectangles → $7x$, three shaded rectangles → $-3x$, two small white boxes → 2, and four shaded small boxes → -4. Combining like terms yields $2x^2 + 4x - 2$.

1.4 Laws of Exponents

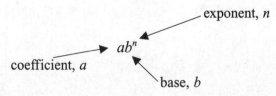

Tip: An exponent can also be referred to as a "power."

An **exponent** is a tricky little number that has different meanings depending on whether it is positive, negative, or zero. Let's look at each of these cases separately.

CASE I: EXPONENT IS POSITIVE INTEGER {1, 2, 3, 4, . . .}.

To show seven 3's multiplied together, we could write:

$$3 \cdot 3 \cdot 3 \cdot 3 \cdot 3 \cdot 3 \cdot 3.$$

or

$$3^7$$

In this form, we call 3 the *base* and 7 the *exponent*.

When the exponent is a positive integer, it tells us *how many times to write the base as a factor*. Below are some examples:

Expression	How It's Read	What It Means
x^2	"x squared" or "x to the 2nd power"	$x \cdot x$
2^3	"2 cubed" or "2 to the 3rd power"	$2 \cdot 2 \cdot 2 = 8$
b^n	"b to the nth power"	$\underbrace{b \cdot b \cdot b \cdot \cdots \cdot b}_{b \text{ written } n \text{ times}}$

CASE II: EXPONENT IS ZERO.

Except for 0, any number (or expression) raised to the zero power is equal to 1.

$$\boxed{b^0 = 1}$$

NOTE: 0^0 is not defined.

Examples:

$x^0 = 1$ (provided that $x \neq 0$)

$5^0 = 1$

$(3xy)^0 = 1$ (provided that $x \neq 0, y \neq 0$)

$(-600 \times 10^5)^0 = 1$

CASE III: EXPONENT IS NEGATIVE INTEGER {−1, −2, −3, . . .}.

A negative exponent tells us to change the form by doing two things:

- Invert the base (change the base to its reciprocal).
- Make the exponent positive.

Examples:

Expression	Change form.	Simplify.
4^{-2}	$\left(\dfrac{1}{4}\right)^2$	$\dfrac{1}{4} \cdot \dfrac{1}{4} = \dfrac{1}{16}$
$\left(\dfrac{1}{2}\right)^{-3}$	2^3	$2 \cdot 2 \cdot 2 = 8$
$2x^{-1}$	$2\left(\dfrac{1}{x}\right)^1$	$\dfrac{2}{x}$
$(2x)^{-1}$	$\left(\dfrac{1}{2x}\right)^1$	$\dfrac{1}{2x}$
$(3x)^{-2}$	$\left(\dfrac{1}{3x}\right)^2$	$\dfrac{1}{3x} \cdot \dfrac{1}{3x} = \dfrac{1}{9x^2}$
$\dfrac{2}{3^{-2}}$	$\dfrac{2}{\left(\frac{1}{3}\right)^2}$	$\dfrac{2}{\frac{1}{9}} = 2 \cdot \dfrac{9}{1} = 18$

Helpful hint: An exponent modifies only what is immediately to its left. Note the use of parentheses.

$$2x^{-1} = \frac{2}{x}$$

$$(2x)^{-1} = \frac{1}{2x}$$

There are some rules you should learn to help you simplify expressions that contain exponents. These "laws of exponents" provide some neat shortcuts.

The Law	What It Means	Examples
$x^a \cdot x^b = x^{a+b}$	When you *multiply* expressions that have the *same base*, **ADD** their exponents.	$x^2 \cdot x^3 = x^{(2+3)} = x^5$ $5^2 \cdot 5^4 = 5^{(2+4)} = 5^6$
$\dfrac{x^a}{x^b} = x^{a-b}$	When you *divide* expressions that have the *same base*, **SUBTRACT** the exponents (top minus bottom).	$\dfrac{x^5}{x^3} = x^{(5-3)} = x^2$ $\dfrac{4^8}{4^6} = 4^2 = 16$ $\dfrac{y^5}{y^7} = y^{-2} = \left(\dfrac{1}{y}\right)^2 = \dfrac{1}{y^2}$
$(x^a)^b = x^{a \cdot b}$	When you raise a "power term" to a power, **MULTIPLY** the exponents.	$(x^4)^3 = x^{(4 \cdot 3)} = x^{12}$ $(x^3)^{-1} = x^{-3} = \dfrac{1}{x^3}$
$(a \cdot b)^n = a^n \cdot b^n$	When the numbers and variables inside the parentheses are *multiplied* together, the exponent will apply to *all* of them.	$5(xy)^4 = 5x^4y^4$ $(3a)^2 = 3^2 \cdot a^2 = 9a^2$ $(-2x^2y)^3 = (-2)^3 \cdot (x^2)^3 \cdot y^3 = -8x^6y^3$
$\left(\dfrac{a}{b}\right)^n = \dfrac{a^n}{b^n}$	When the numbers and variables inside the parentheses are *divided*, the exponent will apply to *all* of them.	$\left(\dfrac{x}{y}\right)^4 = \dfrac{x^4}{y^4}$ $\left(\dfrac{2x}{y^2}\right)^3 = \dfrac{2^3 x^3}{(y^2)^3} = \dfrac{8x^3}{y^6}$

> **Common Error Alert!**
> When adding exponents, be sure you DON'T add the bases!
> $5^2 \cdot 5^4 \neq 10^6$

Example: $(2x^2)^3$ is equivalent to—

A. $6x^6$ **B.** $8x^6$ **C.** $5x^5$ **D.** $6x^5$

Each answer can be checked by choosing a random value (not 0 or ±1) to store for x and then comparing the original expression to the answer choices. In this case, we chose 3 for x and tested all of the choices as shown on the calculator screens below.

A. $6x^6$

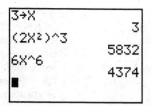

B. $8x^6$

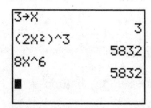

> For more detailed instructions on the use of the **STO** key, refer to A Calculator Tutorial on page 3.

C. $5x^5$

```
3→X
           3
(2X²)^3
        5832
5X^5
        1215
■
```

D. $6x^5$

```
3→X
           3
(2X²)^3
        5832
6X^5
        1458
■
```

Choice B is correct. Notice that the expressions evaluated the same for $x = 3$.

Practice

1. Which expression is equivalent to $m^6 \cdot m^2$?

   A. m^{12} B. m^8 C. m^4 D. m^3

2. Which expression is equivalent to $\dfrac{p^{12}}{p^2}$?

   A. p^{10} B. p^6 C. p^{24} D. p^{14}

3. Which expression is equivalent to $h^8 \cdot h^2$?

   A. $h^4 \cdot h^4$ B. $h^5 \cdot h^3$ C. $h \cdot h^9$ D. $h^{12} \cdot h^6$

4. Simplify $3x^{-2}$.

   A. $9x^2$ B. $\dfrac{1}{9x^2}$ C. $\dfrac{1}{3x^2}$ D. $\dfrac{3}{x^2}$

5. Simplify $(4y)^{-2}$.

   A. $4y^2$ B. $\dfrac{1}{4}y^2$ C. $\dfrac{1}{16y^2}$ D. $\dfrac{4}{y^2}$

6. Simplify $\dfrac{x^5 \cdot x^6}{x^3}$.

   A. x^{10} B. $2x^5$ C. x^{27} D. x^8

7. Which expression is equivalent to $\dfrac{1}{x^{-5}}$?

   A. $\dfrac{1}{x^5}$ B. x^5 C. x^{-5} D. $\dfrac{5}{x}$

8. Simplify $(x^4y^3)^2$.

   A. x^6y^5 B. x^8y^6 C. x^6y^6 D. x^4y^6

9. In the expression $-5m^3$, the base is—

   A. $-5m$ B. m C. 3 D. 5

10. In the expression $2x^7$, the number 2 is called the—

    A. base B. exponent C. factor D. coefficient

11. In the equation $\dfrac{b^{14}}{b^x} = b^7$, what value of x will make the equation true?

    A. 2 B. 7 C. 21 D. −7

12. If $b \neq 0$, $b^{-7} \cdot b^{7} =$

    A. 1   **B.** 0   **C.** $\dfrac{1}{7}$ **D.** 7

13. $(4y^{2})(-3y^{4}) =$

    A. y^{2} **B.** $-12y^{6}$ **C.** $-12y^{8}$ **D.** $-y^{6}$

14. $(3xy^{-2})^{3} =$

    A. $3x^{3}y$ **B.** $\dfrac{3x^{3}}{y^{6}}$ **C.** $\dfrac{27x^{3}}{y^{6}}$ **D.** $\dfrac{27xy}{y^{5}}$

15. $\dfrac{3x^{2}}{x^{-3}} =$

    A. $\dfrac{3}{x}$ **B.** $3x^{5}$ **C.** $3x$ **D.** $3x^{6}$

16. $\dfrac{x^{-2}}{5^{0}} =$

    A. $\dfrac{5}{x^{2}}$ **B.** $\dfrac{1}{x^{2}}$ **C.** $\dfrac{1}{5x^{2}}$ **D.** $\dfrac{5x}{2}$

17. $\left(\dfrac{5x}{10x}\right)^{-1} =$

    A. 2   **B.** $\dfrac{1}{5x}$ **C.** $5x$ **D.** $\dfrac{1}{2}$

18. $\dfrac{9x^{8}}{3x^{4}} =$

    A. $6x^{2}$ **B.** $6x^{4}$ **C.** $3x^{2}$ **D.** $3x^{4}$

19. The total surface area of a cube can be found by using the expression $6s^{2}$, where s equals the length of each edge of the cube. What is the total surface area in square inches of a cube whose edge has a length of 1.5 inches?

    A. 81 in.^{2} **B.** 13.5 in.^{2} **C.** 9 in.^{2} **D.** 18 in.^{2}

20. The volume of a spherical balloon can be determined by using the expression $\dfrac{4}{3}\pi r^{3}$, where r represents the radius. If the radius of the balloon is 5 inches and π is approximately 3.14, which is the closest estimate for the volume of the balloon?

    A. 53 in.^{3} **B.** 60 in.^{3} **C.** 500 in.^{3} **D.** 523 in.^{3}

21. Which expression is equal to 9^{x+y}?

    A. $3^{x} + 3^{y}$ **B.** $3^{x} \cdot 3^{y}$ **C.** $9^{x} + 9^{y}$ **D.** $9^{x} \cdot 9^{y}$

Answers

1. **B**	6. **D**	10. **D**	14. **C**	18. **D**
2. **A**	7. **B**	11. **B**	15. **B**	19. **B**
3. **C**	8. **B**	12. **A**	16. **B**	20. **D**
4. **D**	9. **B**	13. **B**	17. **A**	21. **D**
5. **C**				

Answer Explanations

1. **B** When multiplying terms with the same base, add exponents:

$$m^6 \cdot m^2 = m^{(6+2)} = m^8$$

2. **A** When dividing terms with the same base, subtract exponents:

$$\frac{p^{12}}{p^2} = p^{(12-2)} = p^{10}$$

3. **C** When multiplying terms with the same base, add exponents:

$$h^8 \cdot h^2 = h^{(8+2)} = h^{10}$$

and choice C is $h^1 \cdot h^9 = h^{(1+9)} = h^{10}$.

Since both expressions equal h^{10}, they are equivalent.

4. **D** The expression $3x^{-2}$ can be written as $3\left(\dfrac{1}{x}\right)^2$, which equals $\dfrac{3}{x^2}$.

5. **C** Invert the base, and make the exponent positive to obtain $\left(\dfrac{1}{4y}\right)^2$.

Then: $$\frac{1}{4y} \cdot \frac{1}{4y} = \frac{1}{16y^2}$$

6. **D** The expression $\dfrac{x^5 \cdot x^6}{x^3}$ can be written as $\dfrac{x^{11}}{x^3}$ since the exponents in the numerator can be added. Thus, $\dfrac{x^{11}}{x^3} = x^{(11-3)} = x^8$.

7. **B** The expression $\dfrac{1}{x^{-5}}$ equals $\dfrac{1}{\left(\frac{1}{x}\right)^5}$. This can be written as $\dfrac{1}{\frac{1}{x^5}} = 1 \cdot \dfrac{x^5}{1} = x^5$.

8. **B** The expression $(x^4y^3)^2$ is equivalent to $(x^4)^2 \cdot (y^3)^2 = x^8y^6$.

9. **B** Since $-5m$ is not in parentheses, the exponent, 3, modifies m only. Therefore, the base is m.

10. **D** The coefficient is the number in front of the variable. In this case, 2 precedes x.

11. **B** When dividing terms with the same base, subtract exponents:

$$\frac{b^{14}}{b^x} = b^{(14-x)} = b^7$$

Since $14 - x = 7$, x must equal 7 for the equation to be true.

12. **A** When multiplying terms with the same base, add exponents: $b^{-7} \cdot b^7 = b^0 = 1$ because any variable or number (except 0) raised to the power of 0 equals 1.

13. **B** Through the associative property, the expression can be regrouped as follows:

$$(4 \cdot -3)(y^2 y^4) = -12y^6$$

14. **C** The expression $(3xy^{-2})^3 = 3^3 \cdot x^3 \cdot (y^{-2})^3 = 27x^3 y^{-6}$. Because of the negative exponent on the y variable, $y^{-6} = \frac{1}{y^6}$. Thus the final answer is $\frac{27x^3}{y^6}$.

15. **B** The expression can be simplified as follows:

$$\frac{3x^2}{x^{-3}} = \frac{3x^2}{\left(\frac{1}{x^3}\right)} = 3x^2 \cdot \frac{x^3}{1} = 3x^5$$

16. **B** Since any number (except 0) raised to the power of 0 is 1:

$$\frac{x^{-2}}{5^0} = \frac{x^{-2}}{1} = x^{-2} \quad \text{and} \quad x^{-2} = \frac{1}{x^2}$$

17. **A** The expression $\left(\frac{5x}{10x}\right)^{-1}$ is equivalent to $\left(\frac{10x}{5x}\right)^1$. Simplifying further,

$$\frac{10x}{5x} = \frac{10}{5} \cdot \frac{x}{x} = 2 \cdot 1 = 2.$$

18. **D** The expression $\frac{9x^8}{3x^4} = \frac{9}{3} \cdot \frac{x^8}{x^4}$. Since $9 \div 3 = 3$ and $x^8 \div x^4 = x^4$, the answer is $3x^4$.

19. **B** Substituting $s = 1.5$ into the expression $6s^2$ yields $6(1.5)^2 = 13.5$.

20. **D** Substituting $r = 5$ and $\pi \approx 3.14$ into the expression $\frac{4}{3}\pi r^3$ yields

$$\frac{4}{3}(3.14)(5)^3 = 523.33\ldots \approx 523.$$

21. **D** When multiplying terms with the same base, add exponents: $9^x \cdot 9^y = 9^{x+y}$.

1.5 Operations on Polynomials

In this section, we review how to add, subtract, multiply, and divide polynomial expressions.

A. Addition

To add polynomials, just regroup and combine like terms.

Example 1: Find the perimeter of Rectangle A.

$$3x + 2$$

| $x + 4$ | Rectangle A | $x + 4$ |

$$3x + 2$$

To find the perimeter, add the lengths of the four sides:

$$P = (3x + 2) + (x + 4) + (3x + 2) + (x + 4) \qquad \text{Set it up!}$$
$$= (3x + x + 3x + x) + (2 + 4 + 2 + 4) \qquad \text{Regroup.}$$
$$= \boxed{8x + 12} \qquad \text{Combine like terms.}$$

Sometimes you may need to apply the Distributive Property to simplify polynomials before you add.

Example 2: Find the perimeter of Rectangle B by using the formula $P = 2L + 2W$, where L represents the length and W represents the width of the rectangle.

| Rectangle B | $x + 1$ |

$$2x + 3$$

To find the perimeter of Rectangle B, let $L = 2x + 3$ (the length) and $W = x + 1$ (the width) and plug these values into the formula $P = 2L + 2W$.

$$P = 2(2x + 3) + 2(x + 1) \qquad \text{Substitute for } L \text{ and } W.$$
$$= 4x + 6 + 2x + 2 \qquad \text{Use the distributive property.}$$
$$= (4x + 2x) + (6 + 2) \qquad \text{Regroup.}$$
$$= \boxed{6x + 8} \qquad \text{Combine like terms.}$$

B. Subtraction

Subtraction can be a bit more difficult than addition. By definition, subtraction is the process of "adding the opposite." This means you will actually be performing addition after you change the signs of the second polynomial.

> Definition of subtraction:
>
> $a - b$
>
> is the same as
>
> $a + (-b)$.

Example 3: In Examples 1 and 2, you found expressions for the perimeters of Rectangle A and Rectangle B.

Rectangle A: Perimeter $= 8x + 12$
Rectangle B: Perimeter $= 6x + 8$

How much larger is the perimeter of Rectangle A?

Perimeter A – Perimeter B

$(8x + 12) - (6x + 8)$	Put each polynomial in parentheses.
$(8x + 12) + (-6x - 8)$	Apply the definition of subtraction.
$(8x - 6x) + (12 - 8)$	Regroup.
$\boxed{2x + 4}$	Combine like terms.

> **IMPORTANT!**
>
> When you subtract polynomials, change the sign of <u>every</u> term in the second polynomial. Leave the first polynomial unchanged.

Example 4: Completely simplify: $(3x^3 - 2x^2 + 1) - (x^3 + 3x^2 + x - 1)$.

$(3x^3 - 2x^2 + 1) - (x^3 + 3x^2 + x - 1)$	Given expression.
$(3x^3 - 2x^2 + 1) + (-x^3 - 3x^2 - x + 1)$	Apply definition of subtraction.
$(3x^3 - x^3) + (-2x^2 - 3x^2) - x + (1 + 1)$	Regroup.
$\boxed{2x^3 - 5x^2 - x + 2}$	Combine like terms.

Example 5: Completely simplify: $2(x^2 - 3x) - (x - 7)$.

$2(x^2 - 3x) - (x - 7)$	Given expression.
$2x^2 - 6x - (x - 7)$	Apply the distributive property.
$2x^2 - 6x - x + 7$	Apply definition of subtraction.
$\boxed{2x^2 - 7x + 7}$	Combine like terms.

C. Multiplication

To multiply polynomials, just apply the distributive property.

CASE I: MULTIPLYING BY A MONOMIAL

Example 6: Multiply: $2x^2(x^3 - 5x + 2)$.

$2x^2 (x^3 - 5x + 2)$	Given expression.
$2x^2 \cdot x^3 + 2x^2 (-5x) + 2x^2 \cdot 2$	Apply the distributive property.
$\boxed{2x^5 - 10x^3 + 4x^2}$	When multiplying terms with the same base, add exponents.

CASE II: MULTIPLYING TWO BINOMIALS

Multiplying two binomials together requires a "double application" of the distributive property. This technique is commonly called "FOIL." FOIL is explained below.

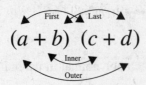

Special Patterns

$(a + b)^2 = a^2 + 2ab + b^2$

$(a - b)^2 = a^2 - 2ab + b^2$

$(a + b)(a - b) = a^2 - b^2$

Letter	What It Stands For	What It Means
F	<u>F</u>irst	Multiply the "first" terms (a and c).
O	<u>O</u>uter	Multiply the "outer" terms (a and d).
I	<u>I</u>nner	Multiply the "inner" terms (b and c).
L	<u>L</u>ast	Multiply the "last" terms (b and d).

You can almost always combine the OI terms (outer and inner) after you multiply.

Example 7: Find the area of Rectangle C.

$$\text{Area} = (2x + 3)(x + 1)$$

$$= \underset{F}{(2x \cdot x)} + \underset{O}{(2x \cdot 1)} + \underset{I}{(3 \cdot x)} + \underset{L}{(3 \cdot 1)}$$

$$= 2x^2 + 2x + 3x + 3 \quad \text{Combine the OI terms.}$$

$$= \boxed{2x^2 + 5x + 3}$$

$x + 1$ ⟶ Rectangle C

$2x + 3$

Example 8: Simplify: $(x - 5)^2$.

$(x - 5)(x - 5)$ — The exponent tells you to write the base twice.

$x^2 - 5x - 5x + 25$ — Use FOIL.

$\boxed{x^2 - 10x + 25}$ — Combine the OI terms.

Common Error Alert!

You *cannot* distribute the exponent!

$(x - 5)^2 \neq x^2 - 25$

D. Division

In Algebra I, you study division only by a monomial. In this case, just split the problem into separate fractions with the same denominator and simplify.

Example 9: Divide: $\dfrac{4x^3 - 10x^2 - x}{2x}$.

$\dfrac{4x^3}{2x} - \dfrac{10x^2}{2x} - \dfrac{x}{2x}$ — Split into three separate fractions with the same denominator.

$\boxed{2x^2 - 5x - \dfrac{1}{2}}$ — Simplify each fraction separately.

Remember:

Subtract exponents when dividing terms with the same base.

Practice

1. Simplify: $(2x^2 + 3x - 1) + (x^2 - 2x + 6)$.

   A. $3x^2 + 5x + 7$ **B.** $3x^2 + 5x + 5$ **C.** $3x^2 + x + 7$ **D.** $3x^2 + x + 5$

2. John has $x + 3$ nickels and twice as many dimes. Which expression represents the total number of coins he has?

   A. $2x + 6$ **B.** $3x + 3$ **C.** $3x + 6$ **D.** $3x + 9$

3. Which polynomial must be added to $7x^2 - 3x + 2$ to get the sum $2x^2 + 6x - 1$?

   A. $-5x^2 + 9x - 3$ **B.** $5x^2 - 3x - 1$
   C. $9x^2 + 3x + 1$ **D.** $-5x^2 + 9x + 3$

4. The physical education department of a school has $3x - 17$ basketballs, $5x^2 + 2x$ soccer balls, and $60 - 2x$ tennis balls. Which of the following is an expression for the sum of all the different balls?

   A. $8x^2 + 43$ **B.** $5x^2 + 7x + 77$ **C.** $65x^2 + 3x - 17$ **D.** $5x^2 + 3x + 43$

5. Find the perimeter of the triangle shown.

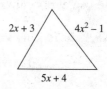

   A. $11x + 6$ **B.** $11x + 8$ **C.** $4x^2 + 7x + 8$ **D.** $4x^2 + 7x + 6$

6. Find the area of a square whose side has a length of $2x + 1$.

   A. $4x + 2$ **B.** $8x + 4$ **C.** $4x^2 + 1$ **D.** $4x^2 + 4x + 1$

7. Simplify: $2(x + 1)(x - 3)$.

   A. $2x^2 - 8x - 12$ **B.** $2x^2 - 4x - 6$ **C.** $2x^2 - 6$ **D.** $4x^2 - 12x$

8. When you divide the polynomial $10x^3 - 5x$ by $5x$, the quotient is—

   A. $5x^2$ **B.** $5x^2 - 1$ **C.** $2x^2 - 1$ **D.** $2x^2 - 5x$

9. To which of the following is $(x - 5)(x - 4)$ equivalent?

   A. $x^2 - 9x + 20$ **B.** $x^2 - 9x - 20$ **C.** $x^2 + 9x + 20$ **D.** $x^2 + 9x - 20$

10. If the product of two binomials is $x^2 + 4x - 5$, and one of the binomials is $x + 5$, what is the other binomial?

   A. $x - 1$ **B.** $x + 1$ **C.** $x - 5$ **D.** $x + 4$

11. To find the area of a triangle, you use the expression $\frac{1}{2}b \cdot h$, where $b = $ base and $h = $ height. If the base of a triangle is $2x + 4$ and its height is x, which of the following represents its area?

    A. $2x^2 + 2$ **B.** $x^2 + 2x$ **C.** $x^2 + 4x$ **D.** $x + 2$

12. Multiply: $(\blacklozenge + \heartsuit)(\blacklozenge - \heartsuit)$.

    A. $\blacklozenge^2 - \heartsuit^2$ **B.** $\blacklozenge^2 + \heartsuit^2$ **C.** $2\blacklozenge - 2\heartsuit$ **D.** $\blacklozenge^2 - 2\blacklozenge\heartsuit + \heartsuit^2$

13. Simplify: $(2x - 3)^2$.

    A. $4x^2 + 9$ **B.** $4x^2 - 6x + 9$ **C.** $4x^2 - 9$ **D.** $4x^2 - 12x + 9$

14. Subtract: $(3x - 2) - (5 + 4x - 2x^2)$.

    A. $2x^2 - x - 7$ **B.** $2x^2 - x + 3$ **C.** $-2x^2 + x - 7$ **D.** $-2x^2 - x - 3$

15. The parallel sides of the trapezoid shown have lengths $2x - 3$ and $x - 1$. Which of the following represents the difference of these lengths?

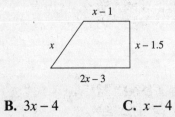

    A. $x - 2$ **B.** $3x - 4$ **C.** $x - 4$ **D.** $3x - 2$

16. Divide: $\dfrac{3x^6 - 6x^3 + 12x^2}{6x^2}$.

    A. $-3x^4 - x + 6$ **B.** $\frac{1}{2}x^3 - 6x + 2$ **C.** $3x^4 - x + 2x^2$ **D.** $\frac{1}{2}x^4 - x + 2$

Answers

1. **D**	5. **D**	9. **A**	13. **D**
2. **D**	6. **D**	10. **A**	14. **A**
3. **A**	7. **B**	11. **B**	15. **A**
4. **D**	8. **C**	12. **A**	16. **D**

Answer Explanations

1. **D**   Group like terms and combine:

$$(2x^2 + 3x - 1) + (x^2 - 2x + 6) = (2x^2 + x^2) + (3x - 2x) + (-1 + 6)$$
$$= 3x^2 + x + 5$$

2. **D**   The number of nickels is $x + 3$.

Multiply $x + 3$ by 2 to find the number of dimes:

Dimes $= 2(x + 3)$

$= 2x + 6$ Apply the distributive property.

Nickels + dimes $= (x + 3) + (2x + 6)$

$= 3x + 9$

3. **A**   Add $7x^2 - 3x + 2$ to choice A, $-5x^2 + 9x - 3$ to get $2x^2 + 6x - 1$:

$$(7x^2 - 3x + 2) + (-5x^2 + 9x - 3) = (7x^2 - 5x^2) + (-3x + 9x) + (2 - 3)$$
$$= 2x^2 + 6x - 1$$

4. **D** $(3x - 17) + (5x^2 + 2x) + (60 - 2x)$ Add.

$= 5x^2 + (3x + 2x - 2x) + (-17 + 60)$ Regroup.

$= 5x^2 + 3x + 43$ Combine like terms.

5. **D** $(2x + 3) + (4x^2 - 1) + (5x + 4)$ Add.

$= 4x^2 + (2x + 5x) + (3 - 1 + 4)$ Regroup.

$= 4x^2 + 7x + 6$ Combine like terms.

6. **D**   The formula for the area of a square is s^2, where s is the length of the side.

$(2x + 1)^2 = (2x + 1)(2x + 1)$

$= 4x^2 + 2x + 2x + 1$ Use FOIL.

$= 4x^2 + 4x + 1$ Combine like terms.

7. **B**   Be sure the 2 is distributed through *one* set of parentheses, not both.

$2(x + 1)(x - 3) = (2x + 2)(x - 3)$ Distribute the 2.

$= 2x^2 - 6x + 2x - 6$ Use FOIL.

$= 2x^2 - 4x - 6$ Simplify.

8. **C**   Write the division as a fraction, split the fraction; then simplify:

$$\frac{10x^3 - 5x}{5x} = \frac{10x^3}{5x} - \frac{5x}{5x} = 2x^2 - 1$$

9. **A** $(x-5)(x-4) = x^2 - 4x - 5x + 20$ Use FOIL.

            $= x^2 - 9x + 20$ Simplify.

10. **A**   The given trinomial, $x^2 + 4x - 5$, can be obtained by multiplying $(x + 5)(x - 1)$:

            $(x + 5)(x - 1) = x^2 - 1x + 5x - 5$ Use FOIL.

            $= x^2 + 4x - 5$ Simplify.

            Therefore choice A, $x - 1$, is correct.

11. **B**   Use the formula $\frac{1}{2} b \cdot h$, with $b = 2x + 4$ and $h = x$:

$$\text{Area} = \frac{1}{2} b \cdot h$$

$$= \frac{1}{2}(2x + 4) \cdot x \qquad \text{Substitute.}$$

$$= (x + 2) \cdot x \qquad \text{Use the distributive property.}$$

$$= x^2 + 2x \qquad \text{Use the distributive property.}$$

12. **A**   This is a special pattern, $(a + b)(a - b) = a^2 - b^2$, where ♦ is a and ♥ is b. Thus:

$$(♦ + ♥)(♦ - ♥) = ♦^2 - ♥^2$$

13. **D**   Rewrite $(2x - 3)^2$ as $(2x - 3)(2x - 3)$ and use FOIL:

            $(2x - 3)^2 = (2x - 3)(2x - 3)$

            $= 4x^2 - 6x - 6x + 9$

            $= 4x^2 - 12x + 9$ Combine like terms.

14. **A**   When subtracting, change the sign of every term of the second polynomial:

            $(3x - 2) - (5 + 4x - 2x^2) = 3x - 2 + (-5 - 4x + 2x^2)$

            $= 2x^2 + (3x - 4x) + (-2 - 5)$

            $= 2x^2 - x - 7$

15. **A**   Subtract:

            $(2x - 3) - (x - 1) = 2x - 3 + (-x + 1)$

            $= (2x - x) + (-3 + 1)$

            $= x - 2$

16. **D**   Split the fraction; then simplify:

$$\frac{3x^6 - 6x^3 + 12x^2}{6x^2} = \frac{3x^6}{6x^2} - \frac{6x^3}{6x^2} + \frac{12x^2}{6x^2} = \frac{1}{2}x^4 - x + 2$$

1.6 Factoring Polynomials

A **factor** is a number or polynomial that is multiplied by another number or polynomial to form a product. You may recall problems from elementary school that were similar to the one shown in Example 1.

Example 1: What are the factors of 12?

1 and 12   2 and 6   3 and 4

These are factors because, when you multiply them together, the product is 12.

In Algebra I, when you are asked to *factor a polynomial*, you need to break down the polynomial into numbers or polynomials whose product is the original expression. There are three types of factoring for which you will be responsible on the Algebra I SOL test:

- Factoring out the greatest common factor (GCF).
- Factoring a difference of perfect squares.
- Factoring a trinomial.

<u>**CASE I:**</u> FACTORING OUT THE GREATEST COMMON FACTOR
(DISTRIBUTIVE PROPERTY)

This type of factoring requires you to "undo" the distributive property or to apply the distributive property "in reverse." You are used to seeing the distributive property written as $a(b + c) = ab + ac$.

If you switch the sides of the equation, the distributive property looks like this:

$$ab + ac = a(b + c).$$

greatest common factor (GCF)

The **greatest common factor (GCF)** of a polynomial is the largest monomial that can be divided evenly into each term of the polynomial. The examples in the table below show how to use the distributive property in reverse to factor a polynomial. Just divide each term of the polynomial by the GCF, insert parentheses, and write the GCF at the front.

Expression	Identify the Greatest Common Factor (GCF)	Divide Each Term by GCF to get Quotient	Write in the Form GCF•Quotient
$15x + 10$	5	$\dfrac{15x}{5} + \dfrac{10}{5}$	$5(3x + 2)$
$9x^2 + 3x$	$3x$	$\dfrac{9x^2}{3x} + \dfrac{3x}{3x}$	$3x(3x + 1)$
$4x^2y - 2xy + 8y$	$2y$	$\dfrac{4x^2y}{2y} - \dfrac{2xy}{2y} + \dfrac{8y}{2y}$	$2y(2x^2 - x + 4)$
$-4x^4 - 8x^3 + 16x^2$	$-4x^2$	$\dfrac{-4x^4}{-4x^2} - \dfrac{8x^3}{-4x^2} + \dfrac{16x^2}{-4x^2}$	$-4x^2(x^2 + 2x - 4)$

Helpful hint: You can always check your answer by redistributing the GCF.

CASE II: FACTORING A DIFFERENCE OF PERFECT SQUARES

A *difference of perfect squares* is a polynomial that fits this form:

"Square" refers to the exponent.

$$a^2 - b^2 = (a + b)(a - b)$$

"Difference" means subtraction.

To factor $a^2 - b^2$, you must first identify a and b. This is easy; a and b are just the values that you must square to get a^2 and b^2, respectively. A difference of perfect squares factors as $a^2 - b^2 = (a + b)(a - b)$ or $a^2 - b^2 = (a - b)(a + b)$. Note that the factors $(a + b)$ and $(a - b)$ are identical except for the signs. Also note that either of the two factors can be written first. In the table below are examples illustrating how to identify and factor a difference of perfect squares.

Expression $a^2 - b^2$	What Is a?	What Is b?	Factored Expression $(a + b)(a - b)$
$x^2 - 100$	x is a.	10 is b.	$(x + 10)(x - 10)$
$9x^2 - 25$	$3x$ is a.	5 is b.	$(3x + 5)(3x - 5)$
$49 - y^2$	7 is a.	y is b.	$(7 + y)(7 - y)$
$9m^2 - 64n^2$	$3m$ is a.	$8n$ is b.	$(3m + 8n)(3m - 8n)$

Helpful hint: You can always check your answer by multiplying the two binomials using FOIL.

Sometimes factoring techniques must be combined to get a *complete* factorization. Consider Example 2.

Example 2: Find the complete factorization of $3x^3 - 27x$.

For this problem, you will need to use both of the preceding techniques (Case I and Case II) to factor *completely*.

Given expression:		$3x^3 - 27x$
Step 1:	Factor out the GCF.	$3x(x^2 - 9)$
Step 2:	Factor the difference of perfect squares.	$3x(x - 3)(x + 3)$

Helpful hint: When factoring, always look for the GCF first.

The complete factorization of $3x^3 - 27x$ is $3x(x - 3)(x + 3)$.

CASE III: FACTORING A TRINOMIAL

A trinomial is a polynomial with three terms. To factor a trinomial, you will need to "undo" FOIL. If a trinomial can be factored, it will break down into two binomials.

Examples 3 and 4 demonstrate a method for factoring a trinomial when the leading coefficient is equal to 1. The *leading coefficient* of a polynomial is the coefficient of the first term when the polynomial is in standard form.

Example 3: Factor $x^2 - 7x + 12$. Check your answer by multiplying.

$$x^2 - \underbrace{3x - 4x} + 12$$

Split the middle term into two monomials such that the product of their coefficients equals the last term.

> Given the expression $x^2 - 7x + 12$, how do you know to split $-7x$ into $-3x - 4x$?
>
> Choose two monomials that:
> - add to equal the middle term: $-3x + -4x = -7x$;
> - have coefficients that multiply to equal the last term: $-3 \cdot -4 = 12$.

$$(x^2 - 3x) + (-4x + 12)$$

Group the terms into pairs.

$$x(x - 3) - 4(x - 3)$$

Factor out the GCF (undo the distributive property) for each pair.

$$(x - 3)(x - 4)$$

Factor $(x - 3)$ from each term, leaving $(x - 4)$.

> This step may seem confusing! Consider the following:
>
> $(x \cdot ♥) - (4 \cdot ♥) = ♥ (x - 4)$
>
> with ♥ as the GCF. Now look back at the problem and think of $(x - 3)$ as ♥.

Check using FOIL:

$$(x - 3)(x - 4) = x^2 - 4x - 3x + 12 = x^2 - 7x + 12 ✔$$

Example 4: Factor $x^2 + 7x + 6$. Check your answer by multiplying.

$$x^2 + \underbrace{6x + 1x} + 6$$

Split the middle term into two monomials such that the product of their coefficients equals the last term.

> Did you choose correctly?
> - $6x + 1x = 7x$ ✔
> - $6 \cdot 1 = 6$ ✔

$$(x^2 + 6x) + (1x + 6)$$

Group the terms into pairs.

$$x(x + 6) + 1(x + 6)$$

Factor out the GCF (undo the distributive property) for each pair.

$$(x + 6)(x + 1)$$

Factor $(x + 6)$ from each term, leaving $(x + 1)$.

Check using FOIL:

$$(x + 6)(x + 1) = x^2 + 1x + 6x + 6 = x^2 + 7x + 6 ✔$$

In Examples 5 and 6, more difficult trinomials are factored. Example 5 introduces a trinomial with two variables. In Example 6 the leading coefficient is greater than 1 but less than 4.

Example 5: Factor $x^2 + 2xy + y^2$. Check your answer by multiplying.

$x^2 + 2xy + y^2$	Given expression.
$(x + y)(x + y)$	x^2 factors as $x \cdot x$. y^2 factors as $y \cdot y$. Both signs are +.

> *Recall* this special pattern from Section 1.5:
> $$(a + b)(a + b) = a^2 + 2ab + b^2$$

Check using FOIL:

$$(x + y)(x + y) = x^2 + xy + xy + y^2 = x^2 + 2xy + y^2 \checkmark$$

Example 6 illustrates a method of factoring that involves setting up possibilities and testing them, one at a time, until the correct factorization is found.

Example 6: Factor $2x^2 + 5x - 3$. Check your answer by multiplying.

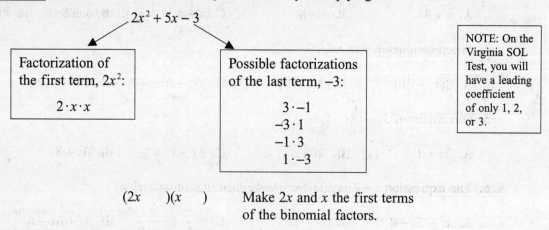

> NOTE: On the Virginia SOL Test, you will have a leading coefficient of only 1, 2, or 3.

Now, through "guess and check," try to determine the correct factors.

First Guess with 3 and −1	Second Guess with −3 and 1	Third Guess with −1 and 3	
$(2x + 3)(x - 1)$	$(2x - 3)(x + 1)$	$(2x - 1)(x + 3)$	Check using FOIL
$2x^2 - 2x + 3x - 3$	$2x^2 + 2x - 3x - 3$	$2x^2 + 6x - 1x - 3$	
$2x^2 + x - 3$ ☻ NO	$2x^2 - x - 3$ ☻ NO	$2x^2 + 5x - 3$ ☺ YES	

On the third guess, when FOIL is applied to $(2x - 1)(x + 3)$, the resulting polynomial, $2x^2 + 5x - 3$, matches the given polynomial. Since a match has been found, there is no need to test the fourth possibility.

Some polynomials cannot be factored.

Helpful hint: Any polynomial of the form $x^2 + a$, where $a > 0$, cannot be factored.

Example 7: Factor $x^2 + 9$.

The natural guess is $(x + 3)(x + 3)$. However, if you use FOIL to multiply, you will get $x^2 + 6x + 9$. This is an example of a polynomial that cannot be factored.

Practice

1. What is the greatest common factor (GCF) of $3x^2 + 6$?

   A. $3x$ **B.** 3   **C.** 6   **D.** $3x^2$

2. Which expression shows $4x + 8$ in completely factored form?

   A. $4(x + 8)$ **B.** $(x + 4)^2$ **C.** $2(2x + 4)$ **D.** $4(x + 2)$

3. Which expression is a factor of $x^2 + 2x - 8$?

   A. $x + 4$ **B.** $x - 4$ **C.** $x + 2$ **D.** $x - 8$

4. When completely factored, $3x^2 - 36 =$

   A. $3(x^2 - 36)$ **B.** $3(x - 12)$ **C.** $3(x - 6)(x + 6)$ **D.** $3(x^2 - 12)$

5. One factor of $3x^2 - 8x - 3$ is—

   A. $3x + 1$ **B.** $3x - 3$ **C.** $3x - 1$ **D.** $3x + 8$

6. The expression $x - 4$ is a factor of which of the following?

   A. $x^2 - 2x + 4$ **B.** $x^3 + 16$ **C.** $x^2 - 16$ **D.** $x^2 + 6x - 8$

7. What is the complete factorization of $3x^2 - 7x - 6$?

   A. $(3x - 3)(x + 2)$ **B.** $(3x - 2)(x + 3)$ **C.** $(3x + 2)(x - 3)$ **D.** $(3x - 1)(x + 6)$

8. In the expression $3x^2 + 7x - 5$, the leading coefficient is—

   A. 2   **B.** 7   **C.** 3   **D.** -5

9. If the area of a square is represented by $x^2 + 8x + 16$, which expression represents the length of one side?

   A. $x + 8$ **B.** $x^2 + 8$ **C.** $x^2 + 4$ **D.** $x + 4$

In questions 10–15, factor completely.

10. $4x^3 - 12x^2 - 8x$

    A. $4x(x-2)(x-1)$ **B.** $4x^3(x^2-3x-2)$ **C.** $4x(x^2-3x-2)$ **D.** $8x(x^2-4)$

11. $81 - 4x^2$

    A. $(9-4x)(9+x)$ **B.** $(3-x)(3+x)(9-2x)$
    C. $(9-2x)^2$ **D.** $(9-2x)(9+2x)$

12. $x^3 - 5x^2 - 6x$

    A. $(x-6)(x+1)$ **B.** $(x^2+1)(x-6)$ **C.** $x(x+1)(x-6)$ **D.** $x(x-3)(x-2)$

13. $2x^2 - 11x + 12$

    A. $(2x-3)(x-4)$ **B.** $(2x-6)(x-2)$ **C.** $(2x-4)(x+3)$ **D.** $(2x-4)(x-3)$

14. $3x^2 - 4xy + y^2$

    A. $(3x-y)^2$ **B.** $(3x-y)(x-y)$
    C. $(3x-2y)(x-2y)$ **D.** $(3x+y)^2$

15. $2x^2y - xy - y$

    A. $y(2x^2-x-1)$ **B.** $y(2x+1)(x-1)$
    C. $(2x+y)^2$ **D.** $y(2x-1)(x+1)$

Answers

1. **B**	4. **D**	7. **C**	10. **C**	13. **A**
2. **D**	5. **A**	8. **C**	11. **D**	14. **B**
3. **A**	6. **C**	9. **D**	12. **C**	15. **B**

Answer Explanations

1. **B**   The expression $3x^2 + 6$ can be divided evenly by 3:

$$\frac{3x^2}{3} + \frac{6}{3} = x^2 + 2$$

       Therefore, $3x^2 + 6$ factors to $3(x^2 + 2)$ with a GCF of 3.

2. **D**   The expression $4x + 8$ has a GCF of 4. Therefore, $4x + 8 = 4(x + 2)$.

3. **A**   The trinomial $x^2 + 2x - 8$ factors to $(x + 4)(x - 2)$, so choice A, $x + 4$, is the correct answer.

4. **D**   The expression $3x^2 - 36$ has a GCF of 3. Therefore, $3x^2 - 36 = 3(x^2 - 12)$. The expression $x^2 - 12$ cannot be factored, so the answer remains $3(x^2 - 12)$.

5. **A**   The expression $3x^2 - 8x - 3$ factors to $(3x + 1)(x - 3)$. Therefore, choice A, $3x + 1$, is the correct answer.

6. **C**   The expression $x^2 - 16$ is a difference of perfect squares and factors to $(x + 4)(x - 4)$. Therefore, choice C is the correct answer.

7. **C**   The trinomial $3x^2 - 7x - 6$ factors to $(3x + 2)(x - 3)$. You can find the answer through "guess and check" using FOIL.

8. **C**   The expression $3x^2 + 7x - 5$ is in standard form, and the leading coefficient is the number, 3, in front of the first term.

9. **D**   The expression $x^2 + 8x + 16$ factors to $(x + 4)(x + 4) = (x + 4)^2$. The lengths of the sides of a square are all equal, as shown in the diagram. Since the area of a square is found by squaring the length of a side, each side must equal $x + 4$.

$x + 4$ Area $= (x + 4)^2 = x^2 + 8x + 16$

$x + 4$

10. **C**   The expression $4x^3 - 12x^2 - 8x$ has a GCF of $4x$. Therefore:

$$4x^3 - 12x^2 - 8x = 4x(x^2 - 3x - 2)$$

       The trinomial $x^2 - 3x - 2$ cannot be factored, so the final result is $4x(x^2 - 3x - 2)$.

11. **D**   The expression $81 - 4x^2$ is a difference of perfect squares where 9 is a and $2x$ is b. Therefore, $81 - 4x^2$ factors to $(9 - 2x)(9 + 2x)$.

12. **C**   The trinomial $x^3 - 5x^2 - 6x$ has a GCF of x. Therefore,

$$x^3 - 5x^2 - 6x = x(x^2 - 5x - 6)$$

       The expression can be factored further to $x(x + 1)(x - 6)$.

> **Common Error Alert:** $81 - 4x^2$ cannot be factored as $(2x + 9)(2x - 9)$, because $4x^2 - 81$ is a different polynomial than $81 - 4x^2$.

13. **A** The trinomial $2x^2 - 11x + 12$ can be factored as $(2x - 3)(x - 4)$. This can be verified using FOIL.

14. **B** In the trinomial $3x^2 - 4xy + y^2$, the first term, $3x^2$, must be split to $3x \cdot x$ and the last term, y^2, must be split to $y \cdot y$. Since the last term is positive and the middle term is negative, both signs must be minuses (−).

   The answer, $(3x - y)(x - y)$, can be verified using FOIL.

15. **B** The expression $2x^2y - xy - y$ has a GCF of y. Therefore:

$$2x^2y - xy - y = y(2x^2 - x - 1)$$

   Since $2x^2 - x - 1$ factors as $(2x + 1)(x - 1)$, the final answer is $y(2x + 1)(x - 1)$.

1.7 From Words to Symbols

Many real-life problems can be made easier by replacing words with mathematical symbols. Some key words will translate into the operations of addition, subtraction, multiplication, and division. These four categories of words are illustrated below.

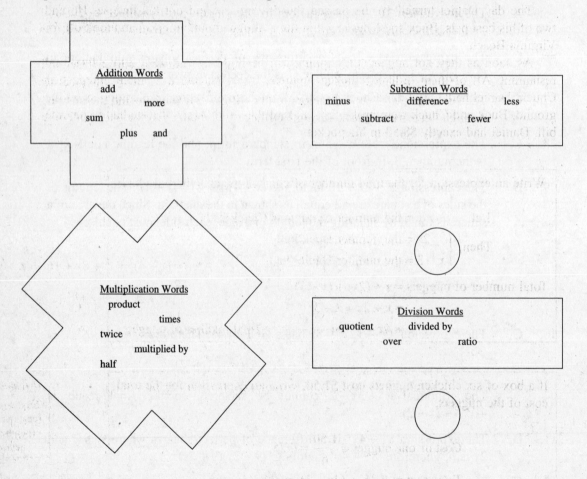

Addition Words
add
more
sum
plus   and

Subtraction Words
minus   difference   less
subtract   fewer

Multiplication Words
product
times
twice
multiplied by
half

Division Words
quotient   divided by
over   ratio

Here are some frequently used phrases translated into symbols:

Phrase	Mathematical Equivalent
Some number (or a number)	x
Twice a number	$2x$
Two less than some number	$x - 2$
Two more than some number	$x + 2$
Half some number	$\dfrac{1}{2}$
Two fewer than some number	$x - 2$
Ratio of some number and 2	$\dfrac{x}{2}$

Common Error Alert: "Less than" expressions can be tricky because the symbols are written in reverse order from the words. For example, "2 less than some number" translates to $x - 2$, NOT $2 - x$. The same is true for "fewer than" expressions.

The rest of this section tells a story about a boy named Daniel and his friends, Buck and Chuck. Throughout the story, you will see how you can use algebra to help in solving real-world problems.

The day Daniel turned 16, he passed the driving test and got his license. He and two of his best pals, Buck and Chuck, got in their "thugged-out" minivan and took off for Virginia Beach.

As soon as they got hungry, they pulled off the highway and went into a fast-food restaurant. All of them ordered chicken nuggets. Buck had twice as many nuggets as Chuck. Daniel had 3 less than Chuck because Daniel dropped three of his nuggets on the ground. Buck and Chuck were broke, as usual, so they told Daniel that he had to pay the bill. Daniel had exactly $8.50 in his pocket.

Write an expression for the total number of chicken nuggets the boys had.

Let x = the number of nuggets Chuck had.

Then: $\begin{cases} 2x = \text{the number Buck had} \\ x - 3 = \text{the number Daniel had} \end{cases}$

Total number of nuggets $= x + (2x) + (x - 3)$
$= x + 2x + x - 3$
$= 4x - 3$ ⟵ Total number of nuggets

If a box of six chicken nuggets cost $1.50, write an expression for the total cost of the nuggets.

Helpful hint:

Total cost = (cost per item) · (number of items)

Cost of one nugget $= \dfrac{1.50}{6} = 0.25$.

Total cost $= \underbrace{0.25}_{\text{Cost per nugget}} \cdot \underbrace{(4x - 3)}_{\text{Total number of nuggets}} = \underbrace{0.25(4x - 3)}_{\text{Total cost}}$

If Chuck ordered nine chicken nuggets, did Daniel have enough money to pay the bill for all three boys?

Since x stands for the number of chicken nuggets Chuck bought, substitute 9 for x into the total cost expression $0.25(4x - 3)$:

$$\text{Total cost} = 0.25(4 \cdot 9 - 3) = \$8.25$$

Daniel could pay the bill since he had $8.50 in his pocket.

The rest of the trip to the beach took the boys 1 hour longer than the time to get from home to the fast-food restaurant. Their average speed going from home to the restaurant was 50 miles per hour. Their average speed for the rest of the trip was only 45 miles per hour.

Write an expression for the total distance the boys traveled.

Let $x =$ the time in hours going from home to the restaurant.

Then:
$\begin{cases} 50 \cdot x = \text{the distance in miles from home to restaurant} \\ x + 1 = \text{the time in hours going from restaurant to beach} \\ 45(x + 1) = \text{the distance in miles from restaurant to beach} \end{cases}$

$$
\begin{aligned}
\text{Total distance} &= 50x + 45(x + 1) \\
&= 50x + 45x + 45 \\
&= 95x + 45 \text{ miles}
\end{aligned}
$$

Remember:

$d = r \cdot t$

distance = rate · time

If the boys were on the road for 30 minutes before they got to the restaurant, how far was the beach from their home?

Substitute $\dfrac{1}{2}$ for x into the expression for total distance:

$$95x + 45 = 95\left(\frac{1}{2}\right) + 45$$
$$= 92.5 \text{ miles}$$

Unit Alert!
Since x is in hours, you must convert 30 minutes to $\dfrac{1}{2}$ hour.

Practice

1. Which expression means 2 less than three times some number?

   A. $2 - 3x$ **B.** $3x - 2$ **C.** $3(x - 2)$ **D.** $3 - 2x$

2. If five objects cost x dollars, which expression represents the cost of fifteen objects?

   A. $15x$ **B.** $3 + 5x$ **C.** $3x$ **D.** $3x + 5$

3. Which expression represents the product of some number and 4 fewer than that number?

   A. $x(x - 4)$ **B.** $4x - 4$ **C.** $4 - 4x$ **D.** $x(4 - x)$

4. Which of the following phrases does *not* represent the expression $2x + 2$?

   A. Twice a number plus 2
   B. 2 more than two times a number
   C. The product of 2 and 1 more than some number
   D. Two times 2 more than some number

5. Five divided by the sum of x and y can be represented as—

   A. $\dfrac{5}{x+y}$　　　B. $\dfrac{5}{x}+y$　　　C. $\dfrac{x+y}{5}$　　　D. $\dfrac{5}{xy}$

6. The product of a number and 5 more than that number can be expressed in simplified form as—

   A. $x^2 + 5$　　　B. $x^2 + 5x$　　　C. $2x + 5$　　　D. $5 + x$

7. If the perimeter of a triangle is $5x - 2$ and two of its sides have lengths of $3x$ and $x + 2$, as shown in the diagram, which expression represents the length of the third side?

   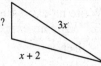

   A. $9x$　　　B. $x - 4$　　　C. $2x - 4$　　　D. x

8. The difference between a number and 5 more than that number is

   A. 5　　　B. $2x - 5$　　　C. $x - 5$　　　D. $5 - x$

9. When Kate took her friend Shelley to the movies, she bought two sodas and a huge bucket of popcorn. If the popcorn cost three times as much as a soda, which expression represents the cost of both sodas and the popcorn?

   A. $7x$　　　B. $6x$　　　C. $5x$　　　D. $2 + 3x$

For questions 10 and 11, use the following information:

Eugene decides to build two adjacent rectangular pens for his sheep and his dogs, as shown in the diagram. He runs fencing all around the perimeter and also puts a piece of fencing as a divider to separate the dogs from the sheep.

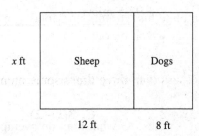

10. Which expression represents the total amount of fencing, in feet, that Eugene will need to build the pens?

    A. $3x + 40$　　　B. $20x$　　　C. $2x + 20$　　　D. $2x + 40$

11. How much greater, in square feet, is the area enclosed for the sheep than the area enclosed for the dogs?

    A. $8x$　　　B. $4x$　　　C. 4　　　D. 80

---

12. When Daniel's brother, Adam, left for college, Daniel moved into Adam's bedroom. He decided to paint the room more to his liking: red walls with a green ceiling. Although Daniel's mom wasn't too pleased with these colors, she bought Daniel the paint he needed. She purchased x gallons of red paint at $10.00 per gallon and y gallons of green paint at $9.50 per gallon. Which expression represents the total cost, in dollars, of the paint?

   A. $19.50(x + y)$ **B.** $19.50xy$ **C.** $10x + 9.50y$ **D.** $9.50x + 10y$

For questions 13 and 14, use the following information:

Susan has two dogs, three cats, and a guinea pig. Each month, she buys 1 bag of food for the guinea pig, 10 cans of dog food, and 15 cans of cat food. The bag of guinea pig food costs $5.50. Each can of dog food costs twice as much as a can of cat food. Let $x =$ the cost of 1 can of cat food.

13. Write an expression for the total cost, in dollars, of the dog food for the month.

   A. $2x$ **B.** $x + 10$ **C.** $20x$ **D.** $2x + 10$

14. How much, in dollars, does Susan spend each month to feed all of her animals?

   A. $5.50 + 25x$ **B.** $5.50 + 10x + 15(2x)$
   C. $5.50 + 25(3x)$ **D.** $5.50 + 10(2x) + 15x$

For questions 15–17, use the following information:

Brandon and Ian work out at the track every day. On Monday, they worked out for 2 hours. Brandon ran 3 miles more than Ian did. Let $x =$ the distance, in miles, that Ian ran on Monday.

15. Write an expression for the distance, in miles, that Brandon ran on Monday.

   A. $3x$ **B.** $3 + x$ **C.** $3 - x$ **D.** $x - 3$

16. If Ian took 2 hours to complete his workout on Monday, which expression represents the rate, in miles per hour, at which he ran?

   A. $\dfrac{2}{x}$ **B.** $\dfrac{x-3}{2}$ **C.** $2x$ **D.** $\dfrac{x}{2}$

17. Suppose Ian ran a total of 7 miles. At what rate, on average, did Brandon run?

   A. $5\,\text{mi/hr}$ **B.** $3.5\,\text{mi/hr}$ **C.** $2\,\text{mi/hr}$ **D.** $7\,\text{mi/hr}$

Answers

1. **B**	5. **A**	9. **C**	12. **C**	15. **B**
2. **C**	6. **B**	10. **A**	13. **C**	16. **D**
3. **A**	7. **B**	11. **B**	14. **D**	17. **A**
4. **D**	8. **A**			

Answer Explanations

1. **B**   Three times some number is $3x$. Two less than that amount is $3x - 2$.

2. **C**   Since 5 objects cost x dollars, 15 objects cost just three times as much. The answer is $3x$.

3. **A**   Let x = some number. Then 4 fewer than that number is $x - 4$. Their product, therefore, is $x(x - 4)$.

4. **D**   Two more than some number is $x + 2$. Two times this amount is $2(x + 2)$, which equals $2x + 4$ using the distributive property. This is not the same as $2x + 2$.

5. **A**   The sum of x and y is $x + y$. Five divided by this sum is $\dfrac{5}{x + y}$.

6. **B**   Let x = a number. Then 5 more than that number is represented by $x + 5$. Product is the result of multiplication: $x(x + 5) = x^2 + 5x$.

7. **B**   The perimeter is the sum of all sides. Since two sides are $3x$ and $x + 2$ and the total must equal $5x - 2$, the third side must be $x - 4$.

   Side 1 + Side 2 + Side 3 = perimeter
   $$3x + (x + 2) + (x - 4) =$$
   $$(3x + x + x) + (2 - 4) = 5x - 2$$

8. **A**   If one number is five more than another number, then the difference between the two numbers must be 5.

9. **C**   Let the cost of a soda = x.

   Kate bought two sodas, $2x$.
   Popcorn cost three times a soda, $3x$.
   Total cost is $2x + 3x = 5x$.

10. **A**   On the diagram, fill in the missing lengths of sides. Be sure to include the length of the fence dividing the pens.

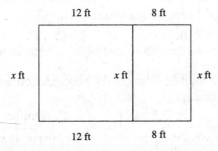

   Total fencing = $12 + 8 + x + x + x + 12 + 8 = 3x + 40$

11. **B**   Area of a rectangle = length · width.

   $\begin{cases} \text{Area of sheep pen} = 12 \cdot x \\ \text{Area of dog pen} = 8 \cdot x \\ \text{Difference in areas} = 12x - 8x = 4x \end{cases}$

12. **C**   Since x gallons of red paint cost $10.00 per gallon and y gallons of green paint costs $9.50 per gallon:

$$\begin{cases} \text{Cost of red paint} = 10.00 \cdot x \\ \text{Cost of green paint} = 9.50 \cdot x \end{cases}$$
$$\text{Total cost} = 10x + 9.50y$$

13. **C**   The cost for 1 can of cat food is x. A can of dog food costs twice as much, $2x$. Since Susan purchases 10 cans of dog food at a cost of $2x$ per can:

$$10 \cdot 2x = 20x$$

14. **D** $\begin{cases} \text{The guinea pig gets 1 bag of food per month at \$5.50} \longrightarrow 5.50 \\ \text{The dog food costs } 10(2x) \text{ per month (from question 13)} \longrightarrow 10(2x) \\ \text{The cats get 15 cans of food at a cost of } x \text{ dollars per can} \longrightarrow 15x \end{cases}$

$$\text{Total cost} = 5.50 + 10(2x) + 15x$$

15. **B**   Since x represents the distance that Ian ran and Brandon ran 3 miles more than Ian, the expression $3 + x$ represents Brandon's distance.

16. **D**   The formula for distance is distance = rate $\cdot$ time $(d = r \cdot t)$

Solve this formula for r: $\quad r = \dfrac{d}{t}$

Since Ian ran x mi in 2 hrs, his rate, r, in miles per hour, is

$$r = \frac{x}{2}$$

17. **A**   Since Brandon ran 3 mi more than Ian, Brandon ran 10 mi. He ran the 10 mi in 2 hr, so his rate was $\dfrac{10 \text{ mi}}{2 \text{ } hr}$, or 5 mi/hr.

1.8 Scientific Notation

Scientific notation is an efficient way of writing very large or very small numbers. To write a number in scientific notation, just place the decimal point after the first nonzero digit and multiply by the appropriate power of 10. Large numbers are written using *positive* powers of 10; very small numbers (between 0 and 1) are written using *negative* powers of 10. This is illustrated in Examples 1 and 2.

Example 1: Write the number 1,360,000 using scientific notation.

Since 1,360,000 is a very large number, 10 must be raised to a <u>positive</u> power.

1,360,000   is the same as 1.36×10^6.

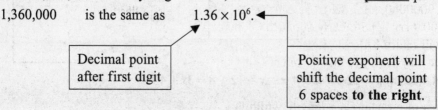

Decimal point after first digit

Positive exponent will shift the decimal point 6 spaces **to the right**.

Check: $1.36 \times 10^6 = 1.360000 \times 10^6 = 1,360,000$

Decimal will move right **6** spaces.

Example 2: Write the number 0.000495 using scientific notation.

Since 0.000495 is a very small number, 10 must be raised to a *negative* power.
0.000495   is the same as 4.95×10^{-4}.

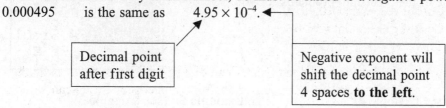

| Decimal point after first digit |
| Negative exponent will shift the decimal point 4 spaces **to the left**. |

Check: $4.95 \times 10^{-4} = 0004.95 \times 10^{-4} = 0.000495$

Decimal will move left **4** spaces.

Sometimes you want to add or subtract numbers that are written in scientific notation. To do this, you need to raise both numbers to the same power of 10.

Example 3: Subtract 7.3×10^8 from 8.42×10^9.

NOTE: Change the number that has the smaller exponent.

Since these numbers have different powers of 10, you must change one of them before you can subtract.

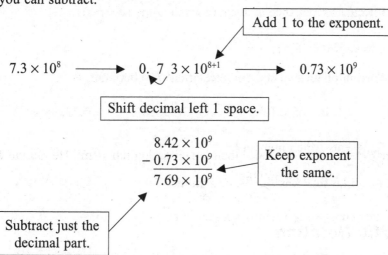

Add 1 to the exponent.

$$7.3 \times 10^8 \longrightarrow 0.\ 7\ 3 \times 10^{8+1} \longrightarrow 0.73 \times 10^9$$

Shift decimal left 1 space.

$$\begin{array}{r} 8.42 \times 10^9 \\ - 0.73 \times 10^9 \\ \hline 7.69 \times 10^9 \end{array}$$

Keep exponent the same.

Subtract just the decimal part.

Problems involving scientific notation can easily be done on your calculator.

Using Your Calculator in Scientific Notation Mode

You may have seen your calculator revert to scientific notation automatically for very large or very small numbers.

For example, if you use the calculator to square the number 9000000, it will return 8.1E13, *not* 81000000000000. (Try it!) Similarly, square 0.0000009, and the calculator will return 8.1E-13.

This answer may look confusing, but it's just the calculator's way of writing powers of 10.

```
9000000²
            8.1E13
.0000009²
            8.1E-13
```

| 8.1 **E** 13 | —— | same as | ⟶ | 8.1×10^{13} |
| 8.1 **E** −13 | —— | same as | ⟶ | 8.1×10^{-13} |

You can force your calculator to use scientific notation all the time by changing the **MODE**. Then your calculator can solve some of the preceding problems for you.

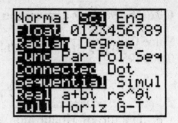

Example 4: (see Example 2):

Write the number 0.000495 using scientific notation.

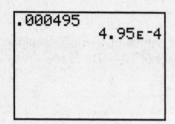

The answer is 4.95×10^{-4}.

Example 5: (see Example 3):

Subtract 7.3×10^8 from 8.42×10^9.

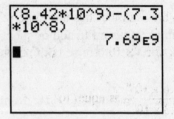

The answer is 7.69×10^9.

Practice

1. Write the following number in scientific notation: 350,000,000.

    A. 3.5×10^7 **B.** 3.5×10^8 **C.** 3.5×10^9 **D.** 3.5×10^{-9}

2. 2.436×10^5 represents which number?

    A. 243,600   **B.** 243,600,000   **C.** 24,360   **D.** 0.02436

3. 0.00297 can be expressed in scientific notation as—

    A. 297×10^{-5} **B.** 2.97×10^{-2} **C.** 2.97×10^{-3} **D.** 2.97×10^{-5}

4. 4.06×10^{-1} is closest in value to which number?

    A. $\dfrac{1}{40}$ **B.** $\dfrac{1}{4}$ **C.** $\dfrac{1}{2}$ **D.** $\dfrac{2}{5}$

5. The product of 2.5×10^3 and 3×10^4 is—

    A. 7.5×10^7 **B.** 7.5×10^{12} **C.** 750,000,000   **D.** 75,000

6. The sum of 2.5×10^3 and 3×10^4 is—

    A. 5.5×10^7 **B.** 3.25×10^4 **C.** 2.8×10^3 **D.** 5.5×10^4

7. The pitch of a musical note depends on the frequency of the vibration that produces it. Middle C vibrates at 2.63×10^2 hertz. The note two octaves above middle C vibrates at 1.052×10^3 hertz. What is the ratio of their frequencies?

   A. $2:1$ **B.** $3:1$ **C.** $4:1$ **D.** $5:1$

8. The top of Mount McKinley is about 6.2×10^3 meters high. If you were flying in a plane over Mount McKinley at an altitude of 1.15×10^4 meters, about how far above Mount McKinley would you be?

   A. 5300 m   **B.** 530 m   **C.** 50,500 m   **D.** 5050 m

9. Which number has the same value as 25.3×10^a?

   A. $2.53 \times 10^{a+1}$ **B.** $2.53 \times 10^{a-1}$ **C.** $253 \times 10^{a+1}$ **D.** $2530\,a$

10. $\dfrac{4.6 \times 10^{10}}{2.3 \times 10^{-5}}$ is equal to—

   A. 2×10^5 **B.** 2×10^{15} **C.** 2.3×10^5 **D.** 2.3×10^{15}

Answers

1. **B**   3. **C**   5. **A**   7. **C**   9. **A**
2. **A**   4. **D**   6. **B**   8. **A**   10. **B**

Answer Explanations

1. **B**   When changing the number 350,000,000 to scientific notation, you must shift the decimal point 8 spaces to the left of its understood position at the end of the number. Thus, the exponent will be positive 8. The answer is 3.5×10^8.

2. **A**   Since the exponent is positive, the number 2.436×10^5 is larger than 2.436. Then $10^5 = 100,000$, and 2.436 times 100,000 equals 243,600.

3. **C**   To express the number 0.00297 in scientific notation, you must move the decimal point 3 spaces to the right. Since it moved right, the exponent will be -3. The answer is 2.97×10^{-3}.

4. **D**   The number 4.06×10^{-1} is equal to 0.406×10^0, which is just 0.406 since any number raised to the power of 0 is 1. The fraction $\dfrac{2}{5}$, which equals 0.4, is closest to 0.406.

5. **A**   Finding a product requires multiplication.

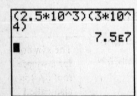

$$(2.5 \times 10^3)(3 \times 10^4) = (2.5 \cdot 3) + (10^3 \cdot 10^4) \qquad \text{Regroup.}$$
$$= 7.5 \times 10^7 \qquad \begin{array}{l}\text{Add exponents}\\ \text{when multiplying.}\end{array}$$

6. **B**   Finding a sum requires addition. In order to add, the numbers must be expressed with the same power of 10.

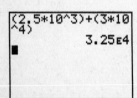

$$(2.5 \times 10^3) + (3 \times 10^4) = (.25 \times 10^4) + (3 \times 10^4)$$
$$= (.25 + 3) \times 10^4 \qquad \text{Get exponents the same.}$$
$$= 3.25 \times 10^4 \qquad \begin{array}{l}\text{Add just the decimal}\\ \text{parts of the numbers.}\end{array}$$

7. **C**   Divide the larger number by the smaller number.

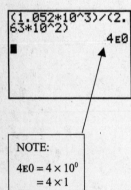

NOTE:
$4\text{E}0 = 4 \times 10^0$
$= 4 \times 1$
$= 4$

$$\frac{1.052 \times 10^3}{2.63 \times 10^2} = \frac{1.052}{2.63} \times \frac{10^3}{10^2} \qquad \text{Split the fraction.}$$
$$= 0.4 \times 10^1 \qquad \begin{array}{l}\text{Use a calculator on the}\\ \text{decimal part.}\end{array}$$
$$= 4 \qquad \begin{array}{l}\text{Remember to subtract}\\ \text{exponents when dividing.}\end{array}$$

The frequency ratio is 4:1.

8. **A**   Since you are looking for the *difference* in height, you must subtract.

$(1.15 \times 10^4) - (6.2 \times 10^3) = (1.15 \times 10^4) - (0.62 \times 10^4)$ Get exponents the same.

$$= (1.15 - 0.62) \times 10^4$$ Subtract only the decimal parts.

$$= 0.53 \times 10^4$$

$$= 0.53 \times 10,000$$ $10^4 = 10,000$

$$= 5300 \text{m}$$

9. **A**   To convert 25.3×10^a, move the decimal point 1 space to the left; then add 1 to the exponent; $2.53 \times 10^{a+1}$.

10. **B**   Divide the expression:

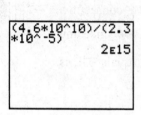

$$\frac{4.6 \times 10^{10}}{2.3 \times 10^{-5}} = \frac{4.6}{2.3} \times \frac{10^{10}}{10^{-5}}$$ Split the fraction.

$$= 2 \times 10^{10-(-5)}$$ Divide. Remember to subtract exponents.

$$= 2 \times 10^{15}$$

1.9 Simplifying and Approximating Radical Expressions

Finding the **square root** of a number is the inverse of squaring a number. The symbol $\sqrt{\ }$ is used for "square root." Let's compare a function machine that "squares" a number with a function machine that "square roots" a number.

> The symbol for a square root ($\sqrt{\ }$) is also called a *radical*.

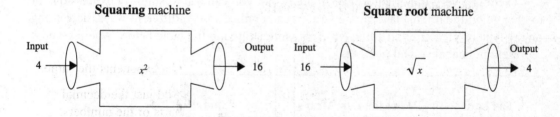

A "square root machine" is just a "squaring machine" that runs in reverse! The **output** of a square root machine is the number that you must **square** to get the **input**.

When you are working with square roots, it helps to know a list of perfect squares:

$$0, 1, 4, 9, 16, 25, 36, 49, 64, 81, 100, \ldots$$

$$2^2 \quad 3^2 \quad 4^2 \quad 5^2 \quad 6^2 \quad 7^2$$

Example 1: Find each square root:

$$\sqrt{9} = 3 \text{ because } 3^2 = 9$$

$$\sqrt{25} = 5 \text{ because } 5^2 = 25$$

$$\sqrt{16} = 4 \text{ because } 4^2 = 16$$

NOTE:
$\sqrt{9} = 3$, *not* ±3
$\sqrt{16} = 4$, *not* ±4
$\sqrt{25} = 5$, *not* ±5
The square root symbol, $\sqrt{}$, yields nonnegative answers only.

Finding square roots of perfect squares such as 9, 16, and 25 is easy because the answer is a whole number. How do you find square roots of numbers that are *not* perfect squares? In this case, you must estimate the value, as shown in Example 2.

Example 2: Locate $\sqrt{42}$ between two consecutive integers.

The number 42 is not a perfect square, so its square root is *not* a whole number. At best, you can try to figure out *about* how big $\sqrt{42}$ is by locating it between two consecutive integers.

Step 1: Locate 42 between consecutive perfect squares:

0, 1, 4, 9, 16, 25, 36, 49, 64, 81, 100, . . .

42

Step 2: Write an inequality to show that 42 is between 36 and 49: $36 < 42 < 49$

Step 3: Take the square root of each part of the inequality: $\sqrt{36} < \sqrt{42} < \sqrt{49}$.

Step 4: Simplify: $6 < \sqrt{42} < 7$

$\sqrt{42}$ is a number between 6 and 7.

There is a very important *law of radicals* that you can use to simplify expressions or to operate on them. This law can be written and applied in two different ways, depending on the type of problem you are given. This is illustrated in the table below, where *a* and *b* represent nonnegative real numbers.

The Law	What the Law Means	Examples
$\sqrt{a \cdot b} = \sqrt{a} \cdot \sqrt{b}$	The square root of two factors can be broken up into the product of their separate square roots. This form of the law is used to simplify radical expressions easily.	$\sqrt{9 \cdot 25} = \sqrt{9} \cdot \sqrt{25}$ $= 3 \cdot 5$ $= 15$ $\sqrt{100 \cdot 3} = \sqrt{100} \cdot \sqrt{3}$ $= 10 \cdot \sqrt{3}$ $= 10\sqrt{3}$ $\sqrt{4 \cdot x^2 \cdot x \cdot y} = 2x\sqrt{xy}$
$\sqrt{a} \cdot \sqrt{b} = \sqrt{ab}$	A product of square roots can be "reassembled" as factors under a single square root symbol. This form of the law is used to multiply radical expressions.	$\sqrt{2} \cdot \sqrt{8} = \sqrt{2 \cdot 8}$ $= \sqrt{16}$ $= 4$ $\sqrt{x} \cdot \sqrt{x^3} = \sqrt{x \cdot x^3}$ $= \sqrt{x^4} = x^2$

Common Error Alert!

$\sqrt{a^2 + b^2} \neq a + b$

For example,

$\sqrt{25 + 4} \neq \sqrt{25} + \sqrt{4}$,

since

$\sqrt{29} \neq 5 + 2$

Examples 3 and 4 show in detail how the law of radicals can be put to work.

Example 3: Simplify $\sqrt{48}$ completely.

| Strategy: | Since 48 is not a perfect square, rewrite it as a product that does contain a perfect square. Then simplify. |

Step 1: Identify all perfect squares that are factors of 48:

$$48 = \mathbf{1} \cdot 48$$
$$\mathbf{4} \cdot 12$$
$$\mathbf{16} \cdot 3$$

> *Reminder:*
> Here again is the list of perfect squares:
>
> 0, 1, 4, 9, 16, 25, 36, 49, 64, 81, 100, . . .

Step 2: Rewrite 48 as a product containing its largest perfect square:

$$48 = 16 \cdot 3$$

Step 3: Take the square root of each side: $\sqrt{48} = \sqrt{16 \cdot 3}$

Step 4: Use the law of radicals: $= \sqrt{16} \cdot \sqrt{3}$

Step 5: Simplify: $= \boxed{4\sqrt{3}}$

Example 4: Simplify $\sqrt{6} \cdot \sqrt{15}$ completely.

| Strategy: | Since neither 6 nor 15 is a perfect square, rewrite the problem, using the law of radicals, as a product that does contain a perfect square. Then simplify. |

$$\sqrt{6} \cdot \sqrt{15} = \sqrt{6 \cdot 15}$$ Apply the Law of radicals.

$$= \sqrt{90}$$ Simplify.

$$= \sqrt{9 \cdot 10}$$ Find largest perfect square factor.

$$= \sqrt{9} \cdot \sqrt{10}$$ Apply the Law of radicals.

$$= \boxed{3\sqrt{10}}$$ Simplify.

Practice

1. $\sqrt{9}$ is equal to which number?

    A. 3   **B.** −3   **C.** 4.5   **D.** 81

2. $3\sqrt{2}$ is the simplified form of which number?

    A. $\sqrt{12}$ **B.** $\sqrt{18}$ **C.** $\sqrt{6}$ **D.** $\sqrt{36}$

3. The simplified form of $\sqrt{75}$ is—

    A. $5\sqrt{3}$ **B.** $3\sqrt{5}$ **C.** $5\sqrt{5}$ **D.** $3\sqrt{3}$

4. Which of the following statements is FALSE?

    A. $\sqrt{a} \cdot \sqrt{b} = \sqrt{ab}$ **B.** $\sqrt{9a} = 3\sqrt{a}$

    C. $\sqrt{a^2} = \pm a$ **D.** $\sqrt{xy} = \sqrt{x} \cdot \sqrt{y}$ (where $x \geq 0$ and $y \geq 0$)

5. What is the smallest number in this set of numbers: $\sqrt{15}, 5, 5\sqrt{2}, 2\sqrt{5}$?

  A. $\sqrt{15}$ B. 5   C. $5\sqrt{2}$ D. $2\sqrt{5}$

6. $\left(\sqrt{x}\right)^2$ is equal to—

  A. $\frac{1}{2}x$ B. x C. x^2 D. $2\sqrt{x}$

7. 9 is the square root of which number?

  A. −3   B. 3   C. 18   D. 81

8. If $7 < \sqrt{x} < 8$, then a possible value for x is:

  A. 4   B. 7.9   C. 15   D. 50

9. Which is the closest approximation of $\sqrt{500}$?

  A. 7.1   B. 22.4   C. 50   D. 250

10. 19.4 is a reasonable approximation of—

  A. $\sqrt{20}$ B. $\sqrt{38}$ C. $\sqrt{200}$ D. $\sqrt{375}$

11. $\sqrt{90}$ is smaller than which number?

  A. $\sqrt{85}$ B. $2\sqrt{10}$ C. 9   D. 9.5

12. If $\sqrt{x} = 4$, then x must equal—

  A. 2   B. 4   C. 8   D. 16

13. Taking a square root is the opposite of—

  A. doubling   B. halving   C. rounding   D. squaring

14. The radius, r, of a circle can be found by using the formula $r = \sqrt{\dfrac{A}{\pi}}$, where A is the circle's area. If a circle has an area of 25 square centimeters, what is its approximate radius?

  A. 8 cm   B. 1.6 cm   C. 2.8 cm   D. 8.9 cm

15. If the area of a square is 500 square units, what is the approximate length of its side?

  A. 22 units   B. 25 units   C. 50 units   D. 125 units

16. The length of the third side of the triangle shown can be found by using the formula $c = \sqrt{a^2 + b^2}$. In this triangle, $a = 7\,\text{cm}$ and $b = 24\,\text{cm}$. What is the length of side c?

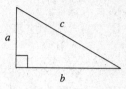

   A. 7.5 cm   **B.** 25 cm   **C.** 31 cm   **D.** $\sqrt{31}$ cm

17. $\sqrt{4} + \sqrt{9}$ is the same as—

   A. $\sqrt{13}$ **B.** $\sqrt{36}$ **C.** $\sqrt{25}$ **D.** $\sqrt{5}$

18. Which expression is in simplest form?

   A. $\sqrt{24}$ **B.** $\sqrt{72}$ **C.** $\sqrt{81}$ **D.** $\sqrt{51}$

19. Which statement is *not* true?

   A. $\sqrt{0} = 0$ **B.** $\sqrt{a \cdot b} = \sqrt{a} \cdot \sqrt{b}$

   C. $\sqrt{a+b} = \sqrt{a} + \sqrt{b}$ **D.** $\left(\sqrt{a}\right)^2 = a$

20. Which number has a square root that is *not* an integer?

   A. 81   **B.** 144   **C.** 200   **D.** 900

Answers

1. A	5. A	9. B	13. D	17. C
2. B	6. B	10. D	14. C	18. D
3. A	7. D	11. D	15. A	19. C
4. C	8. D	12. D	16. B	20. C

Answer Explanations

1. **A** $\sqrt{9} = 3$ because $3^2 = 9$. Remember: the $\sqrt{}$ symbol requires a *nonnegative* answer.

2. **B**   Use the law of radicals: $\sqrt{18} = \sqrt{9 \cdot 2}$
$$= \sqrt{9} \cdot \sqrt{2}$$
$$= 3\sqrt{2}$$

3. **A**   Use the law of radicals: $\sqrt{75} = \sqrt{25 \cdot 3}$
$$= \sqrt{25} \cdot \sqrt{3}$$
$$= 5\sqrt{3}$$

4. **C**   The statement $\sqrt{a^2} = \pm a$ is false because the $\sqrt{}$ symbol means a nonnegative answer only, *not* both a positive and a negative answer.

5. **A** $\sqrt{15} = 3.8729\ldots, 5 = 5, 5\sqrt{2} = 7.071\ldots, 2\sqrt{5} = 4.472\ldots$.

   Therefore, $\sqrt{15}$ is the smallest.

6. **B** $\left(\sqrt{x}\right)^2 = \sqrt{x} \cdot \sqrt{x} = \sqrt{x^2} = x$ because $x \cdot x = x^2$.

7. **D** $\sqrt{81} = 9$ because $9^2 = 81$.

8. **D**   Since $7 < \sqrt{x} < 8$, you can square each term and still get a true inequality:

$$\sqrt{49} < \left(\sqrt{x}\right)^2 < 64 = 49 < x < 64$$

   Thus, x lies between 49 and 64. The answer is 50.

9. **B** $\sqrt{500} = 22.3606\ldots$

   Test the choices in your calculator. The closest approximation is 22.4.

```
√(500)
          22.36067977
█
```

10. **D**   Test the answer choices in your calculator. $\sqrt{375} = 19.3649\ldots$

```
√(375)
          19.36491673
```

11. **D**   Use your calculator to compare values. $\sqrt{90} = 9.486\ldots$, which is less than 9.5.

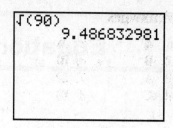

12. **D**   Given the equation $\sqrt{x} = 4$. Since $\sqrt{16} = 4$. x must be 16.

13. **D**   Squaring and taking a square root are opposite operations. See the function machines at the beginning of this section.

14. **C**   Substituting 25 for A into the given formula, $r = \sqrt{\dfrac{A}{\pi}}$, yields

$$r = \sqrt{\frac{25}{\pi}} = 2.8209\ldots$$

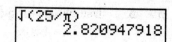

which is approximately 2.8.

15. **A**   Since the area of a square is equal to the square of its side, take the square root of the area to obtain the length of the side. $\sqrt{500} = 22.3606\ldots$, which is approximately 22.

16. **B**   Substitute 7 for a and 24 for b into the given formula, $c = \sqrt{a^2 + b^2}$:

$$c = \sqrt{7^2 + 24^2} = \sqrt{49 + 576} = \sqrt{625} = 25$$

17. **C**   Simplify: $\sqrt{4} + \sqrt{9} = 2 + 3 = 5$. Similarly, $\sqrt{25} = 5$.

18. **D**   The expression $\sqrt{51}$ cannot be simplified because there are no perfect squares (other than 1) that are factors of 51. Therefore, $\sqrt{51}$ is already in simplest form.

19. **C**   The law of radicals does not hold for addition, so $\sqrt{a+b} \neq \sqrt{a} + \sqrt{b}$.

20. **C** $\sqrt{200} = 14.1421\ldots$, which is not an integer.

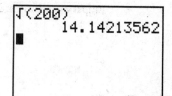

Chapter 2

Equations and Inequalities

2.1 What Is an Equation?

> An **equation** is simply two expressions linked together with an equal sign (=).

Here are some examples of equations:

<table>
<tr><td><u>One-Variable Equations</u></td><td><u>Two-Variable Equations</u></td></tr>
<tr><td>$3x = 2(x - 3)$</td><td>$2x - y = 4$</td></tr>
<tr><td>$x^2 - 3x - 4 = 0$</td><td>$y = x^2 - 4$</td></tr>
</table>

An equation is like a hungry machine that "eats" points. But equation machines are very picky! Only certain points will "satisfy" them.

Example 1: Which of the following points satisfies the equation $2x - y = 4$?

A. $(2, 0)$ 　　　　　　　　　　　　B. $(3, -2)$

Substitute to find out!

A.

(2, 0) FEED ME!

$x = 2$　　$y = 0$

$2x - y = 4$

?
$2(2) - 0 = 4$
$4 - 0 = 4$ ✔

☺ Yummm! The equation machine is satisfied!

B.

(3, –2) FEED ME!

$x = 3$　　$y = -2$

$2x - y = 4$

?
$2(3) - (-2) = 4$
$6 + 4 \neq 4$

☹ Yuckkk! The equation machine is not satisfied!

The point $(2,0)$ satisfies $2x - y = 4$ because it gives a TRUE result.

The point $(3, -2)$ does *not* satisfy $2x - y = 4$ because it gives a FALSE result.

You can also tell whether a point satisfies an equation by looking at the equation's graph.

> A **graph of an equation** is a picture of all of the points that satisfy the equation.

Example 2: The equation $2x - y = 4$ graphs as a line. Use the graph to decide which of the points $A(2, 0)$ and $B(3, -2)$ satisfies this equation.

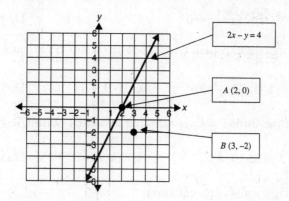

The point $A(2, 0)$ **satisfies** the equation $2x - y = 4$ because it lies on this equation's graph. The point $B(3, -2)$ does not lie on the graph of $2x - y = 4$, so it does *not* satisfy this equation.

You can also solve Example 2 using your calculator.

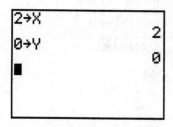

Step 1

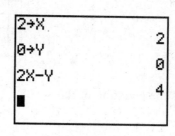

Step 2

For more detail on how to use the **STO** key ($\rightarrow$) on your calculator, refer to A Calculator Tutorial on page 3.

Since the expression $2x - y$ evaluates to 4 when the value of 2 is stored for x and 0 is stored for y, the point $(2, 0)$ satisfies the equation $2x - y = 4$.

What do we do with equations?

- We **graph** them.
- We **solve** them.

That's all we do. And that's what the rest of this chapter is about.

Practice

1. Which point satisfies the equation $3x + 2y = -1$?

    A. $(0, -1)$ B. $(-1, 0)$ C. $(-1, 1)$ D. $(-1, -1)$

2. The point $(2, -1)$ satisfies which equation?

    A. $y = x^2 - 3$ B. $2x - y = 0$ C. $y = -x + 1$ D. $y = 2x - 1$

3. Which point satisfies the equation $y = x^2 - 2$?

    A. $(-1, -3)$ B. $(-1, -2)$ C. $(-1, -1)$ D. $(1, -2)$

4. Every equation of the form $y = kx$ is satisfied by which point?

    A. $(k, 0)$ B. $(0, k)$ C. (k, k) D. $(0, 0)$

5. Which point does <u>not</u> satisfy the equation of the line graphed?

    A. $(2, -2)$ B. $(-2, 2)$

    C. $(0, 2)$ D. $(-2, 6)$

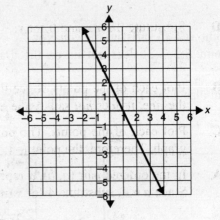

6. Which point satisfies the equation of the graph shown?

    A. $(3, 0)$ B. $(2, 0)$

    C. $(-1, 2)$ D. $(-2, 1)$

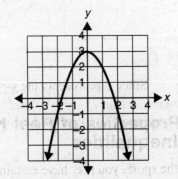

7. If the point (a, b) satisfies the equation $2x - y = 3$ and $a = 4$, then $b =$

    A. 5   B. 4   C. 3   D. -1

Answers

1. **C**	3. **C**	5. **B**	7. **A**
2. **C**	4. **D**	6. **C**	

Answer Explanations

1. **C** Substitute -1 for x and 1 for y:

$$3x + 2y = -1$$
$$3(-1) + 2(1) = -1$$
$$-3 + 2 = -1$$
$$-1 = -1 \; ✔$$

2. **C** Substitute 2 for x and -1 for y:

$$y = -x + 1$$
$$-1 = -(2) + 1$$
$$-1 = -1 \; ✔$$

3. **C** Substitute -1 for x and -1 for y:

$$y = x^2 - 2$$
$$-1 = (-1)^2 - 2$$
$$-1 = 1 - 2$$
$$-1 = -1 \; ✔$$

> **Remember**: Put negative numbers in parentheses when you substitute.

4. **D** Substitute 0 for x and 0 for y:

$$y = kx$$
$$0 = k \cdot 0$$
$$0 = 0 \; ✔$$

5. **B** Plot each of the points. Since the point $(-2, 2)$ does not lie on the graph of the line, it does *not* satisfy the equation of the line graphed.

6. **C** Plot each of the points. The point $(-1, 2)$ is the only point that lies on the graph. Therefore, the point $(-1, 2)$ satisfies the equation of the graph.

7. **A** In the ordered pair (a, b), a represents the x-value.
   Since $a = 4$, substitute 4 for x in the equation $2x - y = 3$ and solve for y:

$$2x - y = 3$$
$$2(4) - y = 3$$
$$8 - y = 3$$
$$y = 5$$

Since b represents the y-value in the ordered pair (a, b), $b = 5$.

2.2 Properties of Real Numbers, Equalities, and Inequalities

Just as the sports you play have certain rules, so does mathematics. For example, in soccer, players are not allowed to use their hands. If some players did not follow this rule, while others did, the game would not go well. Certain basic facts about numbers have been established to ensure consistency. These rules are called *properties*.

When playing a game, you also need to define some vocabulary so that players, officials, and coaches can communicate. Following are some sets of numbers that have been defined to help people communicate mathematically.

Natural numbers are also called "counting numbers."

A. Classifying Numbers

- Natural numbers: {1, 2, 3, 4, ...}
- Whole numbers: {0, 1, 2, 3, ...}
- Integers: {..., −3, −2, −1, 0, 1, 2, 3, ...}
- Real numbers: The set of integers, along with all fractions and decimal numbers

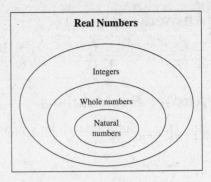

Real Numbers

Integers

Whole numbers

Natural numbers

B. Properties of Real Numbers

A very important "rule" or property is called *closure*. The set of real numbers is said to be "closed" under addition and multiplication. Imagine an infinitely large burlap sack filled with little slips of paper. Each real number in the world is written on one of the slips. The closure property says that, if you grab any two slips of paper and either **add** or **multiply** the two numbers on the slips, the answer will be on one of the slips of paper in the bag or in your hand!

The real numbers are closed for addition.	The real numbers are closed for multiplication.
(real number) + (real number) = (real number)	(real number) · (real number) = (real number)

You may ask, "What is the point of the closure property?" It guarantees that something unpredictable will not happen. For example, since the set of counting numbers is closed under addition, you cannot add two counting numbers such as 5 and 7 and get an answer such as $\frac{1}{3}$, which is *not* a counting number.

The following table shows additional properties (or rules of the game) that apply for all real numbers.

Identity property of addition	$a + 0 = a$	0 is the "identity" for addition.
Identity property of multiplication	$a \cdot 1 = a$	1 is the "identity" for multiplication.
Inverse property of addition	$a + (-a) = 0$	a and $-a$ are "inverses" because their sum is zero.
Inverse property of multiplication	$a \cdot \frac{1}{a} = 1$	a and $\frac{1}{a}$ are inverses because their product is one.

C. Properties of Equality and Inequality

To solve equations or inequalities, certain properties, or rules, have been established to make sure everyone gets the same correct answer. The properties provide consistency and also tactics for finding solutions.

The following properties hold true for all real values a, b, and c.

Name of Property	What It Says	Example	What It Means
Reflexive	$a = a$	$5 = 5$	Any quantity is equal to itself, of course!
Symmetric	If $a = b$, then $b = a$.	If $5 + 2 = x$, then $x = 5 + 2$.	You can switch the expressions on either side of the equal ($=$) sign.
Transitive	If $a = b$ and $b = c$, then $a = c$.	If $x = 5$ and $y = 5$, then $x = y$.	If each of two quantities is equal to the same third quantity, then the two original quantities must equal each other.
Addition • For equality	If $a = b$, then $a + c = b + c$.	If $x - 2 = 5$, then $(x - 2) + 2 = 5 + 2$.	You can add (or subtract) equal quantities to each side of an equation or inequality. For inequalities, you do *not* change the direction of the inequality symbol.
• For inequality	If $a \le b$, then $a + c \le b + c$.	If $y + 1 < 7$, then $(y + 1) + (-1) < 7 + (-1)$.	
Multiplication • For equality	If $a = b$, then $a \cdot c = b \cdot c$.	If $\dfrac{1}{2}x = 5$, then $2\left(\dfrac{1}{2}x\right) = 2 \cdot 5$.	You can multiply or divide both sides of an equation or inequality by the same (nonzero) amount.
• For inequality (2 cases)	If $a > b$ and c is a *positive* number, then $a \cdot c > b \cdot c$. BUT If $a > b$ and c is a *negative* number, then $a \cdot c < b \cdot c$.	$5 > 2$ and since 3 is a *positive* number, $5 \cdot 3 > 2 \cdot 3$, so $15 > 6$. BUT $5 > 2$ and since -1 is a *negative* number, $5(-1) < 2(-1)$, so $-5 < -2$.	If you multiply both sides of an inequality by a *positive number*, the inequality symbol does *not* change direction. SWITCH THE DIRECTION OF THE INEQUALITY SYMBOL WHEN MULTIPLYING BY A NEGATIVE NUMBER.
Substitution • For equality	If $a = b$, then a can be replaced by b (and b can be replaced by a) in any equation or inequality.	If $x = y + 3$ and $x + 5 = 42$, then $(y + 3) + 5 = 42$.	Equal expressions can be used interchangeably.
• For inequality		If $x < 10$ and $z = x$, then $z < 10$.	

Inequality properties hold true for all the inequalities: $<, >, \le, \ge$.

Matching Exercise

In column II below is a list of all the properties you should know. Write in the blank space the letter of each property from column II that is illustrated by its corresponding statement in column I. Some letters may be used more than once.

<u>Column I</u>

_____1. $6 + (-3) = -3 + 6$

_____2. $6 + (-3) = 6 + (-3)$

_____3. If $x + 6 = -3$, then
$x + 6 + (-6) = -3 + (-6)$.

_____4. If $-3 = z + 6$, then
$z + 6 = -3$.

_____5. If $x = -3$ and $-3 = y$, then
$x = y$.

_____6. $-3(2w + 6) = -3(2w) + (-3)(6)$

_____7. $6 + (-6) = 0$

_____8. $6 + 0 = 6$

_____9. If $x + 6 < -3$, then
$x + 6 + (-6) < -3 + (-6)$.

_____10. $6 + (-3)$ is a real number.

_____11. $-3 \cdot 1 = -3$

_____12. $(x + 6) + 3 = x + (6 + 3)$

_____13. If $-2x > 6$, then $-\frac{1}{2}(-2x) < \frac{1}{2} \cdot 6$.

_____14. $-\frac{1}{3} \cdot -3 = 1$

_____15. $2w = w \cdot 2$

_____16. $2 \cdot (-3)$ is an integer.

_____17. $-\frac{1}{2}(2x) = \left(-\frac{1}{2} \cdot 2\right)x$

_____18. If $3x + 6 = 15$, then $3(x + 2) = 15$.

<u>Column II</u>

A. Addition property of equality
B. Addition property of inequality
C. Additive identity
D. Additive inverse

E. Associative property for addition
F. Associative property for multiplication
G. Closure for addition
H. Closure for multiplication

I. Commutative property of addition
J. Commutative property of multiplication

K. Distributive property

L. Multiplicative identity
M. Multiplicative inverse
N. Multiplication property of equality
O. Multiplication property of inequality

P. Reflexive property
Q. Symmetric property
R. Substitution property
S. Transitive property

_____19. If $x + 2 = 8$, then $3(x + 2) = 24$.

_____20. $3y \cdot 6x = 6x \cdot 3y$

_____21. If $3y = 6x$, then $6x = 3y$.

_____22. If $3y = 6x$, then $y = 2x$.

_____23. If $x = 3y$ and $x + 6 = 10$,
            then $3y + 6 = 10$.

Answers

1. **I**	6. **K**	11. **L**	16. **H**	21. **Q**
2. **P**	7. **D**	12. **E**	17. **F**	22. **N**
3. **A**	8. **C**	13. **O**	18. **K**	23. **R**
4. **Q**	9. **B**	14. **M**	19. **N**	
5. **S**	10. **G**	15. **J**	20. **J**	

Practice

NOTE: You may want to review the commutative, associative, and distributive properties
        in Section 1.3 before attempting this practice set.

1. Which of the following is the identity element for multiplication?

    A. 0   **B.** 1   **C.** −1   **D.** 1 and −1

2. The reason that $5 + (-5) = 0$ is that

    A. 5 and −5 are additive inverses
    B. 5 and −5 are multiplicative inverses
    C. 0 is the identity element for addition
    D. the commutative property applies

3. Which property is illustrated by the statement below?

    If $3 = 2x + 1$, then $2x + 1 = 3$.

    A. Commutative property of addition   **B.** Symmetric property
    C. Associative property of addition   **D.** Reflexive property

4. The distributive property is best illustrated by which statement?

    A. If $x = y$ and $y = z$, then $x = z$.
    B. $2x + 6 = 2(x + 3)$
    C. $2(3 + 4) = 2 \cdot 7$
    D. If $2x + 6 = 7$, then $2x + 6 + (-6) = 1$.

5. Which property justifies the statement below?

   If $y = 2x$ and $y + 5 = 3x$, then $2x + 5 = 3x$.

   A. Substitution property
   B. Additive inverse
   C. Associative property of addition
   D. Transitive property

6. If $x = y$ and $x = 3$, then y must also equal 3 because of which property?

   A. Distributive
   B. Closure
   C. Transitive
   D. Commutative

7. You cannot obtain a negative answer when you add positive numbers. This is true because of what property?

   A. Distributive
   B. Closure
   C. Addition property of equality
   D. Commutative

8. Adding 14 to both sides of the equation $3x - 14 = 82$ is acceptable as a first step in solving this equation because of

   A. the commutative property
   B. the symmetric property
   C. the addition property of equality
   D. multiplicative inverses

9. If $2x = y$ and $x = 4y - 7$, which property allows you to conclude that $2(4y - 7) = y$?

   A. Transitive
   B. Symmetric
   C. Substitution
   D. Multiplication property of equality

10. If $y > 5$ and $x > y$, how do you know that x is more than 5?

    A. Because of the reflexive property
    B. Because of the symmetric property
    C. Because of the transitive property
    D. Because of the commutative property

Answers

1. **B**	3. **B**	5. **A**	7. **B**	9. **C**
2. **A**	4. **B**	6. **C**	8. **C**	10. **C**

Answer Explanations

1. **B** The identity element for multiplication is 1 because any number times 1 equals that number: $a \cdot 1 = a$.

2. **A** Additive inverses are two numbers, such as 5 and −5, whose sum is 0.

3. **B** The two equations $3 = 2x + 1$ and $2x + 1 = 3$ are the same except that the expressions have switched sides of the equal sign. This illustrates the symmetric property.

4. **B** The distributive property states that $a(b + c) = ab + ac$. It can also be written in reverse as $ab + ac = a(b + c)$. Choice B is an example of this property; $2x + 6 = 2(x + 3)$.

5. **A** Since $y = 2x$ and $y + 5 = 3x$, $2x$ replaces (substitutes for) y in the equation, resulting in the new equation $2x + 5 = 3x$.

6. **C** The transitive property states that, if each of two different quantities is equal to a third quantity, then the two original quantities are equal. Since $x = y$ and $x = 3$, then $y = 3$.

7. **B** Positive numbers are closed for addition. (Positive number) + (positive number) always equals (positive number).

8. **C** The addition property of equality allows you to add equal quantities to both sides of an equation.

9. **C** Since $x = 4y − 7$, the variable x can be replaced by the quantity $4y − 7$ in the equation $2x = y$. This illustrates the substitution property.

10. **C** Since $x > y$ and $y > 5$, then, because of the transitive property, $x > 5$. If $a > b$ and $b > c$, then $a > c$.

2.3 Solving Linear Equations

A **linear equation** is formed by linking together two linear (or constant) expressions with an equal sign (=). The following examples illustrate the creation of linear equations from linear expressions.

Linear Expressions	Linear Equations
$2x + 7$ $2 - 3x$	$2x + 7 = 2 - 3x$
$\frac{3}{2}(2x - 6)$ $9 - (x + 4)$	$\frac{3}{2}(2x - 6) = 9 - (x + 4)$
$2(x - 1)$	$2(x - 1) = 10$ (10 is a constant)
We **simplify** expressions.	We **solve** equations.

"Solving an equation" means finding all the numbers that satisfy the equation. As explained in Section 2.1, the numbers that satisfy an equation are the ones that make the equation true.

There are three ways to solve a linear equation including: "guess and check," applying the properties of algebra, and graphing with the help of a calculator. This section provides a detailed explanation for each of these three methods.

A. Solving by "Guess and Check"

Example 1: Which number is the solution of the equation $2x + 7 = 2 - 3x$?

A. 0   B. −1   C. 1   D. 2

Try the "guess and check" technique. Substitute the possible choices until you find the one that satisfies the equation.

Try choice A.   Substitute 0 for x: Try choice B.   Substitute −1 for x:

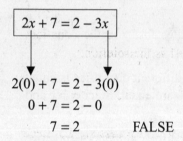   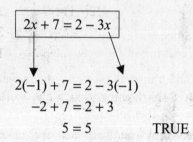

$$2(0) + 7 = 2 - 3(0)$$ $$2(-1) + 7 = 2 - 3(-1)$$
$$0 + 7 = 2 - 0$$ $$-2 + 7 = 2 + 3$$
$$7 = 2 \qquad \text{FALSE}$$ $$5 = 5 \qquad \text{TRUE}$$

Since $7 \neq 2$, choice A, 0, is *not* the solution of $2x + 7 = 2 - 3x$.

Since $5 = 5$, choice B, −1, *is* the solution of $2x + 7 = 2 - 3x$.

You do not need to check choices C and D since only one of the numbers will solve the equation.

B. Solving by Using the Properties of Algebra

Example 2: Solve the equation $2(x - 1) = 10$.

Use the properties of algebra (see Sections 1.3 and 2.2).

Multiplying by $\frac{1}{2}$ is the same as dividing by 2.

Given equation: $2(x - 1) = 10$

$$2x - 2 = 10 \qquad \text{Use the distributive property.}$$
$$2x = 12 \qquad \text{Add 2 to both sides.}$$
$$x = 6 \qquad \text{Multiply both sides by } \frac{1}{2}.$$

Check your answer: See whether the number 6 satisfies the equation $2(x - 1) = 10$.

Substitute 6 for x; then:

$$2(6 - 1) = 10$$
$$2(5) = 10$$
$$10 = 10 \qquad \text{TRUE!} \quad \text{So } x = 6 \text{ is the solution.}$$

Example 3: Find the solution of $2x + 7 = 2 - 3x$.

Here the variable appears on **both** sides of the equation. When this happens, change the equation so that the variable appears on one side only.

Given equation: $\boxed{2x + 7 = 2 - 3x}$

$\underbrace{(3x) + 2x} + 7 = 2 \underbrace{- 3x + (3x)}$ Add $3x$ to both sides.

Zero

$5x + 7 = 2$ Combine like terms.

$5x = -5$ Subtract 7 from both sides.

$x = -1$ Divide both sides by 5.

Check your answer: See whether the number −1 satisfies the equation $2x + 7 = 2 - 3x$.
Substitute −1 for x; then:

$$2(-1) + 7 = 2 - 3(-1)$$
$$-2 + 7 = 2 + 3$$
$$5 = 5 \quad \text{TRUE!} \quad \text{So } x = -1 \text{ is the solution.}$$

Example 4: Solve the equation $\frac{3}{2}(2x - 6) = 9 - (x + 4)$

This problem looks hard because each side of the equation is an expression that needs some work. Start by simplifying each side of the equation separately.

Given equation: $\boxed{\frac{3}{2}(2x - 6) = 9 - (x + 4)}$

Don't forget to subtract *all* the terms in the parentheses.

$\frac{3}{2}(2x) - \frac{3}{2}(6) = 9 - x - 4$ Use the distributive property.

$3x - 9 = 5 - x$ Simplify.

$(x) + 3x - 9 = 5 - x + (x)$ Add x to both sides.

$4x - 9 = 5$ Simplify.

$4x = 14$ Add 9 to both sides.

$x = \frac{14}{4}$ Divide both sides by 4.

$x = 3.5$

C. Solving by Graphing on the Calculator

When you have a really tough equation to solve, as in Example 4, you can let your calculator do it for you! Just graph the two sides of the equation as separate lines, and find the x-coordinate of their point of intersection.

For more detailed information on using your calculator to graph and find intersection points, refer to A Calculator Tutorial on page 3.

Example 5: Find the solution of the equation $\frac{3}{2}(2x-6)=9-(x+4)$

This is the same equation that was solved in Example 4 using the properties of algebra. Here is how to solve it using your calculator:

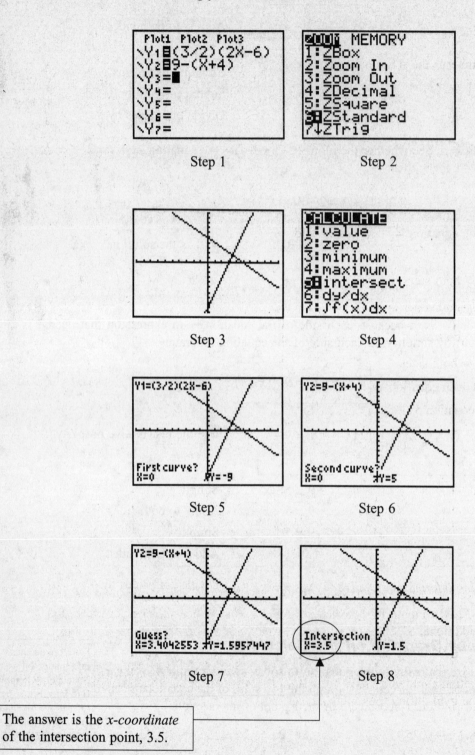

Step 1

Step 2

Step 3

Step 4

Step 5

Step 6

Step 7

Step 8

The answer is the *x-coordinate* of the intersection point, 3.5.

Practice

1. Solve the equation $3x - 7 = -10$.

   A. 1   **B.** -1 **C.** -3 **D.** $\dfrac{-17}{3}$

2. Which number is the solution of the equation $x + 7 = 2(x - 1)$?

   A. 9   **B.** 8   **C.** 6   **D.** 5

3. If $\dfrac{1}{2}x = 7$, then $x =$

   A. 3.5   **B.** 6.5   **C.** 7.5   **D.** 14

4. To solve the equation $\dfrac{y}{-5} = 4$, you should—

   A. multiply both sides by -5
   B. multiply both sides by $-\dfrac{1}{5}$
   C. add 5 to both sides
   D. add $\dfrac{y}{5}$ to both sides

5. Solve the equation $3x - 2 = 6 - x$.

   A. 2   **B.** 4   **C.** 0   **D.** 1

6. Solve $8x - 1.5 = 3x$.

   A. $\dfrac{1}{3}$ **B.** 0.3   **C.** 3   **D.** $\dfrac{15}{11}$

Use the following information to answer questions 7 and 8.

Katryce pays $32.00 a month for her membership at a gym. When she brings a guest, she has to pay an additional $7.25 per visit. Katryce paid $68.25 during the month of April, when a friend was visiting.

7. Which equation could you use to figure out how many times Katryce took her friend to the gym during the month of April?

   A. $32 = 68.25x + 7.25$ **B.** $68.25 = 7.25x + 32$
   C. $68.25 = (32 + 7.25)x$ **D.** $32x = 7.25x - 68.25$

8. How many times did Katryce take her friend with her to the gym during the month of April?

 A. 4   B. 5   C. 7   D. 8

---

9. The value $x = 2.5$ is the solution of all of the following equations *except—*

 A. $2x + 5 = 15 - 2x$ B. $0.4x = 1$
 C. $2(x - 3) = -1$ D. $5x + 7.5 = 9.5$

10. Solve: $\dfrac{x}{5} - 3 = 2 - (8 - x)$

 A. -2.5 B. 3.75 C. -5 D. 5

Answers

1. **B**	3. **D**	5. **A**	7. **B**	9. **D**
2. **A**	4. **A**	6. **B**	8. **B**	10. **B**

Answer Explanations

1. **B**   Solve the given equation:

$$3x - 7 = -10$$
$$3x = -3$$
$$x = -1$$

2. **A**   Solve the given equation:

$$x + 7 = 2(x - 1)$$
$$x + 7 = 2x - 2$$
$$9 = x$$

3. **D**   Multiply both sides by 2 and solve:

$$\frac{1}{2}x = 7$$
$$2\left(\frac{1}{2}x\right) = 2 \cdot 7$$
$$x = 14$$

4. **A**   Since y is divided by -5, you will need to multiply both sides by -5.

5. **A**   Solve the equation:

$$3x - 2 = 6 - x$$
$$4x - 2 = 6$$
$$4x = 8$$
$$x = 2$$

6. **B**   Solve the equation:

$$8x - 1.5 = 3x$$
$$8x = 3x + 1.5$$
$$5x = 1.5$$
$$x = 0.3$$

7. **B**   Katryce's membership fee is set at $32.00. Since she will pay an extra $7.25 per visit when she brings a guest, the additional cost for the month of April can be represented as $7.25x$, where x stands for the number of visits. Katryce paid a total of $68.25. Therefore, the required equation is $68.25 = 7.25x + 32$.

8. **B**   Solve the equation from question 7:

$$68.25 = 7.25x + 32$$
$$36.25 = 7.25x$$
$$\frac{36.25}{7.25} = x$$
$$5 = x$$

9. **D**   Substitute 2.5 for x in choice D:

$$5x + 7.5 = 9.5$$
$$5(2.5) + 7.5 = 9.5$$
$$12.5 + 7.5 = 9.5$$
$$20 = 9.5 \quad \text{FALSE}$$

Therefore, 2.5 is *not* a solution of the equation $5x + 7.5 = 9.5$.

10. **B**   Solve the equation:

$$\frac{x}{5} - 3 = 2 - (8 - x)$$

> You can use your calculator to solve this equation. See Example 5 on page 68.

$$\frac{x}{5} - 3 = 2 - 8 + x$$
$$\frac{x}{5} - 3 = -6 + x$$
$$\frac{x}{5} = -3 + x$$
$$x = 5(-3 + x)$$
$$x = -15 + 5x$$
$$-4x = -15$$
$$x = \frac{-15}{-4}$$
$$x = 3.75$$

2.4 Solving Linear Inequalities

These are **inequality** symbols:

>	greater than
<	less than
≥	greater than or equal to
≤	less than or equal to

When two linear expressions are linked together by any one of the above inequality symbols, we have a **linear inequality**.

Unlike a linear *equation*, which typically has one and only one solution, a linear *inequality* typically has *infinitely many* solutions, as illustrated in Example 1.

Example 1: Compare the solutions for the given linear equation and inequality.

| Equation: $3x + 2 = 5$ | Inequality: $3x + 2 \geq 5$ |

Substituting $x = 1$:

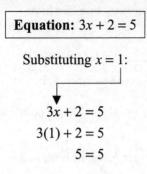

$$3x + 2 = 5$$
$$3(1) + 2 = 5$$
$$5 = 5$$

$x = 1$ is the only solution of $3x + 2 = 5$. No other number can be multiplied by 3 and added to 2 to produce 5.

Substituting $x = 4$:

$$3x + 2 \geq 5$$
$$3(4) + 2 \geq 5$$
$$14 \geq 5 \quad \text{TRUE!}$$

Substituting $x = 10$:

$$3x + 2 \geq 5$$
$$3(10) + 2 \geq 5$$
$$32 \geq 5 \quad \text{TRUE!}$$

Substituting $x = 1$:

$$3x + 2 \geq 5$$
$$3(1) + 2 \geq 5$$
$$5 \geq 5 \quad \text{TRUE!}$$

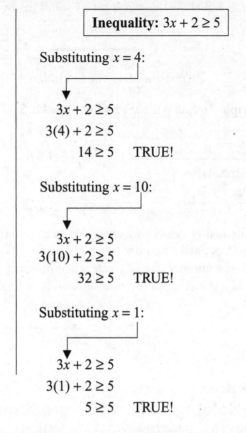

Through substitution, you see that $x = 4$, $x = 10$, and $x = 1$ are all solutions of the inequality $3x + 2 \geq 5$. And there are other solutions, too.

So, if a linear inequality has *infinitely many* solutions, how can you possibly find all of them? It's easy! You solve a linear *inequality* EXACTLY as you solve a linear equation with one very important distinction:

> Whenever you **multiply** or **divide** both sides of an inequality by a **negative** number, you must reverse the direction of the inequality symbol.

"Reversing the direction" of an inequality symbol means switching a "greater than" symbol ($>$ or $\geq$) to a "less than" symbol ($<$ or $\leq$) and vice-versa.

Examples 2 and 3 show how to solve an inequality and then represent the solution set by graphing.

Example 2: Solve the inequality $3(x - 5) < -21$. Then graph the solution set.

Given inequality: $3(x - 5) < -21$	
$3x - 15 < -21$	Use the distributive property.
$3x < -6$	Add 15 to both sides.
$x < -2$	Divide both sides by 3.

Every number smaller than −2 is a solution of the inequality $3(x - 5) < -21$.
You can show the entire set of solutions by graphing on a number line:

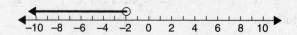

Example 3: Solve the inequality $3x - 4 \leq 5x + 6$. Then graph the set of solutions.

Given inequality: $3x - 4 \leq 5x + 6$

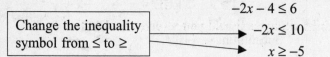

$-2x - 4 \leq 6$	Subtract $5x$ from both sides.
$-2x \leq 10$	Add 4 to both sides.
$x \geq -5$	Divide both sides by -2.

Change the inequality symbol from $\leq$ to $\geq$

The inequality symbol was reversed in the final step from $\leq$ to $\geq$ because you were **dividing** by a **negative** number.

Every number that is greater than or equal to −5 is a solution of the given inequality. Here is a graph of all the solutions of $3x - 4 \leq 5x + 6$:

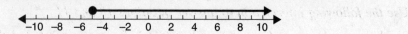

Practice

1. Which number is *not* a solution of the inequality $5 > 2(x - 1)$?

   A. 0   B. 1   C. 3.1   D. 4

2. Which statement is *not* true?

   A. $3 \geq 3$ B. $0 > -4$ C. $-4 > -3$ D. $-1 > -2$

3. Which inequality has the same solution set as $5 - x < -1$?

   A. $x < 6$ B. $x > 6$ C. $x < -6$ D. $x > -6$

4. Which number is a solution of $2(x + 1) < 3x$?

   A. −2   B. 0   C. 1   D. 3

5. The accompanying graph represents the solution set of which inequality?

   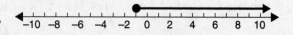

   A. $x - 1 \geq 0$ B. $-x \geq 1$ C. $2x \geq -2$ D. $2x \geq x + 1$

6. Which is the solution to $-\dfrac{3}{2}x + 2 < 8$?

   A. $x > -4$ B. $x > -\dfrac{20}{3}$ C. $x < -4$ D. $x < 4$

7. Which is the solution to $5x - 2 < 2x - 7$?

   A. $x < 3$ **B.** $x < -\dfrac{5}{3}$ **C.** $x > 3$ **D.** $x > -\dfrac{5}{3}$

8. Which is the solution to $3(x - 4) \geq 8x + 1$?

   A. $x \leq -1$ **B.** $x \geq -\dfrac{13}{5}$ **C.** $x \geq -1$ **D.** $x \leq -\dfrac{13}{5}$

9. When solving an inequality, under which situation should you reverse the direction of the inequality symbol?

   A. Whenever you divide
   B. Whenever you add a negative number
   C. Whenever you multiply by a negative number
   D. Whenever you subtract

Use the following information to answer questions 10 and 11.

Siobhan wants to go to Cancun with her friends for winter break, but she needs $350 for the trip. She already has $166 in the bank. She decides to raise the rest of the money by tutoring math students at a rate of $8 an hour. Let $x =$ the number of hours Siobhan will tutor.

10. Which inequality can be used to calculate the minimum number of hours Siobhan will have to tutor to raise the money she needs for the trip?

    A. $166x + 8 \leq 350$ **B.** $8x + 166 \geq 350$
    C. $8x \geq 350 + 166$ **D.** $8(166 + x) \geq 350$

11. What is the minimum number of hours that Siobhan will have to tutor in order to have enough money to go to Cancun?

    A. 15   **B.** 20   **C.** 23   **D.** 32

Answers

1. **D**	3. **B**	5. **C**	7. **B**	9. **C**	11. **C**
2. **C**	4. **D**	6. **A**	8. **D**	10. **B**	

Answer Explanations

1. **D** Substitute 4 for x in the given inequality:

$$5 > 2(x - 1)$$
$$5 > 2(4 - 1)$$
$$5 > 2(3)$$
$$5 > 6 \quad \text{FALSE}$$

2. **C** The statement $-4 > -3$ is false because -4 is a smaller number than -3.

3. **B** Solve the given inequality:

$$5 - x < -1$$

$-x < -1 - 5$ Subtract 5 from both sides.

Reverse the inequality symbol! $\longrightarrow$ $-x < -6$ Simplify.

$x > 6$ Multiply both sides by -1.

4. **D** Substitute 3 for x in the given inequality:

$$2(x + 1) < 3x$$
$$2(3 + 1) < 3(3)$$
$$2(4) < 9$$
$$8 < 9 \quad \text{TRUE}$$

5. **C** The number-line graph illustrates $x \geq -1$. Choice C can be solved to obtain the same result by dividing both sides by 2:

$$2x \geq -2$$
$$\frac{2x}{2} \geq \frac{-2}{2}$$
$$x \geq -1$$

6. **A** Solve the given inequality:

$$-\frac{3}{2}x + 2 < 8$$

$-\frac{3}{2}x < 6$ Subtract 2 from both sides.

Reverse the inequality symbol! $\longrightarrow$ $-3x < 12$ Multiply both sides by 2.

$x > -4$ Divide both sides by -3.

7. **B** Solve the given inequality:

$$5x - 2 < 2x - 7$$

$5x < 2x - 5$ Add 2 to both sides.

$3x < -5$ Subtract $2x$ from both sides.

$x < -\dfrac{5}{3}$ Divide both sides by 3.

8. **D** Solve the given inequality:

$$3(x - 4) \geq 8x + 1$$

$3x - 12 \geq 8x + 1$ Distribute.

$3x \geq 8x + 13$ Add 12 to both sides.

$-5x \geq 13$ Subtract $8x$ from both sides.

Reverse the inequality symbol! $\longrightarrow$ $x \leq -\dfrac{13}{5}$ Divide both sides by -5.

9. **C** Reverse the direction of the inequality symbol whenever you multiply or divide each side of the inequality by a negative number.

10. **B** Siobhan will receive $8 per hour for every hour, x, she tutors: $8x$
    Siobhan has $166 in the bank. $+166$
    Siobhan wants at least $350. ≥ 350
    Therefore the inequality must be $8x + 166 \geq 350$.

11. **C** Solve the inequality from
    question 10: $8x + 166 \geq 350$
    $8x \geq 184$ Subtract 166 from both sides.
    $x \geq 23$ Divide each side by 8.

    Siobhan must tutor for at least 23 hours.

2.5 Solving Literal Equations for a Given Variable

Do you recognize any of the formulas listed below?

$d = r \cdot t$	$A = \dfrac{1}{2} \cdot b \cdot h$	$P = 2(L + W)$	$y = mx + b$
$Ax + By = C$	$E = mc^2$	$A = \pi r^2$	$V = L \cdot W \cdot H$

Formulas like these are *literal equations* because they show how two or more variables are related to each other.

Solving a literal equation is very different from solving an ordinary equation because the answer is *not* a number. When you solve a literal equation, the answer is actually another equation! In fact, the answer is just a scrambled form of the equation you started with.

The point of solving a literal equation is to isolate a particular variable on one side of the equation. This technique is illustrated in Examples 1–3.

Example 1: Solve the equation $d = r \cdot t$ for the variable r.

Circle the variable you want to isolate.

$d = \boxed{r}\, t$ You have to "Move" t away from r.

The t's cancel when you divide!

$\dfrac{d}{t} = \dfrac{r \cdot t}{t}$

$\dfrac{d}{t} = \dfrac{r \cdot t}{t}$ Divide both sides by t ("undo" multiplication by dividing).

$\dfrac{d}{t} = r$ Simplify.

$r = \dfrac{d}{t}$ Switch the sides of the equation (use the symmetric property).

Solution: $r = \dfrac{d}{t}$

Example 2: Solve the equation $P = 2(L + W)$ for L.

Circle the variable you want to isolate.

$P = 2(\textcircled{L} + W)$ You have to "move" W and 2 away from L.

$\dfrac{P}{2} = \dfrac{2(L+W)}{2}$ Divide both sides by 2.

$\dfrac{P}{2} = L + W$ Simplify (the 2's cancel).

$\dfrac{P}{2} - W = L + \underline{W - W}$ Subtract W from both sides ("undo" addition by subtracting).

$\dfrac{P}{2} - W = L$ Simplify.

$L = \dfrac{P}{2} - W$ Switch the sides of the equation.

Solution: $\boxed{L = \dfrac{P}{2} - W}$

If you want to graph a line on your calculator, there's a good chance that it will be given to you in standard form: $Ax + By = C$. If so, you will need to change the form of the equation by isolating y as illustrated in Example 3.

Example 3: Change the equation $4x + 2y = 3$ to slope-intercept form by solving for y.

Circle the variable you want to isolate.

$4x + 2\textcircled{y} = 3$ You have to get y by itself.

$(-4x) + 4x + 2y = (-4x) + 3$ Add $-4x$ to both sides.

$2y = -4x + 3$ Simplify.

$\dfrac{2y}{2} = \dfrac{-4x+3}{2}$ Divide both sides by 2.

$y = \dfrac{-4x}{2} + \dfrac{3}{2}$ Split the fraction.

$y = -2x + 1.5$ Simplify.

> Note: Adding $-4x$ to both sides is equivalent to subtracting $4x$ from both sides.

Solution: $\boxed{y = -2x + 1.5}$ The line in this form can now be graphed on your calculator.

Practice

1. The formula $C = \pi d$ is used to find the circumference of any circle. When solved for π, the formula becomes—

   A. $\dfrac{C}{d}$ 　　　 **B.** $\dfrac{d}{C}$ 　　　 **C.** $C - d$ 　　　 **D.** $C + d$

2. Solving the equation $A = \dfrac{1}{2}bh$ for h yields—

   A. $h = 2A - b$ 　　 **B.** $h = A - \dfrac{1}{2}h$ 　　 **C.** $h = \dfrac{2A}{b}$ 　　 **D.** $h = \dfrac{A}{B} - 2$

3. Given the equation $M = PQR$, solve for R.

   A. $R = M - PQ$ 　　 **B.** $R = \dfrac{PQ}{M}$ 　　 **C.** $R = PQM$ 　　 **D.** $R = \dfrac{M}{PQ}$

4. The formula $A = \dfrac{1}{2}h(b_1 + b_2)$ is used to find the area of a trapezoid. Solve for b_1.

   A. $b_1 = \dfrac{2h}{b_2}$ 　 **B.** $b_1 = \dfrac{2A - h}{b_2}$ 　 **C.** $b_1 = \dfrac{2A}{h} - b_2$ 　 **D.** $b_1 = 2A - hb_2$

5. To solve the literal equation $C = 2\pi r$ for r, you should—

   A. subtract 2π from both sides 　　　　 **B.** divide both sides by 2π
   C. subtract r from both sides 　　　　　 **D.** square both sides

6. Solve $2x - y = 7$ for y.

   A. $y = -2x + 7$ 　 **B.** $y = 2x - 7$ 　 **C.** $y = 2x + 7$ 　 **D.** $y = -2x - 7$

7. Solve $2x + 3y = 6$ for y.

   A. $y = -2x + 2$ 　 **B.** $y = -\dfrac{2}{3}x + 2$ 　 **C.** $y = -\dfrac{2}{3}x + 6$ 　 **D.** $y = \dfrac{2}{3}x - 6$

8. Solve $M = \dfrac{AB}{C}$ for A.

   A. $A = \dfrac{M}{CB}$ 　 **B.** $A = \dfrac{BC}{M}$ 　 **C.** $A = \dfrac{MC}{B}$ 　 **D.** $A = MC + B$

9. The "solution" of a literal equation is—

   A. a number 　　 **B.** a variable 　　 **C.** an equation 　　 **D.** a graph

10. The formula $C = \dfrac{5}{9}(F - 32)$ is used to convert Fahrenheit temperature to Celsius temperature. If you want to convert in the opposite way, you solve the formula for F instead of C. Which formula is correct?

A. $F = \dfrac{5}{9}(C + 32)$ **B.** $F = \dfrac{9}{5}C + 32$ **C.** $F = \dfrac{5}{9}C + 32$ **D.** $F = \dfrac{9}{5}(C + 32)$

11. You know that $d = r \cdot t$ (distance = rate · time). If you know how far you travel and for how long, you can compute your average speed (rate). Which formula is correct for this purpose?

A. $r = d \cdot t$ **B.** $r = \dfrac{t}{d}$ **C.** $r = \dfrac{d}{t}$ **D.** $r = d - t$

Answers

1. **A**	4. **C**	6. **B**	8. **C**	10. **B**
2. **C**	5. **B**	7. **B**	9. **C**	11. **C**
3. **D**				

Answer Explanations

1. **A**   Solve $C = \pi d$ for π.

   Divide both sides by d: $\dfrac{C}{d} = \dfrac{\pi d}{d}$

   Reduce: $\dfrac{C}{d} = \pi \longrightarrow \pi = \dfrac{C}{d}$

   > This problem helps you see the meaning of π. π equals the ratio of circumference to diameter for every circle!

2. **C**   Solve $A = \dfrac{1}{2}bh$ for h.

   Multiply both sides by 2: $2 \cdot A = 2 \cdot \dfrac{1}{2}bh$

   Simplify: $2A = bh$

   Divide both sides by b: $\dfrac{2A}{b} = h \longrightarrow h = \dfrac{2A}{b}$

3. **D**   Solve $M = PQR$ for R.

   Divide both sides by PQ: $\dfrac{M}{PQ} = \dfrac{PQR}{PQ}$

   Reduce: $\dfrac{M}{PQ} = R \longrightarrow R = \dfrac{M}{PQ}$

4. **C**   Solve $A = \dfrac{1}{2}h(b_1 + b_2)$ for b_1.

   Multiply both sides by 2: $2 \cdot A = 2 \cdot \dfrac{1}{2}h(b_1 + b_2)$

   Simplify: $2A = h(b_1 + b_2)$

   Divide both sides by h: $\dfrac{2A}{h} = b_1 + b_2$

   Subtract b_2: $\dfrac{2A}{h} - b_2 = b_1 \longrightarrow b_1 = \dfrac{2A}{h} - b_2$

5. **B**   To solve $C = 2\pi r$ for r, divide both sides by 2π.

   $\dfrac{C}{2\pi} = \dfrac{2\pi r}{2\pi} \longrightarrow \dfrac{C}{2\pi} = r$

6. **B**   Solve $2x - y = 7$ for y.

   Add y to both sides: $2x - y + y = 7 + y$

   Simplify: $2x = 7 + y$

   Subtract 7 from both sides: $2x - 7 = y \longrightarrow y = 2x - 7$

7. **B** Solve $2x + 3y = 6$ for y.

Add $-2x$ to both sides: $(-2x) + 2x + 3y = (-2x) + 6$

Simplify: $3y = -2x + 6$

Divide both sides by 3: $\dfrac{3y}{3} = \dfrac{-2x+6}{3}$

Split the fraction: $y = \dfrac{-2}{3}x + \dfrac{6}{3} \longrightarrow y = \dfrac{-2}{3}x + 2$

8. **C** Solve $M = \dfrac{AB}{C}$ for A.

Multiply both sides by C: $M \cdot C = \dfrac{AB}{C} \cdot C$

Simplify: $MC = AB$

Divide both sides by B: $\dfrac{MC}{B} = A \longrightarrow A = \dfrac{MC}{B}$

9. **C** When "solving" a literal equation, you are rewriting (rearranging) the equation, not coming up with a value. Therefore, the "solution" is an equation.

10. **B** Solve $C = \dfrac{5}{9}(F - 32)$ for F.

Multiply both sides by $\dfrac{9}{5}$: $\dfrac{9}{5} \cdot C = \dfrac{9}{5} \cdot \dfrac{5}{9}(F - 32)$

Simplify: $\dfrac{9}{5}C = F - 32$

Add 32 to both sides: $\dfrac{9}{5}C + 32 = F \longrightarrow F = \dfrac{9}{5}C + 32$

11. **C** Solve $d = r \cdot t$ for r.

Divide both sides by t: $\dfrac{d}{t} = \dfrac{r \cdot t}{t}$

Simplify: $\dfrac{d}{t} = r \longrightarrow r = \dfrac{d}{t}$

2.6 Slope of a Line

The *slope* of a line is a number that tells you how steep a line is. A slope can be positive, negative, 0, or undefined.

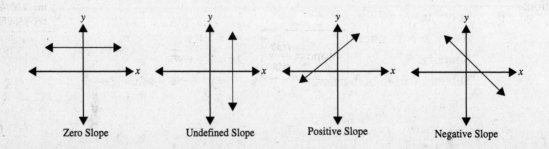

Zero Slope   Undefined Slope   Positive Slope   Negative Slope

- Every *horizontal* line has a slope of 0.
- Every *vertical* line has no slope at all (i.e., its slope is not defined).
- A *diagonal* line has a slope that is either positive or negative depending on which way the line slants.

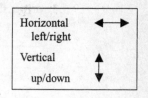

{ A diagonal line that slants *up to the right* has a **positive** slope.
A diagonal line that slants *up to the left* has a **negative** slope.

The steeper the line, the larger its slope (in absolute value).

Example 1: Which line has the greater slope, *A* or *B*?

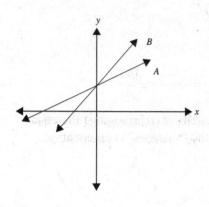

Answer: Line *B* has the greater slope. Both lines slant up to the right, but line *B* is steeper.

Example 2: Which line has slope −5, and which line has slope −2?

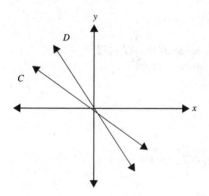

Answer: Line *D* is steeper than line *C*. Since |−5| > |−2|, line *D* has slope −5 and line *C* has slope −2.

You can find the slope of a line by reading a graph, by using a formula, or from an equation for the line. Each of these methods is explained below.

Important Facts
Parallel lines have the **same** slope.

Perpendicular lines have slopes that are **negative reciprocals**.

A. Finding Slope from a Graph

If a line is accurately graphed, you can determine its slope by using this definition:

$$\text{Slope} = \frac{\text{rise}}{\text{run}}$$

Example 3: Find the slope of the line graphed below.

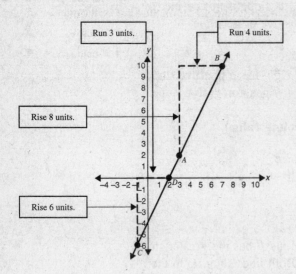

To calculate slope, choose any two points on the line, say *A* and *B*. To move from point *A* to point *B*, you would have to "rise" 8 units, then "run" 4 units.

Answer: Since slope $= \dfrac{\text{rise}}{\text{run}}$,

this line has slope $= \dfrac{8}{4} = 2$.

The slope of a line is <u>constant</u>. Therefore, *any* two points on a line can be used to calculate its slope.

Example 4: Find the slope of the line in Example 3 using a different pair of points (not *A* and *B*).

This time, calculate slope using points *C* and *D*. To move from point *C* to point *D*, you would have to "rise" 6 units and "run" 3 units (see graph for Example 3).

Answer: Slope $= \dfrac{\text{rise}}{\text{run}} = \dfrac{6}{3} = 2$

Of course, you found the same answer as you did in Example 3 since a line has one and only one slope!

Example 5: Find the slope of the line graphed below.

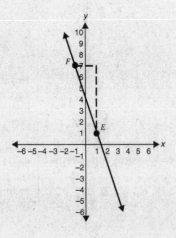

This line slants up to the left, so you expect its slope to be negative.

To move from point *E* to point *F*, you would have to "rise" 6 units, then "run" *to the left* 2 units, so the run is *negative* 2.

Answer: Slope $= \dfrac{\text{rise}}{\text{run}} = \dfrac{6}{-2} = -3$

B. Using a Formula to Find Slope

If you are given two points on a line, you can calculate the slope of the line without seeing its graph. Just use this formula for slope:

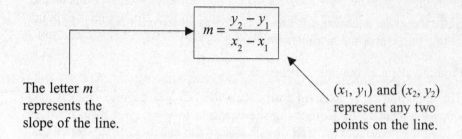

$$m = \frac{y_2 - y_1}{x_2 - x_1}$$

The letter m represents the slope of the line.

(x_1, y_1) and (x_2, y_2) represent any two points on the line.

Example 6: Find the slope of the line that contains the points $(2, -5)$ and $(-6, 11)$.

Label the points:

$(2, -5)$ $(-6, 11)$

(x_1, y_1) (x_2, y_2)

> Note: When using a calculator to determine slope, be sure to put parentheses around both the numerator and denominator of the fraction.

(It doesn't matter which point is (x_1, y_1) and which point is (x_2, y_2).)

Substitute into the formula:

$$m = \frac{y_2 - y_1}{x_2 - x_1}$$

$$= \frac{11 - (-5)}{-6 - 2} = \frac{16}{-8} = -2$$

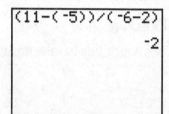

Answer: The slope of the line through the given points is -2.

Knowing the slope of a line can help you to draw its graph, as in Example 7.

Example 7: Graph the line that contains the point $P(-4, -2)$ and has slope $\frac{2}{3}$.

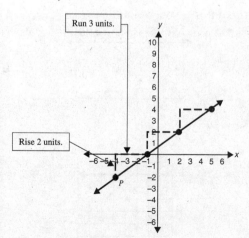

First, plot the given point, $P(-4, -2)$.

Then, since $\text{slope} = \dfrac{\text{rise}}{\text{run}} = \dfrac{2}{3}$, you can "rise" 2 units and "run" 3 units from point P.

Repeat this process (rise 2, run 3) to locate as many points on the line as you want!

C. Finding Slope from an Equation

If a line is written in "slope-intercept" form, $y = mx + b$, the slope of that line is just m, the coefficient of the x-term in the equation.

Example 8: Find the slope of the line $y = 3x + 5$.

Since the given equation, $y = 3x + 5$, is already in $y = mx + b$ form, the slope of this line is just the m value, which is 3.

Example 9: Find the slope of the line $2x + 3y = 6$.

This equation is in standard form: $Ax + By = C$. You have to change it to slope-intercept form. Converting the equation to $y = mx + b$ form involves getting the y-variable by itself on one side of the equation. (See Section 2.5, Example 3.)

$$2x + 3y = 6$$
$$3y = -2x + 6$$
$$y = \left(\frac{-2}{3}\right)x + 2$$

Now you can easily see that the slope of this line is $\dfrac{-2}{3}$.

Practice

1. Which line has the greatest slope?

   A. A **B.** B
   C. C **D.** D

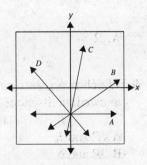

2. Which statement is true about parallel lines A and B as shown in the graph?

   A. Slope of $A >$ slope of B
   B. Slope of $B >$ slope of A
   C. Slope of $A =$ slope of B
   D. Slope of $A = -$(slope of B)

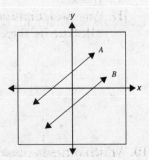

3. What statement about line A is *not* true?

   A. Its equation is $y = 3$.
   B. Its y-intercept is 3.
   C. It has a slope of 0.
   D. It's a vertical line.

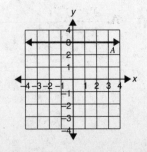

4. What is the slope of the line shown in the graph?

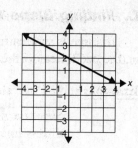

    A. 2   **B.** $\dfrac{1}{2}$

    C. −2   **D.** $-\dfrac{1}{2}$

5. If a line has a slope of 2 and contains the points (2, 4) and (5, k), then k must equal which value?

    A. 2   **B.** 5.5   **C.** 6   **D.** 10

6. What is the slope of the line that passes through the points (−3, 1) and (6, −2)?

    A. $-\dfrac{1}{3}$ **B.** −3   **C.** $\dfrac{1}{3}$ **D.** 3

7. The slope of the line $y = 2x - 5$ is—

    A. $-\dfrac{2}{5}$ **B.** 2   **C.** −5   **D.** $\dfrac{5}{2}$

8. The slope of the line $x + 2y = 7$ is—

    A. 2   **B.** −2   **C.** $\dfrac{1}{2}$ **D.** $-\dfrac{1}{2}$

9. Which two points on the line graphed should be used to calculate its slope?

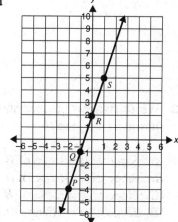

    A. P and R
    B. P and S
    C. Q and S
    D. Any two points on the line can be used to calculate its slope.

10. Which formula *cannot* be used to calculate slope?

    A. $\dfrac{y_2 - y_1}{x_2 - x_1}$ **B.** $\dfrac{y_1 - y_2}{x_1 - x_2}$ **C.** $\dfrac{x_2 - x_1}{y_2 - y_1}$

11. What can be said about the slope of a line that never intersects the *y*-axis?

    A. It's 0.   **B.** It's not defined.

    C. It's negative.   **D.** It's positive.

12. If a line intersects the *x*-axis at 3 and intersects the *y*-axis at −3, then its slope must equal—

    A. 0   **B.** 1   **C.** −1   **D.** 3

13. Which line has the greater slope, *A* or *B*?

Line *A*: $y = 3x + 5$

Line *B*: $-4x + y = 6$

    A. Line *A*   **B.** Line *B*   **C.** Line *A* and Line *B* have the same slope.

    D. The slopes of Lines *A* and *B* cannot be determined.

14. The table below shows several points that lie on some line, *L*. What is the slope of line *L*?

x	−2	−1	0	1	2
y	5	3	1	−1	−3

    A. −2   **B.** 2   **C.** $\dfrac{1}{2}$ **D.** $-\dfrac{1}{2}$

Answers

1. **C**	4. **D**	7. **B**	10. **C**	13. **B**
2. **C**	5. **D**	8. **D**	11. **B**	14. **A**
3. **D**	6. **A**	9. **D**	12. **B**	

Answer Explanations

1. **C**   Line D can be eliminated from consideration because it is negative. Line C is clearly steeper than line A and line B.

2. **C**   The lines are parallel and therefore have the same slope.

3. **D**   The line shown is horizontal, not vertical.

4. **D**   The slope of the line is negative since it falls from left to right. The slope can be determined from the graph by noting that the line falls 1 unit for every 2 units it "runs" to the right. Therefore:

$$m = \frac{\text{rise}}{\text{run}} = \frac{-1}{2} = -\frac{1}{2}$$

5. **D**   Using the slope formula, substitute 2 for m, 2 for x_1, 4 for y_1, 5 for x_2, and k for y_2. Then, solve for k.

$$m = \frac{y_2 - y_1}{x_2 - x_1} \longrightarrow 2 = \frac{k-4}{5-2}$$

$$2 = \frac{k-4}{3}$$

$$6 = k - 4$$

$$10 = k$$

6. **A**   Using the slope formula, substitute -3 for x_1, 1 for y_1, 6 for x_2, and -2 for y_2. Then, solve for m.

$$m = \frac{y_2 - y_1}{x_2 - x_1} \longrightarrow m = \frac{-2-1}{6-(-3)}$$

$$= \frac{-3}{9}$$

$$= -\frac{1}{3}$$

The slope is $-\dfrac{1}{3}$.

7. **B**   The equation $y = 2x - 5$ is in slope-intercept form ($y = mx + b$), so the slope, m, is 2.

8. **D**   The equation $x + 2y = 7$ is in standard form and must be converted to the slope-intercept form by solving for y.

Add $-x$ to both sides: $-x + x + 2y = -x + 7$

Simplify: $2y = -x + 7$

Divide both sides by 2: $\dfrac{2y}{2} = \dfrac{-x + 7}{2}$

Split the fraction: $y = \dfrac{-1}{2}x + \dfrac{7}{2}$

The slope is $-\dfrac{1}{2}$.

9. **D**   Any two points on a line can be used to calculate its slope.

10. **C**   The difference in y-values must be in the numerator, and the difference in x-values must be in the denominator.

11. **B**   If a line does not intersect the y-axis, the line must be vertical. The slope of a vertical line is not defined.

12. **B**   A line that intersects the x-axis at 3 contains the point $(3, 0)$. A line that intersects the y-axis at -3 contains the point $(0, -3)$. Use the slope formula:

$$m = \frac{-3 - 0}{0 - 3} = \frac{-3}{-3} = 1$$

13. **B**   The slope of line A is 3 because the equation is in the form $y = mx + b$, where $m = 3$. The equation of line B can be solved for y.

$$-4x + y = 6$$

Add $4x$ to both sides: $4x + -4x + y = 4x + 6$

Simplify: $y = 4x + 6$

Therefore, the slope of line B is 4. Since $4 > 3$, the slope of line B is greater than the slope of line A.

14. **A**   Choosing any two points, for example, $(-2, 5)$ and $(-1, 3)$, use the slope formula:

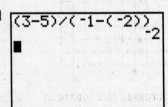

$$m = \frac{3 - 5}{-1 - (-2)} = \frac{-2}{-1 + 2} = \frac{-2}{1} = -2$$

2.7 Finding *x*- and *y*-Intercepts

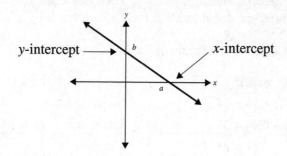

- The ***x*-intercept** of a line is the point where the line crosses the *x*-axis.
- The ***y*-intercept** of a line is the point where the line crosses the *y*-axis.

In the figure above:

The *x*-intercept is *a* or the point (*a*, 0).
The *y*-intercept is *b* or the point (0, *b*).

You can identify *x*- and *y*-intercepts from a graph, from an equation, or from a table of values. These three methods for determining intercepts are explained below.

A. From a Graph

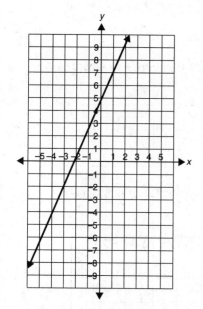 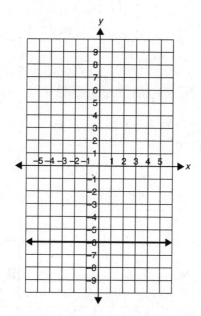 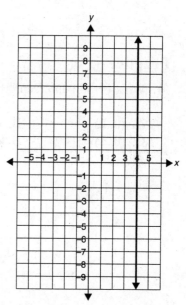

This line crosses the *x*-axis at −2. Its *x*-intercept can be written as −2 or (−2, 0).

The *y*-intercept is 5 or (0, 5) because the line crosses the *y*-axis at 5.

This line is horizontal and has no *x*-intercept. Its *y*-intercept is −6 or (0, −6).

This line is vertical. It has no *y*-intercept. Its *x*-intercept is 4 or (4, 0).

B. From an Equation

- To find the x-intercept, substitute 0 for y. Then, solve for x.
- To find the y-intercept, substitute 0 for x. Then, solve for y.

Example: Find the x- and y-intercepts of the line $3x - 4y = 24$.

For the x-intercept (set $y = 0$):

Given equation:	$3x - 4y = 24$
Substitute:	$3x - 4(0) = 24$
Simplify:	$3x = 24$
Solve for x:	$x = 8$

The x-intercept is 8 or (8, 0).

For the y-intercept (set $x = 0$):

Given equation:	$3x - 4y = 24$
Substitute:	$3(0) - 4y = 24$
Simplify:	$-4y = 24$
Solve for y:	$y = -6$

The y-intercept is −6 or (0, −6).

> **Remember:**
> $y = 0$ for the x-intercept and $x = 0$ for the y-intercept.

C. From a Table of Values

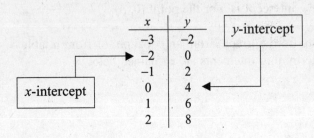

Sometimes you can find the x- and y-intercepts from a table of values. Look for the number 0.

The y-intercept is 4 (because $x = 0$ at this point).

The x-intercept is −2 (because $y = 0$ at this point).

Practice

1. What is the y-intercept of the line that is graphed?

   A. (0, 2) **B.** (2, 0)

   C. (0, 1) **D.** (1, 0)

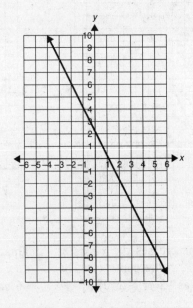

2. Which equation would graph as a line that has no x-intercept?

   A. $y = 2$ **B.** $x = 1$ **C.** $x + y = 1$ **D.** $y = 5x - 2$

3. What is the y-intercept of the line that contains the points shown in the table?

x	−4	−2	0	2	4
y	0	−3	−6	−9	−12

    A. −4   **B.** −6
    C. 0   **D.** The line has no y-intercept.

4. If the y-intercept of a line is 3, the graph of this line would contain which point?

    A. (0, 3)   **B.** (3, 3)   **C.** (3, 0)   **D.** (0, 0)

5. The y-intercept of the line $y = 2x - 4$ is—

    A. 2   **B.** 4   **C.** −4   **D.** (2, −4)

6. The x-intercept of the line $y = 2x - 4$ is—

    A. (2, 0)   **B.** (2, −4)   **C.** (0, −4)   **D.** (−4, 0)

7. A line that has an x-intercept of 2 and a y-intercept of 2 *must* have a slope of—

    A. 2   **B.** −2   **C.** 1   **D.** −1

8. If a line has an x-intercept of 0 and a y-intercept of 0, then the line *must*—

    A. contain the origin   **B.** be vertical
    C. be horizontal   **D.** have a slope of 0

9. The line $3x - 2y = 6$ has the x-intercept—

    A. 3   **B.** 2   **C.** −3   **D.** −2

10. The y-intercept of the line $3x - 2y = 6$ is—

    A. (2, 0)   **B.** (0, 3)   **C.** (0, −3)   **D.** (0, −2)

11. A line that has a positive slope and does *not* contain the origin will have x- and y-intercepts that are—

    A. both positive   **B.** both negative
    C. oppositely signed   **D.** both 0

12. A line that has an x-intercept of −1 and a y-intercept of 2 has the equation—

    A. $y = 2x + 2$ **B.** $y = -x + 2$ **C.** $y = 2x - 1$ **D.** $-x + 2y = 0$

Answers

1. **A**	4. **A**	7. **D**	10. **C**
2. **A**	5. **C**	8. **A**	11. **C**
3. **B**	6. **A**	9. **B**	12. **A**

Answer Explanations

1. **A**   The graph crosses the vertical axis (*y*-axis) at 2, so the *y*-intercept is (0, 2).

2. **A**   Horizontal lines (other than the *x*-axis itself) do not have *x*-intercepts. The equation $y = 2$ graphs as a horizontal line.

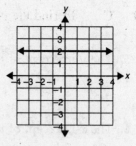

3. **B**   A *y*-intercept always has an *x*-coordinate of 0. The *y*-intercept is −6.

x	−4	−2	0	2	4
y	0	−3	−6	−9	−12

4. **A**   When the graph of an equation has a *y*-intercept of 3, the line must contain the point (0, 3).

5. **C**   Find the *y*-intercept by substituting 0 for *x* in the given equation:

$$y = 2x - 4$$
$$= 2(0) - 4$$
$$= -4$$

6. **A**   Find the *x*-intercept by substituting 0 for *y* in the given equation.

$$y = 2x - 4$$
$$0 = 2x - 4$$
$$4 = 2x$$
$$x = 2$$

An *x*-intercept of 2 is also written as (2, 0).

7. **D**   If a line has an *x*-intercept of 2 and a *y*-intercept of 2, it contains the points (2, 0) and (0, 2). Use the slope formula and the two given points:

$$m = \frac{-2 - 0}{0 - 2} = \frac{-2}{-2} = -1$$

8. **A**   A line that has *x*- and *y*-intercepts of 0 contains the point (0, 0), which is the origin.

9. **B**   To find the x-intercept of $3x - 2y = 6$, substitute 0 for y:

$$3x - 2y = 6$$
$$3x - 2(0) = 6$$
$$3x = 6$$
$$x = 2$$

10. **C**   To find the y-intercept of $3x - 2y = 6$, substitute 0 for x.

$$3x - 2y = 6$$
$$3(0) - 2y = 6$$
$$-2y = 6$$
$$y = -3$$

If the y-intercept is -3, then the line contains the point $(0, -3)$.

11. **C**   There are two possibilities for a line that has a positive slope and does not contain the origin (see graph). Either way, the x- and y-intercepts will have opposite signs (one positive, one negative).

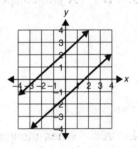

12. **A**   A line that has an x-intercept of -1 and a y-intercept of 2 must contain the points $(-1, 0)$ and $(0, 2)$. Use the slope formula:

$$m = \frac{2-0}{0-(-1)} = \frac{2}{1} = 2$$

Since the y-intercept is 2, use $y = mx + b$ to write the equation of the line: $y = 2x + 2$.

2.8 Graphing Linear Equations

The graph of an equation is a picture of all the points that satisfy that equation. *Linear equations* graph as *lines*. To graph a linear equation, just find two points that satisfy the equation and then connect the points with a straight line.

Linear equations can be written in slope-intercept form or in standard form. Identifying the form in which an equation is written will help you decide which method you should use to graph the line.

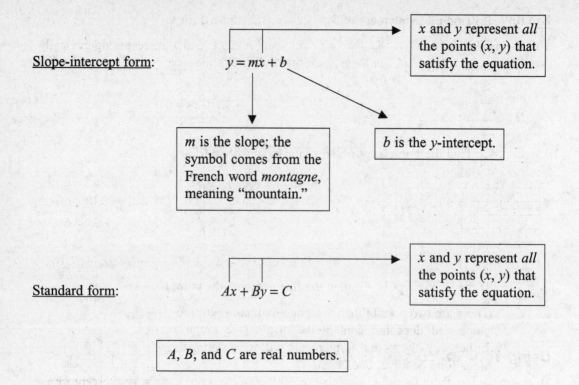

Slope-intercept form: $y = mx + b$

x and y represent *all* the points (x, y) that satisfy the equation.

m is the slope; the symbol comes from the French word *montagne*, meaning "mountain."

b is the y-intercept.

Standard form: $Ax + By = C$

x and y represent *all* the points (x, y) that satisfy the equation.

A, B, and C are real numbers.

Example 1: Graph $y = 2x - 3$.

This line is in slope-intercept form, $y = mx + b$. The y-intercept is one point on the line. Use the slope to find a second point.

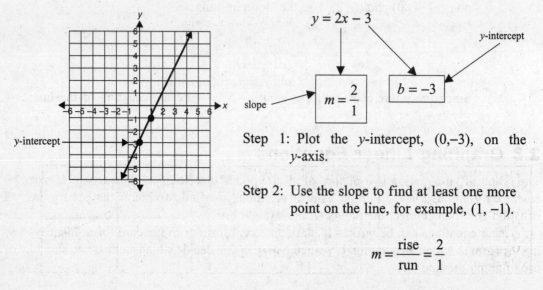

$y = 2x - 3$

y-intercept

slope

$m = \dfrac{2}{1}$

$b = -3$

Step 1: Plot the y-intercept, (0,−3), on the y-axis.

Step 2: Use the slope to find at least one more point on the line, for example, (1, −1).

$$m = \frac{\text{rise}}{\text{run}} = \frac{2}{1}$$

Step 3: Connect the points with a straight line.

Example 2: Graph $2x + 3y = 6$.

This line is in standard form, $Ax + By = C$. You can find its x- and y-intercepts algebraically (see Section 2.7), and then use these coordinates to graph the line.

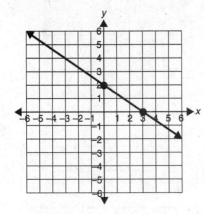

$$\boxed{2x + 3y = 6}$$

Step 1: Find the intercepts:

Let $x = 0$.	Let $y = 0$.
$2(0) + 3y = 6$	$2x + 3(0) = 6$
$3y = 6$	$2x = 6$
$y = 2$	$x = 3$
The y-intercept is $(0, 2)$.	The x-intercept is $(3, 0)$.

Step 2: Plot the intercepts, $(0, 2)$ and $(3, 0)$, and connect them with a straight line.

Using Your Calculator to Graph a Line

To graph the line from Example 2 on your calculator, first write it in slope-intercept form, $y = mx + b$.

$2x + 3y = 6$	Given equation
$3y = -2x + 6$	Add $-2x$ to both sides.
$\dfrac{3y}{3} = \dfrac{-2x + 6}{3}$	Divide both sides by 3.
$y = \dfrac{-2}{3}x + 2$	Split the fraction, and simplify.

Now you can graph the equation on your calculator!

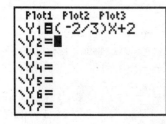

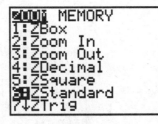

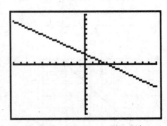

| Step 1 | Step 2 | Step 3 |

Practice

1. Which equation represents the line whose graph is shown?

   A. $y = 2x + 1$ **B.** $y = -2x + 1$
   C. $y = 2x + 2$ **D.** $y = -2x + 2$

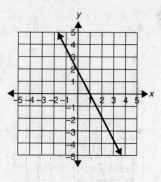

2. Which is the equation of the line graphed?

   A. $2x - 3y = -6$ **B.** $2x + 3y = 6$
   C. $3x + 2y = -6$ **D.** $-3x + 2y = 6$

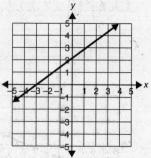

3. Which is the graph of $y = -x + 2$?

   A.

   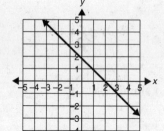

   B.

   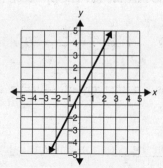

   C.

   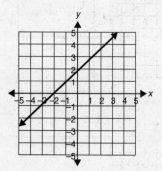

   D.

   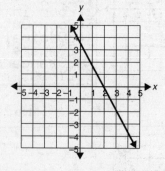

4. Which is the graph of $3x - y = 3$?

A.

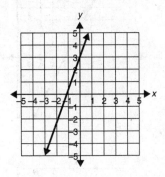

B.

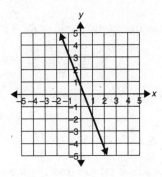

C.

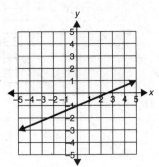

D.

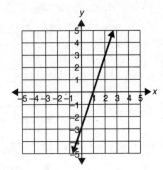

5. Which equation has the same graph as $2x + y = 10$?

    A. $y = 2x - 10$ **B.** $y = -2x + 10$ **C.** $y = -x - 5$ **D.** $y = \frac{1}{2}x + 5$

6. Which line has a y-intercept of -4 and a slope of 2?

A.

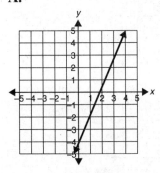

B.

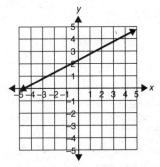

C.

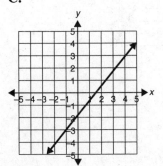

D.

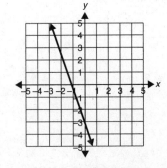

7. Which line contains the same set of points as $y = 3x - 1$?

    A. $3x - y = 1$ **B.** $3x + y = 1$ **C.** $3x - y = -1$ **D.** $x + 3y = 1$

8. Which line has the same slope as $4x + y = 7$?

    A. $x + 4y = 7$ **B.** $4x + y = 8$ **C.** $4x - y = 7$ **D.** $x - 4y = 7$

9. Which line has the same y-intercept as $y = -2x + 5$?

    A. $y = -2x + 6$ **B.** $y = 3x + 5$ **C.** $y = -x + \dfrac{5}{2}$ **D.** $y = -2x - 5$

10. Which line contains the points shown in the table?

x	y
-50	-40
-30	-20
-10	0
10	20
30	40

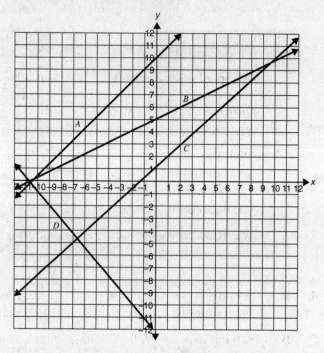

    A. A **B.** B **C.** C **D.** D

11. A line contains the point $(-1, -2)$ and has a slope of $\dfrac{1}{2}$. What is the x-intercept of this line?

    A. -5 **B.** -1.5 **C.** 0 **D.** 3

Answers

1. **D**   4. **D**   6. **A**   8. **B**   10. **A**
2. **A**   5. **B**   7. **A**   9. **B**   11. **D**
3. **A**

Answer Explanations

1. **D**   The graph has a y-intercept of 2 and a slope of -2. Therefore, using $y = mx + b$, the equation is $y = -2x + 2$.

2. **A**   The graph has a y-intercept of 2 and a slope of $\frac{2}{3}$. Therefore, using $y = mx + b$, the equation is $y = \frac{2}{3}x + 2$. Change to standard form:

$$y = \frac{2}{3}x + 2$$

Multiply both sides by 3: $3 \cdot y = 3\left(\frac{2}{3}x + 2\right)$

Distribute: $3y = 2x + 6$
Add -6 to both sides: $-6 + 3y = 2x + 6 + (-6)$
Simplify: $-6 + 3y = 2x$
Add $-3y$ to both sides: $-6 = 2x - 3y$

The equation is $2x - 3y = -6$.

3. **A**   The equation $y = -x + 2$ is in slope-intercept form. Therefore, the slope is -1 and the y-intercept is 2. A is the only graph with a y-intercept of 2 and a slope of -1.

4. **D**   Solving $3x - y = 3$ for y results in the equation $y = 3x - 3$. Therefore, the line has a slope of 3 and a y-intercept of -3, matching graph D.

5. **B**   Solving $2x + y = 10$ for y results in the equation $y = -2x + 10$.

6. **A**   Only graphs A and D have y-intercepts of -4. Only graph A has a slope of 2. Therefore, the answer is A.

7. **A** You need to match an equation to $y = 3x - 1$. Solve choice A, $3x - y = 1$, for y.

$$3x - y = 1$$

Add $-3x$ to both sides:	$-3x + 3x - y = -3x + 1$
Simplify:	$-y = -3x + 1$
Multiply both sides by -1:	$(-1)(-y) = -1(-3x + 1)$
Distribute and simplify:	$y = 3x - 1$

Choice A matches the original equation.

8. **B** Solving $4x + y = 7$ for y results in the equation $y = -4x + 7$, which has a slope of -4. Solving choice B for y results in the equation $y = -4x + 8$, which also has a slope of -4.

9. **B** The line $y = -2x + 5$ has a y-intercept of 5 because it is in the form $y = mx + b$, where b represents the y-intercept. Choice B has the equation $y = 3x + 5$, which also has a y-intercept of 5.

10. **A** You can find the slope, m, of the line from the table:

$$m = \frac{40 - 20}{30 - 10} = \frac{20}{20} = 1$$

Only lines A and C have slope 1, so choices B and D can be eliminated. From the table, you can also see that the line has x-intercept $(-10, 0)$. Since choice C has x-intercept $(-1, 0)$; choice A must be the correct answer.

11. **D** Find the answer by using graph paper! Plot the point $(-1, -2)$. Then, using the given slope, $\frac{1}{2}$, you can "rise 1" and "run 2" twice, landing on the x-axis at 3.

2.9 Graphing Linear Inequalities in Two Variables

The graph of an inequality is a picture representing all the points that satisfy that inequality. To graph a *linear inequality*, you must graph a line that divides the xy-plane into two parts and then shade either above that line or below it. The shaded region represents all the points that satisfy the inequality.

Examples 1 and 2 will help you understand how to graph a linear inequality.

Steps

1. Convert the inequality to slope-intercept form. This tells you the "boundary line" for your graph.

2. Graph the boundary line as either a solid or a dashed line according to this rule:

   • < and >, line will be **dashed**.
   • ≤ and ≥, line will be **solid**.

3. a. Choose any point *not* on the boundary line to use as a test point. Label its coordinates on your graph.

   b. Substitute the test point into the given inequality, and simplify.

4. *Shade* your graph.

Notice that, in the true result for Example 1, the test point lies in the shaded region. In the false result of Example 2, the test point lies outside the shaded region.

Example 1:

Graph $2x + y \leq 5$.

$$y \leq -2x + 5$$

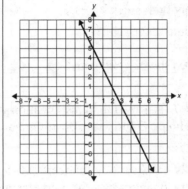

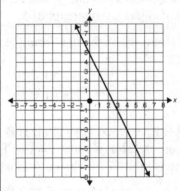

Test point: (0, 0)

$$2x + y \leq 5$$
$$2(0) + 0 \leq 5$$
$$0 \leq 5 \quad \text{TRUE}$$

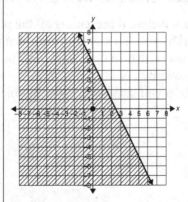

Test point *worked*!
Shade to include test point.

Example 2:

Graph $2y > x$.

$$y > \frac{1}{2}x$$

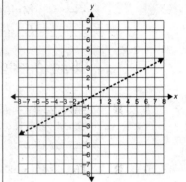

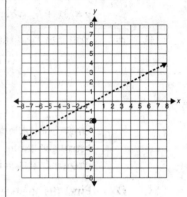

Test point: (0, −2)

$$2y > x$$
$$2(-2) > 0$$
$$-4 > 0 \quad \text{FALSE}$$

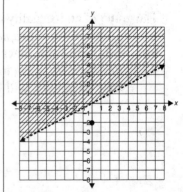

Test point *failed*!
Shade away from test point.

Practice

1. Which graph correctly represents the solution region for $3x + y \leq 4$?

A.

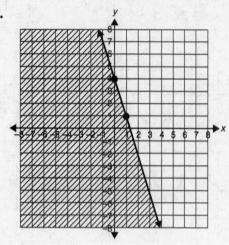

B.

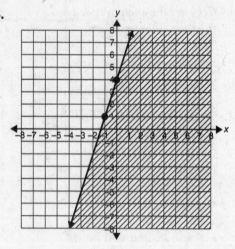

C.

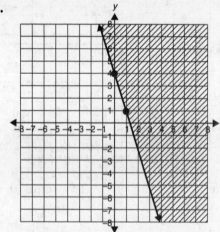

D.

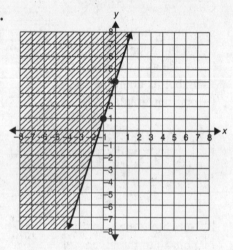

Use the graph to answer questions 2 and 3.

2. Which point does *not* satisfy the inequality whose graph is shown?

    A. (0, 0)   **B.** (−1, 0)
    C. (0, 1)   **D.** (1, 2)

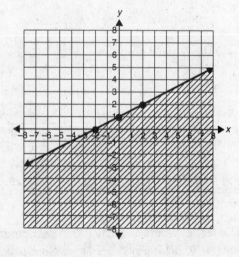

3. Which inequality is represented by the graph?

    A. $y > 2x + 1$ **B.** $y \geq \dfrac{1}{2}x + 1$ **C.** $y \leq \dfrac{1}{2}x + 1$ **D.** $y \leq 2x + 1$

4. Which is the correct graph for $x - y > 0$?

A.

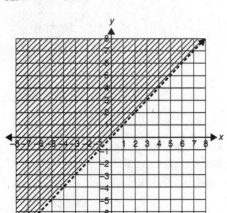

B.

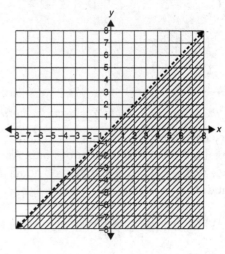

C.

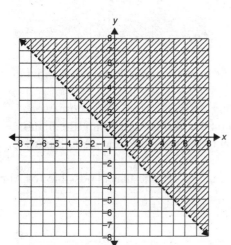

D.

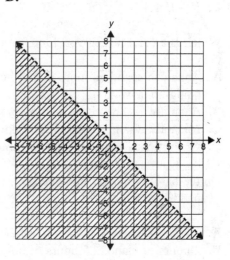

5. Which inequality symbol will produce a boundary line that is dashed, *not* solid?

A. $\leq$ **B.** $\geq$ **C.** $\neq$ **D.** $<$

6. Steve loves to eat Twix and Kit Kat. Suppose an ordered pair (T, K) on the graph represents a Twix/Kit Kat combo that Steve might eat on any given day. Let T = the number of Twix bars, and K = the number of Kit Kat bars. Assume the scale is the same on both axes. Because the shaded region is *below* the boundary line, you know that—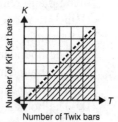

A. Steve always eats more Twix than Kit Kat
B. Steve always eats more Kit Kat than Twix
C. Steve always eats equal numbers of Twix and Kit Kat
D. Steve eats candy and no other food ever

7. Which inequality correctly represents the graph?

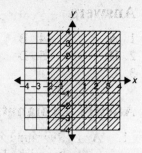

A. $x > 2$ **B.** $x > -2$
C. $y > -2$ **D.** $y \leq -2$

Use the graph and the following information to answer questions 8–11.

Every day after school, Anna has to do her homework and practice the piano. Let P = the number of hours Anna spends practicing the piano, and let H = the number of hours Anna spends doing her homework.

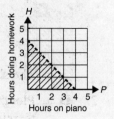

8. Which inequality properly represents the graph?

    A. $4P + 4H \leq 0$ **B.** $P \leq H$
    C. $H + P \leq 4$ **D.** $P \leq H + 4$

9. Which is a correct real-world interpretation of the graph?

    A. Anna can spend no more than 4 hours of total time practicing the piano and doing homework.
    B. Anna always spends more time practicing the piano than doing homework.
    C. Anna always spends more time doing homework than practicing the piano.
    D. Anna spends equal amounts of time practicing the piano and doing homework.

10. On the basis of the graph, which is a combination of time that is possible for Anna to spend?

    A. 1 hour of piano, 4 hours of homework
    B. 2 hours of piano, 2.5 hours of homework
    C. 3 hours of homework, 0 hours of piano
    D. 4 hours of homework, 4 hours of piano.

11. Anna also rows crew. Once the crew season was over, Anna increased the maximum number of hours she could spend on homework. The maximum time she spent practicing piano remained unchanged. How would the boundary line on the graph have to change to reflect these facts?

    A. The boundary line would become dashed.
    B. The boundary line would become vertical.
    C. The boundary line would move parallel to itself.
    D. The boundary line would become steeper.

Answers

1. **A**	4. **B**	6. **A**	8. **C**	10. **C**
2. **D**	5. **D**	7. **B**	9. **A**	11. **D**
3. **C**				

Answer Explanations

1. **A** Rewriting $3x + y \le 4$ in slope-intercept form, $y \le -3x + 4$, shows that the boundary line has a negative slope, so the answer cannot be choice B or D. Test the point $(0, 0)$:

$$3(0) + 0 \le 4$$
$$0 \le 4 \quad ✔$$

The shading needs to cover the point $(0, 0)$ as in choice A.

2. **D** Plot the point $(1, 2)$, and you find that it does not lie in the shaded region and therefore does not satisfy the inequality.

3. **C** The boundary line has a slope of $\dfrac{1}{2}$ and a y-intercept of 1, so the answer cannot be choice A or D. Since the point $(0, 0)$ lies in the shaded region, it must satisfy the correct inequality. Test choice C:

$$y \le \frac{1}{2}x + 1$$
$$0 \le \frac{1}{2}(0) + 1$$
$$0 \le 1 \quad ✔$$

4. **B** Rewriting $x - y > 0$ in slope-intercept form $(y < x)$ shows a positive slope, so the answer cannot be choice C or D. Test a point such as $(2, 0)$:

$$x - y > 0$$
$$2 - 0 > 0$$
$$2 > 0 \quad ✔$$

Therefore, the point $(2, 0)$ should be included in the shaded region. The correct answer must be choice B.

5. **D** Boundary lines are dashed when either $<$ or $>$ is used.

6. **A** Pick a sample point (T, K) in the shaded region, for example, the point $(3, 2)$. Here, $T = 3$ and $K = 2$. Since $T =$ the number of Twix bars (3) and $K =$ the number of Kit Kat bars (2), you can see that Steve eats more Twix than Kit Kat. For every point (T, K) in the shaded region, T will be greater than K, so Steve always eats more Twix bars than Kit Kat.

7. **B**   The boundary line is a vertical line with the equation $x = -2$. The test point, $(0, 0)$, lies in the shaded region and satisfies choice B, $x > -2$, because $0 > -2$.

8. **C**   The boundary line has the equation $y = -x + 4$. In this case, x is represented by P and y is represented by H. Substituting into the boundary equation gives $H = -P + 4$. Rewriting gives $H + P = 4$. Choice C has this boundary equation. Test a point from the shaded region, for example $(2, 1)$, to see that the inequality $H + P \leq 4$ holds true:

$$H + P \leq 4$$
$$2 + 1 \leq 4$$
$$3 \leq 4$$

9. **A**   Since the correct inequality is $H + P \leq 4$, the total number of hours that Anna can spend on homework and on the piano is less than or equal to 4.

10. **C**   Since the number of total hours spent on homework and piano must be less than or equal to 4 (see question 9), the only combination that satisfies this inequality is $(P, H) = (0, 3)$. Additionally, this point lies in the shaded region.

11. **D**   If Anna could increase her maximum time spent on homework but not on piano, the y-intercept would increase while the x-intercept would remain unchanged. Thus, the boundary line would become steeper.

2.10 Writing Equations of Lines

Every line can be described by an *equation*. This is important because, if you have an equation for a line, you can draw its graph. You can also use the equation to determine whether any particular point lies on that line. An equation is an algebraic way of representing all the points that lie on a given line.

As you have learned, a line can be written in *standard* form, $Ax + By = C$, or in *slope-intercept* form, $y = mx + b$. Slope-intercept form is generally the easier one to use when writing an equation of a line. To write an equation in this form, you need two pieces of information about the line:

- Its slope, m.
- Its y-intercept, b.

Examples 1–6 show how to write an equation of a line given any of the following:

- The graph of the line.
- The slope and a point on the line.
- Two arbitrary points on the line.

A. Writing an Equation from a Graph of a Line

Example 1: Write the equation of the line shown.

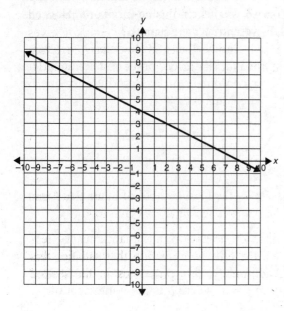

Step 1: Find the slope using any two points on the line

$$m = \frac{\text{rise}}{\text{run}} = \frac{-2}{4} = -\frac{1}{2}.$$

Step 2: Find the y-intercept, $b = 4$, or the point $(0, 4)$.

Step 3: Substitute these values for m and b into $y = mx + b$:

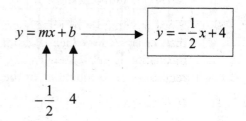

$$y = mx + b \longrightarrow \boxed{y = -\frac{1}{2}x + 4}$$

$$-\frac{1}{2} \qquad 4$$

Example 2: Write the equation of the line shown.

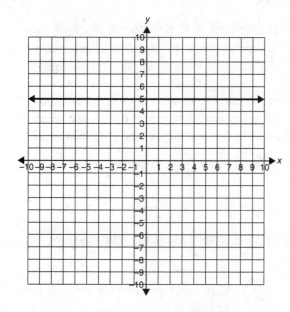

• The slope is zero, $m = 0$.
• The y-intercept is 5, $b = 5$.

Substitute these values for m and b into $y = mx + b$:

$$y = 0x + 5 \longrightarrow \boxed{y = 5}$$

Example 3: Write the equation of the line shown.

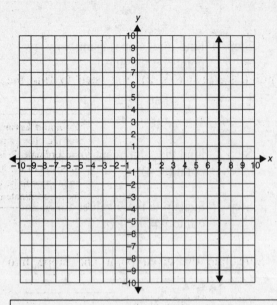

This line has no slope and no y-intercept, so you have no value for m or b. How can you write the equation?

Notice that every point on the line has an x-coordinate of 7. Describe this line by the equation $x = 7$.

$$x = 7$$

All horizontal lines have equations of the form **$y = b$**, where b is the y-intercept of the line.

All vertical lines have equations of the form **$x = a$**, where a is the x-intercept of the line.

B. Writing an Equation Given the Slope and a Point on a Line

Example 4: Find an equation for the line that has slope $\frac{1}{3}$ and contains the point $(-3, 2)$. There are two ways to solve this problem.

Method 1: Find the equation by graphing. *Use graph paper!*

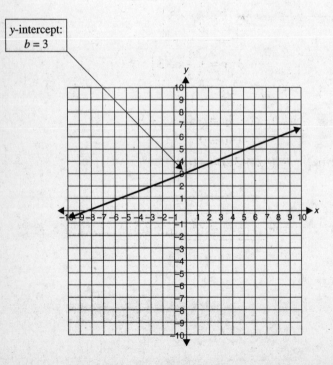

y-intercept: $b = 3$

Step 1: Plot the given point $(-3, 2)$.

Step 2: Use the slope, $m = \frac{1}{3}$ ("rise" 1, "run" 3) to find more points on the line.

Step 3: Carefully draw the line through the points.

Step 4: Find the y-intercept of the line by reading your graph.

Step 5: Write the equation of the line.

$$y = \frac{1}{3}x + 3$$

Sometimes graphing is not an easy method to use. In that case, use algebraic techniques as shown in Method 2.

Method 2:   Find the equation algebraically.

You are given the slope $\left(m = \dfrac{1}{3} \right)$ and a point, $(x, y) = (-3, 2)$. You need to find the y-intercept.

$$\left. \begin{array}{l} m = \dfrac{1}{3} \\[2mm] x = -3 \\[1mm] y = 2 \end{array} \right\} \longrightarrow y = mx + b$$

> **Common Error Alert!**
> For the ordered pair $(-3, 2)$, the y-coordinate, 2, is *not* the y-intercept of the line. For the y-coordinate to be the y-intercept, the x-coordinate must be 0.

$2 = \dfrac{1}{3}(-3) + b$ Step 1: Substitute the given point and slope into $y = mx + b$.

$2 = -1 + b$ Step 2: Solve the equation for b.

$3 = b$ Step 3: Write the equation of the line using slope-intercept form.

$$\boxed{y = \dfrac{1}{3}x + 3}$$

Although it is easier to write equations using slope-intercept form, some problems will ask you to put the final answer in standard form.

Example 5: Write the equation $y = \dfrac{1}{3}x + 3$ in standard form, $Ax + By = C$.

Slope intercept form $\longrightarrow$ $\boxed{y = \dfrac{1}{3}x + 3}$

Step 1:   Multiply both sides by 3 to clear the fraction: $3 \cdot y = 3\left(\dfrac{1}{3}x + 3 \right)$

$3y = x + 9$

Step 2:   Add $-x$ to both sides $(-x) + 3y = (-x) + x + 9$

$-x + 3y = 9$

Step 3:   Since the coefficient of the x-term is negative, multiply both sides by -1: $-1(-x + 3y) = -1(9)$

$x - 3y = -9$

Standard form $\longrightarrow$ $\boxed{x - 3y = -9}$

C. Writing an Equation Given Two Points on a Line

This is a little harder than the preceding problem because you have to find both the *y*-intercept *and* the slope.

Example 6: Find the equation of the line that contains the points (2, 9) and (−2, 3).

Again, there are two methods you can use to solve this problem.

Method 1: Algebraically

Step 1: Find the slope using the slope formula:

$$m = \frac{y_2 - y_1}{x_2 - x_1}$$

$$\underbrace{(2, 9)}_{(x_1, y_1)} \quad \underbrace{(-2, 3)}_{(x_2, y_2)}$$

$$= \frac{3-9}{-2-2} = \frac{-6}{-4} = \frac{3}{2}$$

Step 2: Find the *y*-intercept by substituting the slope and either of the two given points into $y = mx + b$:

$$9 = \frac{3}{2}(2) + b \qquad \text{Substitute (2, 9).}$$

$$9 = 3 + b \qquad \text{Solve for } b.$$
$$6 = b$$

Step 3: Write the equation using slope-intercept form, $y = mx + b$.

$$\boxed{y = \frac{3}{2}x + 6}$$

Method 2: Graphically

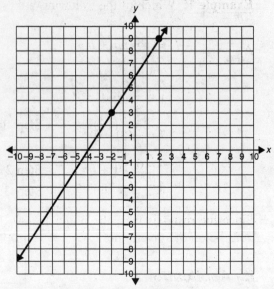

Step 1: Carefully graph the two given points on graph paper.

Step 2: Draw the line through the two points.

Step 3: Now find the slope and the *y*-intercept from the graph:

$$\text{Slope, } m = \frac{\text{rise}}{\text{run}} = \frac{6}{4} = \frac{3}{2}$$

y-intercept, $b = 6$

Step 4: Write the equation using slope-intercept form, $y = mx + b$.

$$\boxed{y = \frac{3}{2}x + 6}$$

D. Determining Whether a Point Lies on a Given Line

You can use an equation of a line to see which points lie on the line and which points do not. Just substitute the given point into the equation, simplify, and see whether the result is true or false.

- A TRUE result means the point *does* lie on the line.
- A FALSE result means the point does *not* lie on the line.

Example 7: Which of the following points lies on the line $y = \frac{3}{4}x - 10$?

| | Determining whether a point lies on a line is the same procedure as deciding whether a point "satisfies" an equation. See Section 2.1. |

A.   (8, −4)

$$y = \frac{3}{4}x - 10$$

$$-4 = \frac{3}{4}(8) - 10$$

$$-4 = 6 - 10$$

$$-4 = -4 \quad \text{TRUE} \quad ☺$$

Since the result is true, the point (8, −4) *does* lie on the given line.

B.   (4, −6)

$$y = \frac{3}{4}x - 10$$

$$-6 = \frac{3}{4}(4) - 10$$

$$-6 = 3 - 10$$

$$-6 = -7 \quad \text{FALSE} \quad ☹$$

Since the result is false, the point (8, −4) does *not* lie on the given line.

E. Applications

Many real-life problems can be modeled and solved using an equation of a line. Cost problems, in particular, lend themselves nicely to this approach. Whether to use slope-intercept or standard form depends on the type of information given in the problem, as illustrated below.

Slope-intercept form: $y = mx + b$

This form is great when only *one* type of item is being bought/sold.

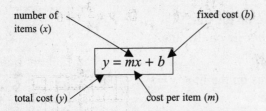

Example 8: To earn a little extra money, Angela goes to people's houses after school to take care of their dogs while they are at work. For each visit to a person's house, she charges $5 plus an additional $1.50 for each dog she has to walk.

A. Write an equation to model the amount Angela charges for a visit.

$$y = mx + b$$

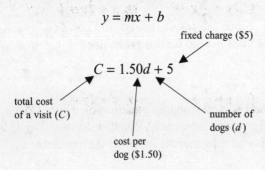

B. How much would Angela charge for one visit to a house that had three dogs?

$$C = 1.50d + 5$$
$$= 1.50(3) + 5 \quad \text{(3 dogs means } d = 3\text{)}$$
$$= 9.50$$

Angela would charge $9.50.

Standard form: $Ax + By = C$

This form is great when *two* different kinds of items are being bought/sold.

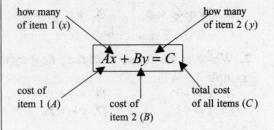

Example 9: Nick takes care of people's animals after school. He charges $1.50 for each dog he walks. He charges $0.50 for each cat he cares for (cats are easier!). On Monday, he earned $13.00 by taking care of animals.

A. Write an equation to model Nick's earnings on Monday.

$$Ax + By = C$$

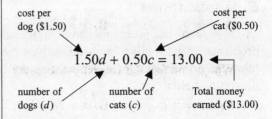

B. If Nick walked seven dogs on Monday, how many cats did he take care of?

$$1.50d + 0.50c = 13.00$$
$$1.50(7) + 0.50c = 13.00 \quad \text{(7 dogs means } d = 7\text{)}$$
$$10.50 + 0.50c = 13.00$$
$$0.50c = 2.50$$
$$c = 5$$

Nick took care of 5 cats.

Practice

1. Which is a correct equation for the line that has slope $\frac{3}{4}$ and y-intercept 6?

   A. $3x + 4y = 6$ **B.** $y = \frac{3}{4}x - 6$ **C.** $x + \frac{3}{4}y = 6$ **D.** $y = \frac{3}{4}x + 6$

2. Which is the equation of the line graphed?

   A. $x = -3$ **B.** $x + y = -3$
   C. $y = -3$ **D.** $y = -3x$

   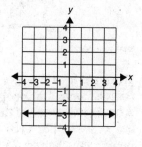

3. If a line has slope $\frac{1}{2}$ and x-intercept 4, which is a correct equation for the line?

   A. $y = \frac{1}{2}x + 4$ **B.** $y = \frac{1}{2}x - 2$ **C.** $y = \frac{1}{2}x - 8$ **D.** $x + 2y = 4$

4. Which line has the greatest slope?

   A. $y = 0$ **B.** $y = x$ **C.** $y = \frac{1}{2}x$ **D.** $x + 2y = 0$

5. Which line has the largest y-intercept?

   A. $x + y = 1$ **B.** $x + 2y = 1$ **C.** $x + 3y = 1$ **D.** $x - 4y = 1$

6. The equation of a *vertical* line always takes on which form?

   A. $x =$ some number   **B.** $y =$ some number
   C. $x + y =$ some number   **D.** $y = mx + b$

7. Which is a correct equation for the line that contains the points $(0, 2)$ and $(102, -100)$?

   A. $y = 2x + 2$ **B.** $y = -x + 2$
   C. $102x - 100y = 0$ **D.** $x + 2y = -4$

8. Which is a correct equation for the line graphed?

   A. $2x + 3y = 0$ **B.** $2x = 3y$

   C. $y = \frac{2}{3}x + 3$ **D.** $y = -\frac{3}{2}x + 3$

   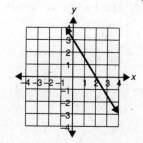

9. If a line has x-intercept $= k$ and y-intercept $= k$, where $k \neq 0$, its equation could be written as—

   A. $y = k$ **B.** $x + y = k$ **C.** $y = kx$ **D.** $kx + ky = 0$

10. A line has a slope of $\dfrac{5}{7}$ and contains the point $(14, -10)$. Which is the correct equations for this line?

   A. $y = \dfrac{5}{7}x - 10$ **B.** $y = -\dfrac{5}{7}x + 10$ **C.** $y = \dfrac{5}{7}x - 20$ **D.** $y = -\dfrac{5}{7}x + 20$

11. A line has a slope of $-\dfrac{1}{2}$ and contains the point $(-4, 5)$. What is its y-intercept?

   A. 3   **B.** 5   **C.** 7   **D.** -3

12. A line contains the points $(1, -4)$ and $(-3, 2)$. Which is the correct value to substitute for m when writing the equation of this line in $y = mx + b$ form?

   A. -4 **B.** -1.5 **C.** 1   **D.** $\dfrac{3}{2}$

13. The line $y = \dfrac{1}{2}x - 3$ can be rewritten in standard form as—

   A. $x - 2y = 6$ **B.** $-x + 2y = -6$ **C.** $x + 2y = 6$ **D.** $2x + y = -6$

14. Which equation does *not* have a y-intercept of 2?

   A. $y = -x + 2$ **B.** $2x + 3y = 6$ **C.** $x + 2y = 0$ **D.** $y = 2$

Use the following information to answer questions 15–18.

Beth's parents want her to improve her grades. They agree to give her $5 for showing them her report card and an additional $2.50 for every A or B she receives.

15. If x represents the number of A's and B's that Beth brings home, which equation represents the total sum, S, of money Beth's parents will give her?

   A. $S = (5 + 2.50)x$ **B.** $S = 5x + 2.50$ **C.** $S = 2.50x + 5$ **D.** $S + 5 = 2.50x$

16. If all seven of Beth's grades are A's or B's, how much money will she get from her parents?

   A. $14.50   **B.** $17.50   **C.** $20.00   **D.** $22.50

17. If Beth gets only $15.00, how many of her grades were either A's or B's?

   A. 3   **B.** 4   **C.** 5   **D.** 6

18. Beth's parents decide to get tough and change the deal. She will still get $5.00 for showing them her report card and $2.50 for each A or B she receives. But now *she* will have to pay *them* $3.00 for every C, D, or F! If Beth receives seven grades in all and x of them are A's or B's, which equation represents the amount of money, S, Beth will receive (or pay)?

   A. $S = 5 + 2.50x - 3.00(7 - x)$ B. $S = 5 - 0.50x$
   C. $S = 7.50x + 3.00(7 - x)$ D. $S = 7.50x - 3.00$

Use the following information to answer questions 19 and 20.

Linda is a basketball player. She never makes 3-point shots, but does make 2-point shots and 1-point free throws. Let x = the number of 2-point shots, and y = the number of 1-point free throws.

19. If Linda scored 27 points in her best game ever, which equation properly models the situation?

   A. $x + 2y = 27$ B. $3(x + y) = 27$ C. $2x + y = 27$ D. $y = 3x + 27$

20. Suppose Linda's team scored 47 points in the last game. They missed ALL of their free throws but did make 2-point and 3-point shots from the floor. If the team landed seven 3-point shots, how many 2-point shots did they make?

   A. 10   B. 13   C. 21   D. 26

Answers

1. D	5. A	9. B	13. A	17. B
2. C	6. A	10. C	14. C	18. A
3. B	7. B	11. A	15. C	19. C
4. B	8. D	12. B	16. D	20. B

Answer Explanations

1. **D**   Use $y = mx + b$, where the slope is $m = \dfrac{3}{4}$ and the y-intercept is $b = 6$.

   Therefore, the equation of the line is $y = \dfrac{3}{4}x + 6$.

2. **C**   A horizontal line always has the form $y = b$, where b is the y-intercept. From the graph, the y-intercept is -3. Therefore, the equation is $y = -3$.

3. **B**   Use the form $y = mx + b$, where the slope is $m = \dfrac{1}{2}$. The x-intercept of 4 means that the line contains the point $(4, 0)$. Substitute this information to find the y-intercept, b.

$$y = mx + b$$

$$0 = \frac{1}{2}(4) + b$$

$$0 = 2 + b \longrightarrow b = -2$$

   Therefore, the equation of the line is $y = \dfrac{1}{2}x - 2$.

4. **B**   Write the slope of each of the lines:

Choice A:	$y = 0$	slope $= 0$
Choice B:	$y = x$	slope $= 1$
Choice C:	$y = \dfrac{1}{2}x$	slope $= \dfrac{1}{2}$
Choice D:	Rewrite in slope-intercept form.	
Then	$x + 2y = 0$, same as $y = -\dfrac{1}{2}x$.	slope $= -\dfrac{1}{2}$

   Therefore, choice B, $y = x$, has the largest slope, $m = 1$.

5. **A** Rewrite all the lines in slope-intercept form.

Choice A: $y = -x + 1$ y-intercept = 1

Choice B: $y = -\dfrac{1}{2}x + \dfrac{1}{2}$ y-intercept = $\dfrac{1}{2}$

Choice C: $y = -\dfrac{1}{3}x + \dfrac{1}{3}$ y-intercept = $\dfrac{1}{3}$

Choice D: $y = \dfrac{1}{4}x - \dfrac{1}{4}$ y-intercept = $-\dfrac{1}{4}$

Therefore, choice A, $x + y = 1$, has the largest y-intercept, $b = 1$.

6. **A** The equation of a vertical line always takes on the form $x =$ some number.

7. **B** Use the slope formula with the points (0, 2) and (102, −100):

$$m = \frac{-100 - 2}{102 - 0} = \frac{-102}{102} = -1$$

Choice B, $y = -x + 2$, is the only correct equation for a line with a slope of −1.

8. **D** From the graph, the line contains the points (0, 3) and (2, 0). Use the slope formula:

$$m = \frac{0 - 3}{2 - 0} = \frac{-3}{2}$$

The point (0, 3) indicates a y-intercept of $b = 3$. Use $y = mx + b$, and substitute $-\dfrac{3}{2}$ for m and 3 for b. Then

$$y = -\frac{3}{2}x + 3$$

9. **B** The line contains the points $(k, 0)$ and $(0, k)$. Substitute these values into choice B:

$$x + y = k$$

$k + 0 = k$ $0 + k = k$
$\quad k = k$ $\quad k = k$

Since both points satisfy the equation, choice B is correct.

Alternative solution:

Calculate the slope:
$m = \dfrac{k - 0}{0 - k} = -1$

Only choice B, $x + y = k$, has a slope of −1.

10. **C** Use the form $y = mx + b$, where the slope is $m = \dfrac{5}{7}$ and the point is (14, −10). Substitute this information to find the y-intercept, b:

$$y = mx + b$$
$$-10 = \frac{5}{7}(14) + b$$
$$-10 = 10 + b \longrightarrow b = -20$$

Therefore, the equation of the line is $y = \dfrac{5}{7}x - 20$.

11. **A** Use the form $y = mx + b$, where the slope is $m = -\dfrac{1}{2}$ and the point is (−4, 5). Substitute this information to find the y-intercept, b:

$$y = mx + b$$
$$5 = -\frac{1}{2}(-4) + b$$
$$5 = 2 + b \longrightarrow b = 3$$

The y-intercept of the line is 3.

12. **B** Use the slope formula with the points (1, −4) and (−3, 2):

$$m = \frac{2 - (-4)}{-3 - 1} = \frac{6}{-4} = -1.5$$

Choice B is the correct value, −1.5, to substitute for m.

13. **A** Rewrite the given equation, $y = \dfrac{1}{2}x - 3$, in standard form.

$$y = \frac{1}{2}x - 3$$

Multiply both sides by 2: $\qquad 2 \cdot y = 2\left(\dfrac{1}{2}x - 3\right)$

Distribute: $\qquad\qquad\qquad 2y = x - 6$

Add −x to both sides: $\qquad -x + 2y = -6$

Multiply both sides by −1: $\qquad x - 2y = 6$

The standard form is $x - 2y = 6$.

14. **C** Rewrite choice C in slope-intercept form:

$$x + 2y = 0$$
$$2y = -x$$
$$y = -\frac{1}{2}x$$

This line has a y-intercept of 0, not 2.

15. **C** S represents total earnings, $2.50 is money per grade of A or B, x is the number of A's or B's, and $5 is a fixed amount:

$$S = 2.50x + 5$$

16. **D**   Substitute 7 for x into the equation $S = 2.50x + 5$ from question 15:

$$S = 2.50(7) + 5 = \$22.50$$

17. **B**   Substitute \$15.00 for total earnings (S) in the equation $S = 2.50x + 5$, and solve for x:

$$15 = 2.50x + 5$$
$$10 = 2.50x$$
$$4 = x$$

18. **A**   Beth still earns through the equation $S = 2.50x + 5$. However, now you must subtract the amount she will need to pay her parents. If x represents the number of A's or B's, then $7 - x$ represents the number of grades that are not A's or B's (she has 7 classes). Beth will have to pay her parents \$3.00 for each grade that is not A or B. The amount of money she will receive (or pay) is represented by the equation

> Note: If S were to evaluate as a negative quantity, Beth would have to pay her parents!

$$S = 5 + 2.50x - 3.00(7 - x)$$

19. **C**   The value of each 2-point shot (x) is 2. The value of each 1-point shot (y) is 1. The total number of points is 27. The equation that models this situation is

$$2x + y = 27$$

20. **B**   Seven 3-point goals total 21 points. Let x = the number of 2-point goals. Then the total points scored can be represented by the equation

$$2x + 21 = 47$$
$$2x = 26$$
$$x = 13$$

Therefore, the number of 2-point shots the team made was 13.

2.11 Graphing Linear Functions by Transformations

The equation $y = x$ is the simplest but perhaps the most important of all the linear functions. Because all other linear functions arise from this one, we sometimes refer to $y = x$ as the "granddaddy" of the linear functions.

In this section, we examine how small changes to the granddaddy function, $y = x$, affect its graph and produce new linear functions.

This process is referred to as graphing linear functions *by transformation.*

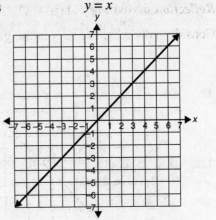

$y = x$

Vertical Shifts

Let's see how adding or subtracting a number from x affects the graph of $y = x$.

$y = x + 1$

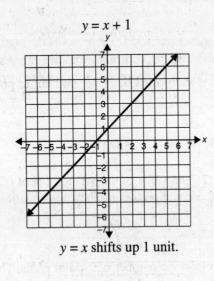

$y = x$ shifts up 1 unit.

$y = x - 2$

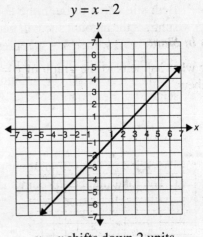

$y = x$ shifts down 2 units.

$y = x + 4$

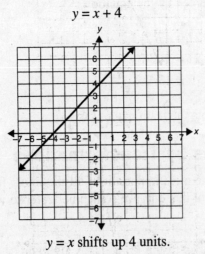

$y = x$ shifts up 4 units.

$y = x - 3$

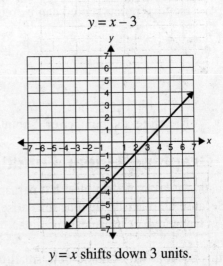

$y = x$ shifts down 3 units.

Given the equation $y = x + b$:

- If $b > 0$, the graph of $y = x$ shifts UP b units.
- If $b < 0$, the graph of $y = x$ shifts DOWN b units.

Reflection across the y-Axis

Consider now what happens to the graph of $y = x$ when x is changed to $-x$.

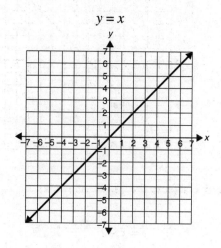

$y = x$

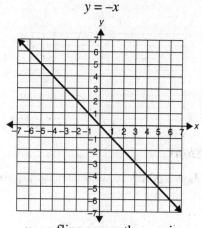

$y = -x$

$y = x$ flips across the y-axis.

Changes in Slant

Consider what happens to the graph of $y = x$ as x is multiplied by larger and larger positive numbers.

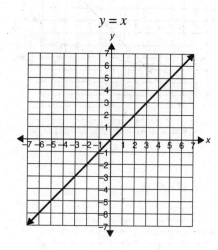

$y = x$

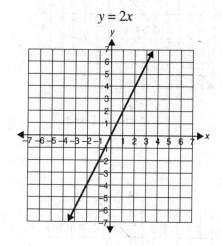

$y = 2x$

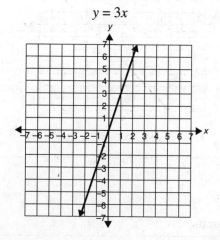

$y = 3x$

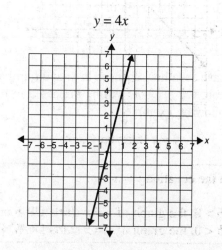

$y = 4x$

Now consider what happens to the graph of $y = x$ as x is multiplied by smaller and smaller fractions.

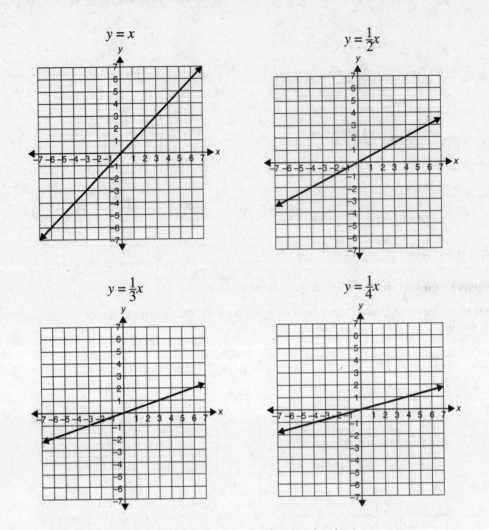

For $m > 0$, the larger the value of m, the steeper the graph of $y = mx$.

Given the equation $y = mx$, with $m > 0$,

- If $m > 1$, the graph of $y = mx$ is STEEPER than the graph of $y = x$.
- If $0 < m < 1$, the graph of $y = mx$ is LESS STEEP than the graph of $y = x$.

You have seen how changes in m and b impact the graph of $y = x$. The graph of *any* linear function, $y = mx + b$, will be impacted in the same way by changes in m or b. Consider the following example.

Example: Given line L whose equation is $y = \frac{1}{2}x + 1$. Changing this equation to

$y = \frac{1}{2}x + 3$ (by adding 2 to the right-hand side) will cause the graph of

$y = \frac{1}{2}x + 1$ to shift up 2 units.

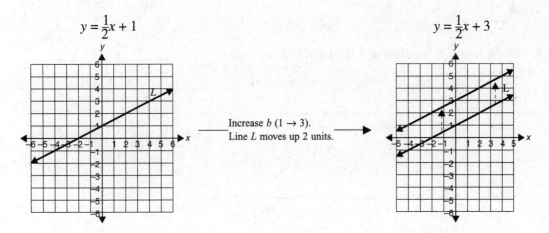

Practice

1. If $f(x) = \frac{1}{2}x$, which is a graph of $y = f(x) + 1$?

A.

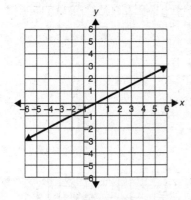

B.

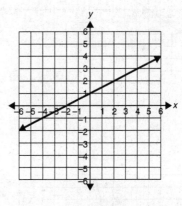

C.

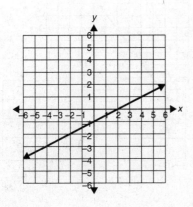

D.

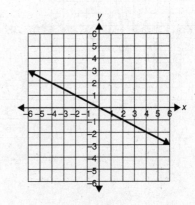

2. If the graph of $y = x$ is shifted down 3 units, which is the equation of the resulting graph?

   A. $y = x + 3$ **B.** $y = 3x$ **C.** $y = -3x$ **D.** $y = x - 3$

3. By how many units must the graph of $y = 4x + 2$ be shifted down to be equivalent to the graph of $y = 4x - 3$?

   A. 4   **B.** 3   **C.** 2   **D.** 5

4. If the line $y = \dfrac{2}{3}x$ shown at the right is made twice as steep, which of the following is the resulting graph?

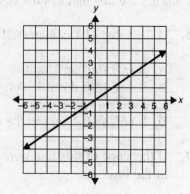

A.

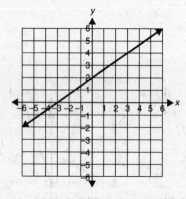

B.

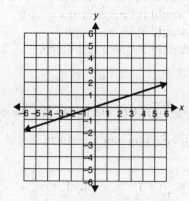

C.

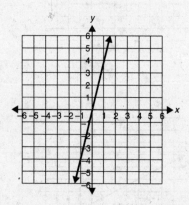

D.

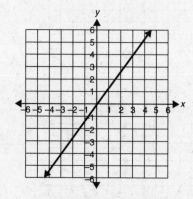

5. For the line $Ax + By = C$, if you doubled the values of A and B but left C alone, what would happen to the graph of the line?

   A. Its slope would double.
   C. Its slope would increase by a factor of 4.
   B. Its slope would be cut in half.
   D. Its slope would not change.

Use the following information for questions 6 and 7.

Consider the line that has the equation $y = 2x + k$.

6. If the value of k is increased by 1, what will happen to the graph of this line?

   A. It will shift up 1 unit.
   B. It will shift down 1 unit.
   C. Its slope will increase.
   D. It will shift 1 unit to the right.

7. If the slope of this line were changed from 2 to 3, what would happen to the graph of the line?

   A. It would become steeper.
   B. It would reflect over the y-axis.
   C. It would shift up 1 unit.
   D. It would become less steep.

---

8. Suppose line A in the figure has the equation $y = \dfrac{4}{3}x$.

   Which equation can transform line A into line B?

   A. $y = \dfrac{1}{3}x + 7$ **B.** $y = -\dfrac{4}{3}x$

   C. $y = \dfrac{4}{3}$ **D.** $y = \dfrac{1}{3}x$

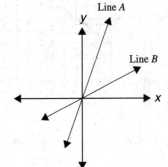

Answers

1. **B**   3. **D**   5. **D**   7. **A**
2. **D**   4. **D**   6. **A**   8. **D**

Answer Explanations

1. **B** Adding 1 to $f(x)=\dfrac{1}{2}x$ changes the y-intercept from 0 to 1. Graph B has a y-intercept of 1.

2. **D** Shifting $y = x$ down 3 units changes the y-intercept from 0 to −3. The equation $y = x - 3$ has a y-intercept of −3.

3. **D** For a y-intercept to change from 2 to −3, the graph must be shifted down 5 units.

4. **D** The line becomes twice as steep, so the slope doubles from $\dfrac{2}{3}$ to $\dfrac{4}{3}$. The y-intercept does not change. Choice D has a slope of $\dfrac{4}{3}$.

5. **D** Converting the line $Ax + By = C$ to slope-intercept form, you have

$y = \dfrac{-A}{B}x + \dfrac{C}{B}$. This line has slope $\dfrac{-A}{B}$. If you doubled the values of A and B, you would get the equation $(2A)x + (2B)y = C$

Solve this for y:
$$2Ax + 2By = C$$
$$2By = -2Ax + C$$
$$y = \dfrac{-2Ax + C}{2B}$$
$$y = \dfrac{-A}{B}x + \dfrac{C}{2B}$$

Notice that the 2's canceled, so the slope did not change.

6. **A** Increasing k (the y-intercept) by 1 will raise the line $y = 2x + k$ by 1 unit. The slope will be unaffected.

7. **A** Changing the slope from 2 to 3 would make the graph rise faster, so the line would become steeper.

8. **D** The only change to the graph is that line A has become less steep as it is transformed into line B. The y-intercept has not changed, nor has the slope become negative. The equation of choice D shows a smaller slope with the y-intercept still at 0.

2.12 Solving Systems of Linear Equations in Two Variables

What Is a System of Two Linear Equations?

When we consider two linear equations at the same time, we refer to the two equations as a *system*. Solving a system involves finding the point (if any) that the lines have in common.

Shown at the right is the graph of the following system:

$$\begin{cases} y = -3x + 2 \\ y = x - 2 \end{cases}$$

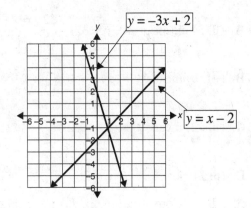

Here are two facts about this system:

- The point where the two lines intersect, $(1, -1)$, is called the *solution* of the system.
- The coordinates of this point, $(1, -1)$, satisfy both equations in the system. Substituting 1 for x and -1 for y gives:

$$
\begin{array}{ll}
y = -3x + 2 & y = x - 2 \\
-1 = -3(1) + 2 & -1 = 1 - 2 \\
-1 = -3 + 2 & -1 = -1 \quad \checkmark \\
-1 = -1 \quad \checkmark &
\end{array}
$$

How Many Solutions Does a System of Linear Equations Have?

A system of linear equations can have exactly one solution, no solution, or infinitely many solutions, as illustrated below.

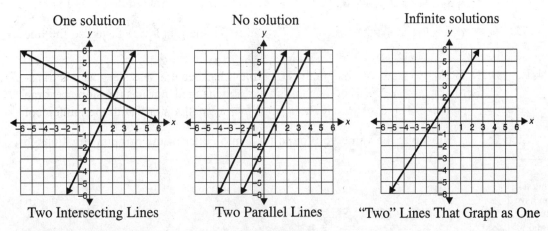

How Do You Solve a System of Linear Equations?

There are many ways to solve a system, including: guess and check, substitution, elimination, and graphing. Examples for these methods follow.

A. Solving by Guess and Check

Example 1: Which is a solution to the system $\begin{cases} 2y = x+6 \\ 2x+y = -2 \end{cases}$?

A. $(0, 3)$ B. $(-1, 0)$ C. $(-2, 2)$ D. $(6, 2)$

To be a solution, the ordered pair must satisfy BOTH equations. Test each point by substituting for x and y in both equations.

A. $(0, 3)$ means $x = 0$, $y = 3$. $\begin{cases} 2y = x+6 & 2(3)+0=6 & 6=6 & \text{YES} \\ 2x+y = -2 & 2(0)+3=-2 & 0+3 \neq -2 & \text{NO} \end{cases}$

B. $(-1, 0)$ means $x = -1$, $y = 0$. $\begin{cases} 2y = x+6 & 2(0) = -1+6 & 0 \neq 5 & \text{NO} \\ 2x+y = -2 & 2(-1)+0 = -2 & -2 = -2 & \text{YES} \end{cases}$

C. $(-2, 2)$ means $x = -2$, $y = 2$. $\begin{cases} 2y = x+6 & 2(2) = -2+6 & 4=4 & \text{YES} \\ 2x+y = -2 & 2(-2)+2 = -2 & -4+2 = -2 & \text{YES} \end{cases}$

D. $(6, 2)$ means $x = 6$, $y = 2$. $\begin{cases} 2y = x+6 & 2(2) = 6+6 & 4=12 & \text{NO} \\ 2x+y = -2 & 2(6)+2 = -2 & 12+2 \neq -2 & \text{NO} \end{cases}$

The correct answer must be choice C, $(-2, 2)$, because that point satisfies BOTH equations.

B. Solving by Substitution

The substitution method is easy to use when one of the equations already has a variable isolated, as illustrated in Example 2.

Example 2: Solve the system $\begin{cases} y = 2x-15 \\ 3x+2y = 12 \end{cases}$ using substitution.

Step 1:   Since y is isolated in the first equation, you can immediately substitute $(2x - 15)$ for y in the second equation.

> Don't forget to put parentheses around the quantity you are substituting.

$y = \boxed{2x - 15}$

$3x + 2y = 12 \longrightarrow 3x + 2(2x - 15) = 12$ Substitute $(2x - 15)$ for y.

$3x + 4x - 30 = 12$ Simplify, using the distributive property.

$7x - 30 = 12$ Solve for x.

$7x = 42$

$x = 6$

Step 2:   Substitute the value you found for x into either of the original equations to get y.

> NOTE: when solving a system, you have to find values for both x and y.

$y = 2x - 15$

$= 2(6) - 15$ Substitute 6 for x.

$= 12 - 15$ Simplify.

$= -3$

Step 3: Write your final answer as an ordered pair (x, y).

The solution to the system $\begin{cases} 3x+2y=12 \\ y=2x-15 \end{cases}$ is the point $(6, -3)$.

The substitution method is more difficult to use when neither equation has an isolated variable. In this case, you must begin by isolating a variable.

Example 3: Solve the system $\begin{cases} 5x+2y=10 \\ x+4y=-16 \end{cases}$ using substitution.

Step 1: For this problem, it is easiest to isolate x in the second equation since the coefficient of this variable is 1.

Solve $x + 4y = -16$ for x:
$$x + 4y = -16$$
$$\underline{-4y \quad -4y}$$
$$x = -16 - 4y$$

$$\begin{cases} 5x+2y=10 \\ x+4y=-16 \end{cases} \longrightarrow \boxed{\text{same as}} \longrightarrow \begin{cases} 5x+2y=10 \\ x=-16-4y \end{cases}$$

Step 2: Now that you have an isolated variable, proceed as in Example 2. Substitute $(-16 - 4y)$ for x in the first equation.

$$\begin{cases} 5x+\boxed{2y}=10 \\ x=\boxed{-16-4y} \end{cases} \qquad 5x+2y=10 \longrightarrow 5(-16-4y)+2y=10$$

Solving, you find $y = -5$.

Step 3: Substitute the value you found for y into either of the original equations to get x.

$$5x + 2y = 10$$
$$5x + 2(-5) = 10 \qquad \text{Substitute } -5 \text{ for } y.$$
$$5x - 10 = 10 \qquad \text{Solve for } x.$$
$$5x = 20$$
$$x = 4$$

Step 4: Write your final answer as an ordered pair (x, y).

The solution to the system $\begin{cases} 5x+2y=10 \\ x+4y=-16 \end{cases}$ is the point $(4, -5)$.

C. Solving by Elimination

Solving by the elimination method is easy when (a) both equations are in standard form, and (b) the coefficients of x (or of y) are opposites, as illustrated in Example 4.

Example 4: Solve the system $\begin{cases} 2x+6y=12 \\ 4x-6y=18 \end{cases}$.

Step 1: Draw a line under the second equation and add vertically:

$$\begin{array}{r} 2x + 6y = 12 \\ + \underline{4x - 6y = 18} \\ 6x + 0 = 30 \end{array}$$

Step 2:   Solve the resulting equation: $6x = 30$

$$x = 5$$

Step 3:   Substitute the value you found for x into either of the original equations to get y:

$$2x + 6y = 12$$

$2(5) + 6y = 12$ Substitute 5 for x.

$y = \dfrac{1}{3}$ Solve for y.

Step 4:   Write your final answer as an ordered pair (x, y).

The solution to the system $\begin{cases} 2x + 6y = 12 \\ 4x - 6y = 18 \end{cases}$ is the point $\left(5, \dfrac{1}{3}\right)$.

Example 5 illustrates the more difficult situation in which the coefficients are not opposites for either variable.

Example 5: Solve the system $\begin{cases} x + y = 6 \\ -2x + 6y = 12 \end{cases}$ using elimination.

Step 1:   To use elimination effectively, when you add the two equations, a variable must disappear. In this case, that will not happen unless you first multiply one of the equations by an appropriate number. Multiplying the first equation by 2 will cause one of the variables (x) to disappear when you add.

> NOTE: You also could have multiplied the first equation by −6 (that would make the y's disappear).

$$\begin{cases} x + y = 6 \\ -2x + 6y = 12 \end{cases} \longrightarrow \begin{cases} 2(x + y = 6) \\ -2x + 6y = 12 \end{cases} \longrightarrow \begin{cases} 2x + 2y = 12 \\ -2x + 6y = 12 \end{cases}$$

Step 2:   Now proceed as in step 1 of Example 4. Draw a line under the second equation, and add vertically:

$$\begin{array}{r} 2x + 2y = 12 \\ -2x + 6y = 12 \\ \hline 0 + 8y = 24 \end{array}$$

Step 3:   Solve the resulting equation:

$$8y = 24$$
$$y = 3$$

Step 4:   Substitute the value you found for y into either of the original equations to get x:

$$x + y = 6, \text{ where } y = 3$$
$$x + 3 = 6$$
$$x = 3$$

Step 5:   Write your final answer as an ordered pair (x, y).

The solution to the system $\begin{cases} x + y = 6 \\ -2x + 6y = 12 \end{cases}$ is the point $(3, 3)$.

D. Solving by Graphing

Your calculator can find the solution of a system!

Example 6: Solve the system $\begin{cases} y = \dfrac{1}{3}x + 5 \\ y = -\dfrac{2}{3}x + 2 \end{cases}$ graphically.

For more detailed explanations of using your calculator to graph and find intersections, refer to A Calculator Tutorial on page 3.

Since the equations are already in the form $y = mx + b$, they can easily be entered into your graphing calculator.

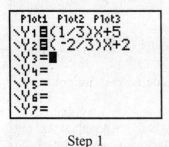

Step 1

ZOOM MEMORY
1: ZBox
2: Zoom In
3: Zoom Out
4: ZDecimal
5: ZSquare
6: ZStandard
7↓ZTrig

Step 2

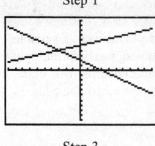

Step 3

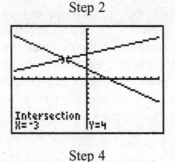

Step 4

The solution to the system $\begin{cases} y = \dfrac{1}{3}x + 5 \\ y = -\dfrac{2}{3}x + 2 \end{cases}$ is the point $(-3, 4)$.

If the equations in a given system are not in $y = mx + b$ form, you must convert them algebraically before you can use a calculator to solve the system.

Example 7: Solve the system $\begin{cases} 2x + 6y = 22 \\ x = 3 + y \end{cases}$ graphically.

Step 1:   Change each equation to $y = mx + b$ form. (See Section 2.5, Example 3.)

$$2x + 6y = 22 \quad \text{becomes} \quad y = -\frac{1}{3}x + \frac{11}{3}$$

$$x = 3 + y \quad \text{becomes} \quad y = x - 3$$

Step 2:   Now that the equations are in $y = mx + b$ form they can easily be entered into your graphing calculator. Follow the steps shown in Example 6.

Step 3: The point of intersection provides the solution.

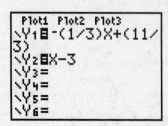 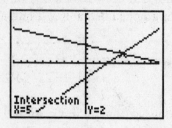

> If you don't see the intersection point when you use ZOOM 6, you will have to adjust the window on your calculator. Refer to A Calculator Tutorial on page 3.

Step 4: Write your final answer as an ordered pair.

The solution to the system $\begin{cases} 2x + 6y = 22 \\ x = 3 + y \end{cases}$ is the point (5, 2).

E. Applications

Just for fun, let's see how we might use a system of equations to solve a word problem. Jack Sprat and his wife, Plumpy, went out for dinner. Plumpy had a 3-pound steak, but Jack ate only vegetables. The bill for their dinner was $42.00. Jack was outraged. He said to Plumpy, "Gosh darn it, Plumpy! If you hadn't ordered that huge steak, our bill would have been a whole lot less than $42.00. Your share of the bill is $13.26 more than twice my share!" Plumpy said, "Why do you have to speak in riddles, you meanie? Can't you just tell me how much I owe?" Help Plumpy figure out her share of the bill.

Step 1: Assign variables. Let x = Jack's share of the bill
and y = Plumpy's share.

Step 2: Translate words into equations.

- The total bill was $42.00. $x + y = 42.00$
- Plumpy's share was $13.26 $y = 2x + 13.26$
  more than twice Jack's share.

Step 3: Choose a solution method.   Here, the substitution method
                                           is a good choice since y is
                                           already isolated.

Step 4: Find the value of one of the $x + y = 42$
variables. $x + (2x + 13.26) = 42$
                                                    $3x + 13.26 = 42$
                                                              $x = 9.58$

Step 5: Answer the question posed $9.58 was Jack's share of the bill.
by the problem.

                                           To find Plumpy's share,
                                           subtract $9.58 from $42.00:

                                           $\$42.00 - 9.58 = \$32.42$

Plumpy's share of the bill was
$32.42.

Practice

1. Which system graphed below has solution (1,1)?

A.

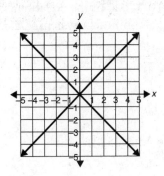

B.

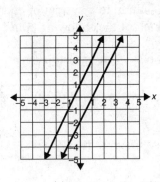

C.

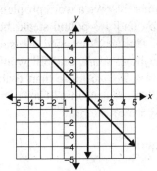

D.

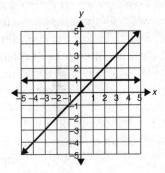

2. Which system has solution (3, −1)?

A. $\begin{cases} 3x - y = 0 \\ x - 3y = 0 \end{cases}$ 　　**B.** $\begin{cases} x + 3y = 0 \\ 5x - 3y = 8 \end{cases}$ 　　**C.** $\begin{cases} x = -3y \\ x - y = 4 \end{cases}$ 　　**D.** $\begin{cases} 2x + 3y = 3 \\ 3x - 4y = 9 \end{cases}$

3. What is the solution of the system of equations graphed at the right?

A. (3, −1)　　　　**B.** (−3, 3)
C. (−1, 2)　　　　**D.** (−1, 3)

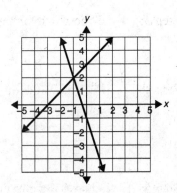

4. If $x + 3 = 5$, what is the product of x and $x + 3$?

A. 6　　　　　**B.** 10　　　　　**C.** 15　　　　　**D.** 40

5. Which system of equations has no solution?

A. $\begin{cases} y = 2x \\ 4x - 2y = 0 \end{cases}$
B. $\begin{cases} y = x+1 \\ x - y = 2 \end{cases}$
C. $\begin{cases} x = 0 \\ y = 0 \end{cases}$
D. $\begin{cases} x = 3y \\ y = 3x \end{cases}$

6. Suppose the solution to a system of equations is (−2, 0) and one of the equations is $y = x + 2$. Which of the following *could* be the other equation in this system?

A. $-2x + y = 0$
B. $2x - 2y = 0$
C. $x + 2y = -2$
D. $2x - y = -2$

7. Which system does *not* have (0, 0) as its solution?

A. $\begin{cases} 2x + 3y = 0 \\ 3x + 4y = 0 \end{cases}$
B. $\begin{cases} x - y = 0 \\ x + y = 0 \end{cases}$

C. $\begin{cases} y = ax \\ y = bx \end{cases}$ where a and b are real numbers
D. $\begin{cases} y = ax + 1 \\ y = bx + 1 \end{cases}$ where $a \neq b$

8. If a system of equations has no solution, the graph of the system is

A. a single line
B. intersecting lines
C. parallel lines
D. nonexistent (cannot be drawn)

9. The solution of a system of equations

A. is the point of intersection of the lines on the graph of the system
B. must satisfy *both* equations in the system
C. does not exist if the lines are parallel
D. All of the above are true.

10. The y-coordinate of the solution point of the system $\begin{cases} 2x + 5y = 3 \\ x - 5y = 9 \end{cases}$ is—

A. 4
B. −1
C. $\dfrac{1}{5}$
D. $\dfrac{3}{5}$

11. Which system lends itself *most* readily to solution by the substitution method?

A. $\begin{cases} y - 4 = \dfrac{1}{2}(x - 3) \\ 3x - 4y = 0 \end{cases}$
B. $\begin{cases} 2x - 3y = 6 \\ x + 3y = 3 \end{cases}$

C. $\begin{cases} 2x - 3y = 6 \\ y = 2x \end{cases}$
D. $\begin{cases} x + y = 10 \\ -x + 6y = 4 \end{cases}$

12. If $Ax + By = C$ and $y = x$, then, by substitution, it follows that—

    A. $Ax = By$ **B.** $(A + B)x = C$

    C. $A = B$ **D.** $(AB)x = C$

13. When John tried to solve the system $\begin{cases} 2x - 3y = 23 \\ x = 14 + 2y \end{cases}$, he correctly found that x had a value of 4. He needs you to finish the problem by finding the corresponding value of y, which is

    A. −5   **B.** 15   **C.** 22   **D.** 23

14. Shown here is the graph of line L_1, one of two lines that make up a system of equations. The point shown, (3, 2), represents the solution of the system. Which could be the equation of the other line, which is not shown?

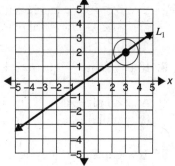

    A. $y = \dfrac{7}{5}x - \dfrac{11}{5}$ **B.** $y = \dfrac{8}{3}x - \dfrac{7}{4}$

    C. $y = \dfrac{3}{5}x - 1$ **D.** $y = \dfrac{1}{2}(x - 3) + \dfrac{3}{4}$

15. Find the x-coordinate of the solution to the system $\begin{cases} y = -x + 4 \\ y = \dfrac{2}{3}x - 1 \end{cases}$.

    A. −3   **B.** −1   **C.** 3   **D.** 4

16. Pasha was supposed to make a square poster for his Spanish class. By mistake, he made his poster 4 inches longer than it was wide. If the total perimeter of his poster was 56 inches, what was the length of the longer side of the poster?

    A. 8 in.   **B.** 10 in.   **C.** 12 in.   **D.** 16 in.

Use the following information to answer questions 17–19.

Beatrice got spring fever and went on a mad shopping spree. She bought T-shirts at $9.50 each and several pairs of pants. The T-shirts cost $9.50 apiece; each pair of pants cost 3 times as much as a T-shirt. She bought two more T-shirts than pairs of pants, and her total bill was $133.00.

Let x = the number of T-shirts,
and y = the number of pairs of pants.

17. Which equation shows the correct relationship between x and y?

    A. $x = y + 2$ **B.** $y = x + 2$ **C.** $y = 9.50x$ **D.** $y = 3x$

18. Which equation correctly represents the total cost of Beatrice's purchases?

A. $9.50x + 3y = 133.00$

B. $9.50x + 28.50y = 133.00$

C. $9.50y + 28.50x = 133.00$

D. $x + 3y = 9.50$

19. How much money did Beatrice spend on T-shirts?

A. $28.50   **B.** $38.00   **C.** $47.50   **D.** $57.00

Answers

1. **D**	5. **B**	9. **D**	13. **A**	17. **A**
2. **C**	6. **C**	10. **B**	14. **A**	18. **B**
3. **C**	7. **D**	11. **C**	15. **C**	19. **C**
4. **B**	8. **C**	12. **B**	16. **D**	

Answer Explanations

1. **D**   The solution to a system of equations is the point of intersection. The lines in graph D intersect at the point (1, 1).

2. **C**   Substitute 3 for x and -1 for y into the system $\begin{cases} x = 3y \\ x - y = 4 \end{cases}$:

$$x = -3y \qquad\qquad x - y = 4$$
$$3 = -3(-1) \qquad 3 - (-1) = 4$$
$$3 = 3 \;\checkmark \qquad\qquad 3 + 1 = 4 \;\checkmark$$

3. **C**   The solution to a system of equations is the point of intersection. The lines in graph C intersect at the point $(-1, 2)$.

4. **B**   If $x + 3 = 5$, then $x = 2$. Substitute 2 for x and find the product:

$$x(x + 3) = 2(2 + 3) = 10$$

5. **B**   Put the second equation of the system $\begin{cases} y = x + 1 \\ x - y = 2 \end{cases}$ into $y = mx + b$ form:

$$x - y = 2 \longrightarrow y = x - 2$$

Both lines have slopes of 1 and their y-intercepts are different, so the lines are parallel. Since parallel lines do not intersect, the system has no solution.

6. **C**   Substitute -2 for x and 0 for y into the equation $x + 2y = -2$:

$$-2 + 2(0) = -2$$
$$-2 = -2 \;\checkmark$$

Since $(-2, 0)$ satisfies the equation, $x + 2y = -2$ must be the other equation in the system.

7. **D**   Substitute 0 for y and 0 for x into the system $\begin{cases} y = ax + 1 \\ y = bx + 1 \end{cases}$:

$$0 = a(0) + 1 \qquad 0 = b(0) + 1$$
$$0 \neq 1 \qquad\qquad 0 \neq 1$$

To be a solution to a system, a point must satisfy both equations. The point (0, 0) does not satisfy either equation.

8. **C**   A system that has no solution graphs as parallel lines.

9. **D**   All the statements are true. The solution of a system is the point tof intersection, must satisfy both equations, and does not exist if the lines are parallel.

10. **B** The given system, $\begin{cases} 2x+5y=3 \\ x-5y=9 \end{cases}$, can be solved most easily by elimination:

$$2x + 5y = 3$$
$$\underline{x - 5y = 9}$$
$$3x + 0 = 12$$
$$x = 4$$

Substitute 4 for x into the first equation:

$$2(4) + 5y = 3$$
$$8 + 5y = 3$$
$$5y = -5 \longrightarrow y = -1$$

11. **C** The system $\begin{cases} 2x-3y=6 \\ y=2x \end{cases}$ is most easily solved by substitution because one of the variables, y, is isolated.

12. **B** Since $y = x$, substitute x for y into the equation $Ax + By = C$ and add like terms:

$$Ax + Bx = C \longrightarrow (A + B)x = C$$

13. **A** Since you know $x = 4$, substitute 4 for x into the equation $x = 14 + 2y$:

$$4 = 14 + 2y$$
$$-10 = 2y$$
$$y = -5$$

14. **A** Substitute 3 for x and 2 for y into the equation $y = \dfrac{7}{5}x - \dfrac{11}{5}$:

$$2 = \frac{7}{5}(3) - \frac{11}{5}$$
$$2 = \frac{21}{5} - \frac{11}{5}$$
$$2 = \frac{10}{5} \quad \checkmark$$

15. **C** Solve by graphing; the point of intersection is (3, 1). The x-coordinate is 3.

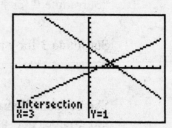

16. **D**   The length is 4 in. more than the width: $L = W + 4$

The perimeter of the rectangle is: $P = 2L + 2W$

By substitution: $P = 2(W + 4) + 2W$

$= 4W + 8$

Substitute 56 for the perimeter: $56 = 4W + 8$

$48 = 4W$

$12 = W$

The problem asks you to find the length: $L = W + 4$

$= 12 + 4 = 16$

The poster is 16 in. long.

17. **A**   Beatrice bought two more T-shirts than pairs of pants:

$$\text{T-shirts} = \text{pants} + 2 \longrightarrow x = y + 2$$

The correct equation is choice A.

18. **B**   T-shirts = $9.50 each

Pants = 3(price of a T-shirt) = 3(9.50) = 28.50 each

Total spent = $133.00

Let

x = the number of T-shirts,

y = the number of pairs of pants.

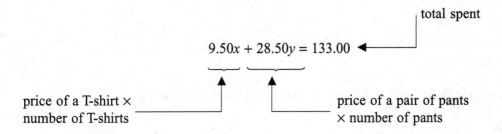

19. **C**   Since $x = y + 2$ (from question 17), substitute $(y + 2)$ for x into the cost equation (from question 18):

$$9.50x + 28.50y = 133.00$$
$$9.50(y + 2) + 28.50y = 133.00$$
$$9.50\ y + 19.00 + 28.50y = 133.00$$
$$38y = 114$$
$$y = 3 \qquad \text{Beatrice bought 3 pairs of pants.}$$

Substitute 3 for y into $x = y + 2$:

$$x = 3 + 2$$
$$= 5$$

She bought 5 T-shirts.

Since T-shirts cost $9.50 each:

$$9.50(5) = 47.50$$

Beatrice spent $47.50 on T-shirts.

2.13 Solving Quadratic Equations

WHAT IS A QUADRATIC EQUATION?

Quadratic equations in standard form can be modeled by the equation

$$Ax^2 + Bx + C = 0$$

> If A equaled 0, the equation
>
> $Ax^2 + Bx + C = 0$
>
> would be *linear*, not quadratic.

where $A \neq 0$. The main objective of this section is to **solve** quadratic equations. There are a variety of methods you can use, including:

- Guess and check.
- Graphing on the calculator.
- Isolating the square.
- Factoring.
- Quadratic formula.

Examples for each of these methods are discussed in this section.

A. Guess and Check

Example 1: Which is a solution to the equation $x^2 + 3x - 10 = 0$?

A.   −2   B.   −5   C.   5   D.   7

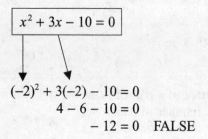

Try choice A: Substitute −2 for x.

$$x^2 + 3x - 10 = 0$$

$$(-2)^2 + 3(-2) - 10 = 0$$
$$4 - 6 - 10 = 0$$
$$-12 = 0 \quad \text{FALSE}$$

Since $-12 \neq 0$, choice A, −2, is *not* a solution of $x^2 + 3x - 10 = 0$.

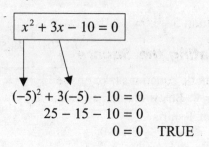

Try choice B: Substitute −5 for x.

$$x^2 + 3x - 10 = 0$$

$$(-5)^2 + 3(-5) - 10 = 0$$
$$25 - 15 - 10 = 0$$
$$0 = 0 \quad \text{TRUE}$$

> *Reminder*:
> Put negative numbers in parentheses when you substitute.

Since $0 = 0$, choice B, −5, *is* a solution of $x^2 + 3x - 10 = 0$.

B. Graphing on the Calculator

Quadratic equations have U-shaped graphs, called parabolas, that can intersect the x-axis exactly twice, once, or not at all. Therefore, the number of possible solutions for a quadratic equation is two, one, or none. The solutions will be the x-intercepts of the graph.

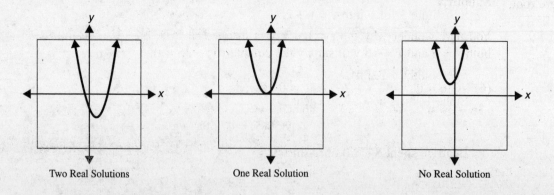

Two Real Solutions   One Real Solution   No Real Solution

To use the graphing method, you must do two things before picking up your calculator:

- Get the equation equal to 0.
- Replace the 0 with y.

These steps are illustrated in Example 2.

Example 2: Solve $5 - x^2 = -4x$.

$$5 - x^2 + 4x = 0 \quad \text{Get the equation equal to 0 by adding } 4x \text{ to both sides.}$$

$$5 - x^2 + 4x = y \quad \text{Replace 0 with } y.$$

> For a more detailed explanation of graphing and finding x-intercepts, refer to *A Calculator Tutorial* on pages 3.

Now use your calculator to find the x-intercepts of the graph. These will be the solutions of the equation.

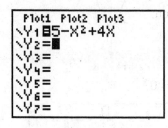

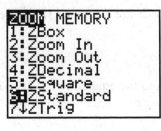

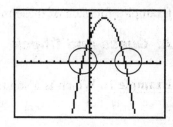

Step 1   Step 2   Step 3

The equation $5 - x^2 = -4x$ has two solutions, $x = -1$ and $x = 4$.

C. Isolating the Square

Quadratic equations take on the form $Ax^2 + Bx + C = 0$. If $B = 0$, the equation becomes $Ax^2 + C = 0$. Below are some examples of quadratic equations of this form or a variation.

$$x^2 - 36 = 0 \qquad 98 = 2x^2 \qquad 3x^2 = 21 \qquad 3 - x^2 = -22$$

To solve these equations, **isolate** the squared variable (i.e., get it by itself) and then take the square roots of both sides.

> Remember to take both the positive *and* the negative square root.

Example 3: Solve $x^2 - 36 = 0$.

Given equation: $\qquad\qquad\qquad\qquad x^2 - 36 = 0$

Add 36 to both sides: $\qquad\qquad\qquad\quad x^2 = 36$

Take the square root of both sides: $\qquad \sqrt{x^2} = \pm\sqrt{36}$

Simplify: $\qquad\qquad\qquad\qquad\qquad x = \pm 6$

You may wonder why the symbol $\pm$ was inserted in front of $\sqrt{36}$. In this case, both $x = 6$ and $x = -6$ will satisfy the equation $x^2 - 36 = 0$:

$$(6)^2 - 36 = 0 \qquad\qquad (-6)^2 - 36 = 0$$

$$36 - 36 = 0 \ \checkmark \qquad\quad 36 - 36 = 0 \ \checkmark$$

The graph of $y = x^2 - 36$ further supports two answers. Notice that the graph crosses the x-axis at 6 and −6.

Not all quadratic equations have neat integer solutions, as Example 4 illustrates.

Example 4: Solve $3x^2 = 21$.

Given equation: $\qquad\qquad\qquad\quad 3x^2 = 21$

Divide both sides by 3: $\qquad\qquad\quad x^2 = 7$

Take the square root of both sides: $\quad \sqrt{x^2} = \pm\sqrt{7}$

Simplify: $\qquad\qquad\qquad\qquad\quad x = \pm\sqrt{7}$

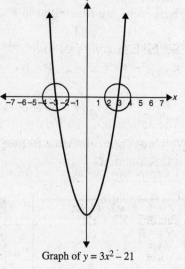

Graph of $y = 3x^2 - 21$

Since 7 is not a perfect square, the exact answers are $x = \pm\sqrt{7}$.

The approximate answers are $\pm 2.64575\ldots$.

```
√(7)
          2.645751311
```

D. Factoring

In Section 1.6 you learned how to factor polynomials. You will need to review this section before continuing with the factoring method for solving quadratic equations. Also, you will be making use of the **zero product property** explained in the table below.

The Zero Product Property	What It Means	Example
If $ab = 0$, then either $a = 0$ or $b = 0$.	If the *product* of two expressions is 0, then *at least* one of those expressions must itself be 0.	If $(x + 2)(x - 2) = 0$ then either $x + 2 = 0$ or $x - 2 = 0$.

To solve a quadratic equation by factoring, follow these steps:

- Get the equation equal to 0.
- Factor the equation completely.
- Set each factor equal to 0.
- Solve each new equation for x.

> The zero product property tells you what happens when a product is equal to 0, not any other number. For example, if $a \cdot b = 16$, it is *not* necessarily true that either $a = 16$ or $b = 16$.

Examples 5 and 6 illustrate the factoring method.

Example 5: Solve $x^2 + 7x = -10$

Given equation:	$x^2 + 7x = -10$
Add 10 to both sides:	$x^2 + 7x + 10 = 0$
Factor:	$(x + 5)(x + 2) = 0$

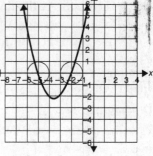

Set each factor equal to 0:	$x + 5 = 0$	$x + 2 = 0$
Solve:	$x = -5$	$x = -2$

Graph of $y = x^2 + 7x + 10$

The solutions of $x^2 + 7x = -10$ are $x = -5$ and $x = -2$. Notice that these values are the x-intercepts of the corresponding graph.

Example 6: Solve $x^2 + 10x + 25 = 0$ by factoring.

Given equation:	$x^2 + 10x + 25 = 0$
Factor:	$(x + 5)(x + 5) = 0$

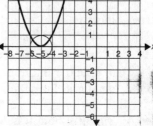

Set each factor equal to 0:	$x + 5 = 0$	$x + 5 = 0$
Solve:	$x = -5$	

Graph of $y = x^2 + 10x + 25$

This quadratic equation has only one solution, $x = -5$. Notice that the graph of $y = x^2 + 10x + 25$ has only one x-intercept.

E. Quadratic Formula

Many quadratic equations cannot be solved by factoring or by isolating the square. However, there is a method for solving quadratic equations that always works. This method makes use of the quadratic formula.

The Quadratic Formula

Given the quadratic equation $ax^2 + bx + c = 0$, $a \neq 0$, you can find its solutions by substituting the values for a, b, and c into this formula:

$$x = \frac{-b \pm \sqrt{b^2 - 4ac}}{2a} \quad \text{also written as} \quad x = \frac{-b}{2a} \pm \frac{\sqrt{b^2 - 4ac}}{2a}$$

You may be familiar with the first version of the quadratic formula, but the second version shown above is much easier to evaluate. In Examples 7 and 8 the second version will be used to solve the given quadratic equations.

When you use the quadratic formula, one of three things will happen. The number under the square root symbol will be negative, 0, or positive.

• If the number under the square root symbol is negative, the quadratic equation will have **no real solutions**.

- If the number under the square root symbol is 0, the quadratic equation will have exactly **one real solution**.
- If the number under the square root symbol is positive, the quadratic equation will have **two real solutions**.

Example 7: Solve $x^2 - 6x - 3 = 0$.

Try factoring:

$$x^2 - 6x - 3 = 0$$
$$(x - 3)(x + 1) = 0$$
$$x^2 + 1x - 3x - 3 = 0$$
$$x^2 - 2x - 3 = 0$$

NO! Doesn't factor!

Since factoring doesn't work, use the quadratic formula.

> The quadratic formula:
> $$x = \frac{-b}{2a} \pm \frac{\sqrt{b^2 - 4ac}}{2a}$$

Step 1: Get one side equal to 0: $\qquad x^2 - 6x - 3 = 0$

Step 2: Identify a, b, and c: $\qquad a = 1, b = -6, c = -3$

Step 3: Substitute values for a, b, and c into the quadratic formula: $\qquad x = \frac{-(-6)}{2(1)} \pm \frac{\sqrt{(-6)^2 - 4(1)(-3)}}{2(1)}$

Step 4: Simplify both fractions (before and after the $\pm$ signs): $\qquad x = \frac{6}{2} \pm \frac{\sqrt{36 + 12}}{2}$

> Recall from Section 1.9 that
> $$\frac{\sqrt{48}}{2} = \frac{\sqrt{16} \cdot \sqrt{3}}{2}$$
> $$= \frac{4\sqrt{3}}{2} = 2\sqrt{3}$$

Step 5: Split into two equations, one with $+$ and one with $-$: $\qquad x = 3 + \frac{\sqrt{48}}{2} \qquad x = 3 - \frac{\sqrt{48}}{2}$

Step 6: Simplify: $\qquad x = 3 + 2\sqrt{3} \qquad x = 3 - 2\sqrt{3}$

The exact solutions of $x^2 - 6x - 3 = 0$ are $x = 3 + 2\sqrt{3}$ and $x = 3 - 2\sqrt{3}$ (or approximately 6.464 or −0.046). You could never have found these by factoring.

Here's another example of a quadratic equation that will not factor.

Example 8: Solve $x^2 + x = -4$.

Get one side equal to 0: $\qquad\qquad x^2 + x + 4 = 0$
Identify a, b, and c $\qquad\qquad a = 1, b = 1, c = 4$

Plug the values into the quadratic formula: $\qquad x = \frac{-(1)}{2(1)} \pm \frac{\sqrt{(1)^2 - 4(1)(4)}}{2(1)}$

Simplify: $\qquad = \frac{-1}{2} \pm \frac{\sqrt{1 - 16}}{2}$

$\qquad = \frac{-1}{2} \pm \frac{\sqrt{-15}}{2}$

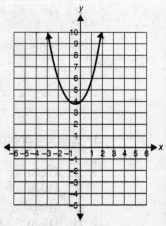

Graph of $y = x^2 + x + 4$

$x = \frac{-1}{2} \pm \frac{\sqrt{-15}}{2}$ actually are solutions of the equation $x^2 + x = -4$, but we call them "imaginary" solutions!

Whoops! A negative number under a radical symbol! Since the number under the square root sign is negative, this quadratic equation has **no real solution**. Notice that the graph of the corresponding equation, $y = x^2 + x + 4$, does not intersect the x-axis.

F. Applications of Quadratics

When Gilligan, the Skipper, and all the rest were shipwrecked on "Gilligan's Island," the Skipper decided to fire an emergency flare in the hope that someone would see it and rescue them. (Of course, they were never rescued. Too bad!) Because the Professor was a physicist, he figured out that, if the flare were fired upward with an initial velocity of 25 meters per second, then its height, h, in meters, after t seconds could be roughly calculated using this equation: $h(t) = -5t^2 + 25t$. Gilligan, being smarter than you might think, correctly used this equation to figure out when the flare would hit the ground. Here's what Gilligan did:

Gilligan let $h(t) = 0$: $h(t) = -5t^2 + 25t$

Then he solved for t, $0 = -5t^2 + 25t$

(using the factoring $0 = -5t \, (t - 5)$

method): $-5t = 0$ or $t - 5 = 0$

$t = 0$ or $t = 5$

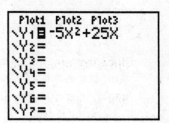

Gilligan determined what these values meant:

- $t = 0$ was the time, in seconds, when the flare was fired.
- $t = 5$ was the time, in seconds, that the flare took to hit the ground.

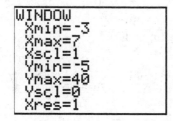

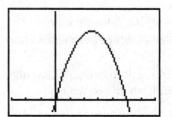

Practice

1. A quadratic equation can be written in the form—

A. $y = mx + b$
C. $Ax^2 + Bx + C = 0$

B. $Ax + By = C$
D. $Ax^3 + Bx^2 + Cx = 0$

2. Solve the equation $(2x - 1)^2 = 9$.

A. $x = \pm\dfrac{1}{2}$ **B.** $x = \pm 3$ **C.** $x = 2, x = -1$ **D.** $x = -1, x = \dfrac{1}{2}$

3. Find the approximate solutions of $0 = -x^2 + x + 5$ using your graphing calculator.

A. About −1 and 1
B. About −3 and 3
C. About −2 and 3
D. About 2 and −3

4. Which quadratic equation has no real solution?

A. $x^2 = 0$ **B.** $x^2 = 1$ **C.** $(x - 1)^2 = 0$ **D.** $x^2 + 1 = 0$

Use this graph of a quadratic function to answer questions 5 and 6.

5. What are the zeros of this function?

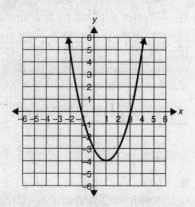

    A. −1, −3, and 3

    B. −1, −3, 1, and 3

    C. 1 and −3

    D. −1 and 3

6. The graph allows you to find the solutions of which quadratic equation?

    A. $(x - 1)(x + 3) = 0$ **B.** $(x + 1)(x - 3) = 0$
    C. $x^2 + x - 3 = 0$ **D.** $x^2 - x + 3 = 0$

7. The solutions of the equation $50x^2 = 100$ are—

    A. $x = \pm 2$ **B.** $x = \pm\sqrt{2}$ **C.** $x = \pm\sqrt{50}$ **D.** $x = \pm 50$

8. Which table has points that follow a quadratic pattern?

A.

x	−2	−1	0	1	2
y	−3	−2	−1	0	1

B.

x	−2	−1	0	1	2
y	2	1	0	1	2

C.

x	−2	−1	0	1	2
y	4	1	0	1	4

D.

x	−2	−1	0	1	2
y	2	2	2	2	2

Given the equation $x^2 - 3.494x + 1 = 0$. Without a calculator, this would be a very hard equation to solve. *Use this equation and your calculator to answer questions 9 and 10.*

9. Use the guess and check method to see which number is the closest to an actual solution of the given equation.

    A. 0   **B.** 0.315   **C.** 1.249   **D.** 3.962

10. Find a zero of the corresponding quadratic function to the *nearest tenth*.

    A. 3   **B.** 3.2   **C.** 3.4   **D.** 3.5

11. Which number is a solution of $x^2 - 5x + 6 = 0$?

    A. –5   **B.** –3   **C.** 2   **D.** 6

12. By factoring, you can see that the equation $x^2 + 4x - 12 = 0$ has the same solutions as which pair of linear equations?

    A. $x - 6 = 0$ and $x - 2 = 0$
    B. $x + 6 = 0$ and $x - 2 = 0$
    C. $x + 4 = 0$ and $x - 12 = 0$
    D. $x - 4 = 0$ and $x + 12 = 0$

13. When Jack tried to solve the equation $x^2 - x = 6$ by the guess and check method, he substituted the number 3 into the equation and got $6 = 6$ for his result. This tells us that—

    A. 3 is a solution of the equation
    B. 3 is *not* a solution of the equation
    C. 6 is a solution of the equation
    D. 3 and 6 are both solutions of the equation

14. To solve the equation $x^2 - 4x = 21$ by the factoring method, you should begin by—

    A. changing $x^2 - 4x$ to $x(x - 4)$
    B. subtracting 21 from both sides of the equation
    C. squaring both sides of the equation
    D. adding $4x$ to both sides of the equation

15. Which of the following is a correct setup for solving the equation $2x^2 + 3x - 1 = 0$ by using the quadratic formula?

    A. $x = \dfrac{-3}{4} \pm \dfrac{\sqrt{9 - (4)(2)(-1)}}{4}$ **B.** $x = \dfrac{-3}{2} \pm \dfrac{\sqrt{9 - (4)(2)(-1)}}{2}$

    C. $\dfrac{-3}{4} \pm \dfrac{\sqrt{3 - (4)(2)(-1)}}{4}$ **D.** $\dfrac{-3}{2} \pm \dfrac{\sqrt{9 + (4)(2)(-1)}}{2}$

16. John set up the quadratic formula to solve a particular quadratic equation. Here is his setup:

$$x = \frac{-3 \pm \sqrt{9 - 16}}{2}$$

What conclusion can you draw about the solution of John's equation based on this setup?

    A. The equation has no real solution.
    B. The equation has infinitely many solutions.
    C. The equation has exactly one real solution.
    D. The equation has exactly two real solutions.

Use the following information to answer questions 17 and 18.

Joan had a rectangular garden plot that was 5 meters longer than it was wide. The area of the garden was 14 square meters.

17. Which equation correctly models this situation?

    A. $x(14 - x) = 5$ **B.** $5x^2 + 14 = 0$ **C.** $x(x + 5) = 14$ **D.** $x^2 + 5 = 14$

18. What was the longer dimension of Joan's garden?

    A. 2 m   **B.** 5 m   **C.** 7 m   **D.** 9 m

---

19. Bruce dropped his calculator out of his bedroom window by accident. Sadly, it broke, so he had to do his entire SOL exam without it. (Don't worry; he passed anyway!) The equation $h = -16t^2 + 20$ models his calculator's height, h, above the ground as a function of time, t, in seconds. To the *nearest tenth*, how much time passed before the calculator struck the ground?

    A. 0.8 sec   **B.** 1.1 sec   **C.** 1.5 sec   **D.** 2.1 sec

Answers

1. **C**	5. **D**	9. **B**	13. **A**	17. **C**
2. **C**	6. **B**	10. **B**	14. **B**	18. **C**
3. **C**	7. **B**	11. **C**	15. **A**	19. **B**
4. **D**	8. **C**	12. **B**	16. **A**	

Answers Explanations

1. **C** This is the definition of a quadratic equation, where $A \neq 0$.

2. **C** Take the square roots of both sides: $2x - 1 = \pm 3$.
   When $2x - 1 = 3$, $x = 2$. When $2x - 1 = -3$, $x = -1$.

3. **C** Graph $y = -x^2 + x + 5$. The x-intercepts are about -2 and 3.

4. **D** The graph of $y = x^2 + 1$ does not intersect the x-axis.

5. **D** The zeros of the function are the x-intercepts, -1 and 3, of the graph.

6. **B** Work backwards: $x = -1$ and $x = 3$ are the solutions of $(x + 1)(x - 3) = 0$.
   These solutions correspond to the x-intercepts of the graph.

7. **B** Divide both sides by 50; $x^2 - 2$. Then take the ($\pm$) square roots of both sides.

8. **C** Each y-value in table C is produced by squaring the corresponding x-value, and $y = x^2$ is quadratic.

9. **B** Substituting 0.315 for x in the given equation, $x^2 - 3.464x + 3 = 0$, gives a result of -0.001385, which is very close to 0.

10. **B** The zero of the function is the x-intercept of the graph. Use your calculator to find the answer: 3.2.

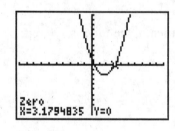

11. **C** Factor the given equation, $x^2 - 5x + 6 = 0$:

$$(x - 3)(x - 2) = 0$$

   Then $x - 3 = 0$ or $x - 2 = 0$.
   The solutions are $x = 3$ and $x = 2$ (choice C).

12. **B** Factor the given equation $x^2 + 4x - 12 = 0$:

$$(x + 6)(x - 2) = 0$$

   By the zero product property, either $(x + 6) = 0$ or $(x - 2) = 0$.

13. **A** The number 3 is a solution because it satisfied the given equation by producing a true result ($6 = 6$) when substituted. The value of 6 is irrelevant.

14. **B**   First, get one side equal to 0 and simplify. Only then should you factor.

15. **A**   Choices B and D have the wrong denominator. Choice C has the wrong value under the radical symbol because 3, the value for b, was not squared.

16. **A** $(9 - 16)$ gives a negative number under the radical. You cannot get a "real" value when you take the square root of a negative number.

17. **C**   Let x = width of Joan's garden. Then $x + 5$ = length. For a rectangle, area = length $\times$ width. The area is given as $14\,m^2$. Substitute: $14 = x(x + 5)$.

18. **C**   Solve the equation from question 17. Use the distributive property; then subtract 14 from both sides:

$$x^2 + 5x - 14 = 0$$

Factoring gives $(x + 7)(x - 2) = 0$; then, $x = -7$ or $x = 2$. Can't have a negative width, so eliminate $x = -7$. Then $x = 2$ is the width. The longer dimension, the length, is $x + 5 = 7\,m$.

19. **B**   You can enter the equation $h = -16t^2 + 20$ into your calculator as $y = -16x^2 + 20$. Graph the equation $y = -16x^2 + 20$ on your calculator, and find the zero of the function.

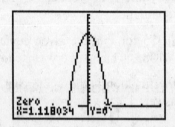

To the nearest tenth, the time is 1.1 sec.

Chapter 3

Relations and Functions

3.1 What Is a Function?

A **function** is a special way of matching the members of one set, called the *domain*, with the members of a second set, called the *range*. You can think of a function as a machine that takes the domain elements as *inputs*, and transforms them into range elements as *outputs*. But a function must also follow this important rule: ***Each input must be paired with exactly one output.***

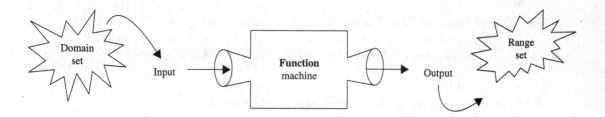

There are many ways of representing functions. You may see a function in the form of a graph, a mapping, a table, or a listing of ordered pairs.

A. Recognizing a Function from a Graph

To be a function, a graph must pass the "**vertical line test**": *No vertical line can cross the graph of a function in more than one point!*

<u>**Example 1:**</u> These *are* functions. Each one passes the vertical line test.

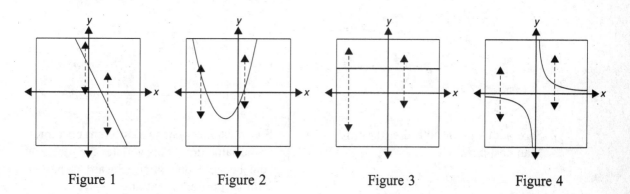

| Figure 1 | Figure 2 | Figure 3 | Figure 4 |

Example 2: These are *not* functions. Each one fails the vertical line test.

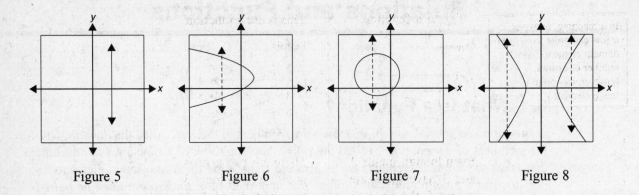

Figure 5   Figure 6   Figure 7   Figure 8

Here are three rules about graphs of functions:

- All lines are functions except vertical lines. (See Figures 1 and 5.)
- All parabolas that open upward or downward are functions. (See Figure 2.) All parabolas that open sideways are *not* functions. (See Figure 6.)
- Closed figures such as circles are *not* functions. (See Figure 7.)

B. Recognizing a Function from a Mapping

Any set of ordered pairs is referred to as a *relation*. For a relation to be a function, however, each input from the domain set must have **exactly one** partner, or output, in the range set.

Example 3:

This *is* a function.

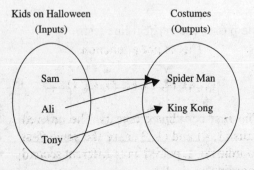

Sam and Ali can both dress up in Spider Man costumes.

This is *not* a function.

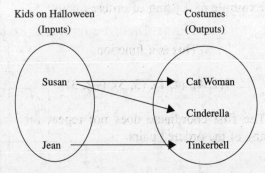

Susan cannot wear two different costumes at the same time. This violates the function rule because one input (Susan) is paired with two different outputs.

Example 4:

In a mapping, only *one* arrow can point *from* each domain element. (Any number of arrows, however, can point *to* a range element.)

This *is* a function.

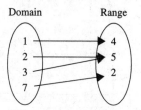

Even though inputs 2 and 3 have the same output, 5, the function rule is not violated.

This is *not* a function.

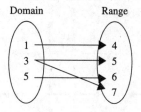

There are two arrows pointing from input 3 to outputs 5 and 7.

C. Recognizing a Function from a Table or a Listing of Ordered Pairs

Example 5: Table

This *is* a function.

input	−3	−1	1	2
output	2	1	−1	−3

Each input has just one partner, and no input is listed twice.

This is *not* a function.

input	−3	2	1	−3
output	−4	−2	0	2

Input −3 has two outputs, −4 and 2.

Example 6: Listing of ordered pairs

This *is* a function.

{(1, 4), (4, 1), (3, 3), (−2, 3)}

The first coordinate does not repeat for any of the ordered pairs.

This is *not* a function.

{(1, 4), (4, 1), (1, 3), (3, 1)}

The first coordinate repeats. The ordered pairs (1, 4) and (1, 3) have the same first coordinate, 1, paired with different second coordinates.

Here are three rules about functions represented as a table or a listing of ordered pairs:

- In a table, input elements can be listed only once (assuming no input/output pairs are identical).
- In a listing, different ordered pairs cannot have the same first coordinate.
- You can plot the points given in a table or listing, and then use the vertical line test.

Practice

1. Which represents the graph of a function?

A. 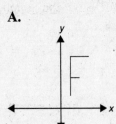   B. 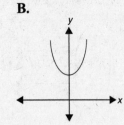   C. 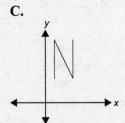   D.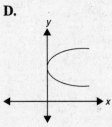

2. Which graph is a function?

A. 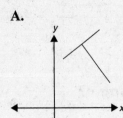   B. 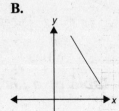   C. 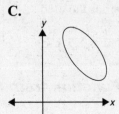   D.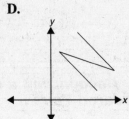

3. Which line does *NOT* represent the graph of a function?

A. 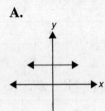   B. 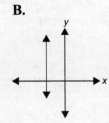   C. 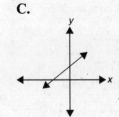   D.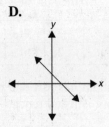

4. Which of these graphs is a function?

A. 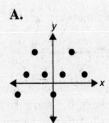   B. 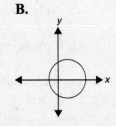   C. 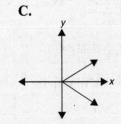   D.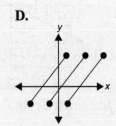

5. Which table of values represents a function?

A.

x	y
2	−1
4	0
6	−1
8	0

B.

x	y
−1	2
0	4
−1	6
0	8

C.

x	y
9	3
9	5
9	7
9	9

D.

x	y
2	5
1	4
0	3
1	2

6. Which mapping does *not* represent a function?

A.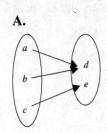

B.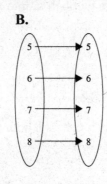

C.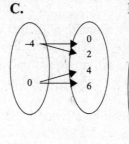

D.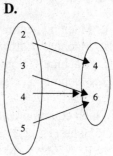

7. Which is *not* a function?

A.

x	y
−2	4
−1	1
0	0
1	1
2	4
3	9

B. {(2, 0), (0, 2), (3, 4), (4, 3), (5, 2)}

C.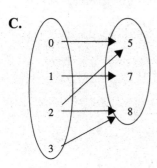

D.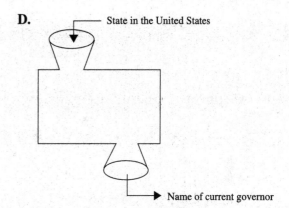

8. Which set of ordered pairs represents a function?

A. {(2, 5), (3, 7), (−3, 4), (3, −2)} **B.** {(1, 5), (5, 7), (−3, 4), (5, −2)}
C. {(2, 5), (3, 5), (−3, 5), (5, 5)} **D.** {(2, 5), (2, 7), (2, 4), (2, −2)}

9. Which value for *k* will make this table of values a function?

x	−1	2	k	−3
y	4	5	−1	2

A. −1   **B.** 5   **C.** 2   **D.** −3

10. Julie is trying to decide which of the following machines is *not* a function machine. Each machine transforms the input, a positive number, k, into a particular shape.

    A. Machine A draws a square with area $= k$.
    B. Machine B draws a circle with radius $= k$.
    C. Machine C draws a triangle with perimeter $= k$.
    D. Machine D draws a cube with volume $= k$.

11. Which equation *cannot* be a function because it contains both the point (1, 2) and the point (1, −2)?

    A. $x = \dfrac{1}{2}y$ **B.** $y = 2^x$ **C.** $y = 2x^2$ **D.** $x = \left(\dfrac{y}{2}\right)^2$

12. Which choice represents a *different* function from the one given by the graph?

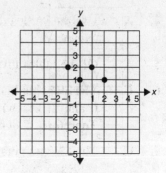

    A. $y = |x| + 1$ for $x = -1, 0, 1, 2$ **B.**

x	−1	0	1	2
y	2	1	2	1

    C. $\{(0, 1), (2, 1), (-1, 2), (1, 2)\}$ **D.**

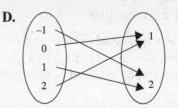

13. Which equation does *not* represent a function?

    A. $y = 5$ **B.** $y = x + 5$ **C.** $y = x^2 + 5$ **D.** $x = 5$

14. If the point (2, −3) lies on the graph of some function, which point *cannot* also lie on the graph?

    A. (−3, 2)   **B.** (−3, −3)   **C.** (5, −3)   **D.** (2, 5)

15. Which operation on the set of positive integers $\{1,2,3,4, \ldots\}$ will *not* produce a function?

    A. Squaring   **B.** Doubling
    C. Finding the prime factors   **D.** Decreasing by 5

Answers

1. **B**	4. **A**	7. **C**	10. **C**	13. **D**
2. **B**	5. **A**	8. **C**	11. **D**	14. **D**
3. **B**	6. **C**	9. **B**	12. **A**	15. **C**

Answers Explanations

1. **B**   Use the vertical line test. Vertical lines intersect more than once in all graphs except B.

2. **B**   Use the vertical line test. Vertical lines intersect more than once in all graphs except B.

3. **B**   All lines are functions unless they are vertical. Since B is a vertical line, it is not a function.

4. **A**   Use the vertical line test. Vertical lines intersect more than once in all graphs except A.

5. **A**   Of the tables given, only A does not repeat an x-value.

6. **C**   The mapping in choice C has the input value -4 pointing to two output values, 0 and 2. Likewise, the input value 0 points to two output values, 4 and 6. Therefore, C does not represent a function.

7. **C**   The mapping diagram in choice C has input 2 paired with two different output values, 5 and 8. Therefore, C is not a function.

8. **C**   Choice C is a function because each first coordinate (i.e., input value) is paired with one second coordinate (i.e., output value).

9. **B**   Since the table of values already has x-values of -1, 2, and -3, the table will be a function only if k has a different value. Thus, k must be 5.

10. **C**   For a relationship to be a function, no input can produce multiple outputs. Consider the case of a triangle with a perimeter of 12. Many different triangles can be drawn that have perimeters of 12 (see figures below).

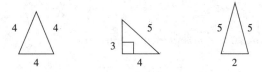

11. **D**   In equation D, both points are solutions. Since $(2/2)^2$ and $(-2/2)^2$ both equal 1, an input of $x = 1$ yields two different outputs. Therefore, $x = \left(\dfrac{y}{2}\right)^2$ cannot be a function.

12. **A**   For equation A, $y = |x| + 1$, the last value, $x = 2$, yields $y = |2| + 1 = 3$. The point $(2, 3)$ does not correspond to the given graph.

13. **D**   The graph of equation D, $x = 5$, is a vertical line. All lines are functions *unless* they are vertical.

        Alternative solution: Using your graphing calculator, enter each of the equations and graph in the standard window. Notice that you cannot enter $x = 5$ into your calculator. Only functions can be entered into the Y = screen. Thus, $x = 5$ is not a function.

14. **D**   Since the given point (2, –3), and (2, 5) have the same first coordinate but different second coordinates, these two points must lie on a vertical line. The vertical line test would fail.

15. **C**   Finding the prime factors of the set will not produce a function. For example, the prime factors of 6 are both 2 and 3. Since the input value, 6, has two output values, 2 and 3, a function is not generated.

3.2 Function Notation

Mathematicians have a clever way of referring to the output of a function. Consider the following function machine:

Be careful! $f(\star)$ does NOT mean f times $\star$.

In this diagram, the name of the function is f and the input is $\star$. The output is written as $f(\star)$.

If the input to this function were 5, for example, the output would be written as $f(5)$.
If the input were –2, the output would be expressed as $f(-2)$.
If the input were x, the output would be $f(x)$.

Example 1: Suppose $g(x) = 2x + 1$. This single statement tells us *all* of the following things:

- This is an equation for a function whose name is g.
- When the input to this function is x, the output is $g(x)$.
- Given an input, this function multiplies it by 2 and then adds 1.
- As a function machine, $g(x) = 2x + 1$ diagrams like this:

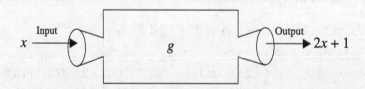

Once you have an equation for a function, you can use rules of algebra to determine the output for a given input and the input(s) for a given output. Examples 2 and 3 illustrate how this can be done.

Example 2: Given $h(x) = 3x - 2$, find $h(5)$.

This example asks for the *output* when the input is 5.

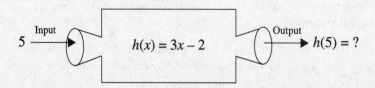

To find the answer, just substitute 5 for x and simplify:

$$h(x) = 3x - 2$$
$$h(5) = 3(5) - 2$$
$$= 13$$

The output is 13.

Example 3: Use the function $h(x) = 3x - 2$ again. This time, find x when $h(x) = 10$.

This example asks for the *input* when the output is 10.

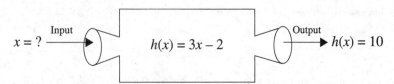

To find the answer, substitute 10 for $h(x)$ and solve for x.

$$h(x) = 3x - 2$$
$$10 = 3x - 2$$
$$12 = 3x$$
$$x = 4$$

The input is 4.

Finding inputs and outputs is easy when you are given a table or a listing of function values. You just need to choose the right number from the table or list, as shown in examples 4–7.

Example 4: Given the following table of values for some function, f. Find $f(6)$.

x	−3	0	3	6	9
$f(x)$	6	2	−1	4	2

This example asks for the *output* when the input is 6. The answer is 4 because the ordered pair (6, 4) has an input of 6 and an output of 4.

Example 5: Using the table from Example 4, find x when $f(x) = 2$.

This example asks for the *input* when the output is 2. There are two answers; $x = 0$ and $x = 9$ are both inputs that produce an output of 2. (Recall that a function must have a unique output for each input, but any number of inputs can share the same output.)

Example 6: Given the function $g = \{(1, 3), (-5, 7), (6, 2), (-3, 1)\}$, find $g(1)$.

Ordered pairs are always listed in the form (input, output). Therefore, the ordered pairs in this example must be in the form $(x, g(x))$.

To find $g(1)$, use the ordered pair (1, 3), which has 1 for an input. The output, $g(1)$, is 3.

Example 7: Using the function g given in Example 6, find x when $g(x) = 1$.

This time, use the ordered pair (−3, 1), which has 1 for the output. The input, x, is −3 because $g(-3) = 1$.

From a graph, you can determine input and output values by remembering that points on the graph of a function always have the form (input, output).

Example 8: Use the graph of the function f to find $f(2)$.

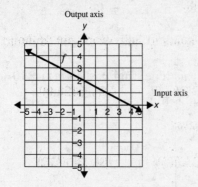

Since 2 is an input, locate the ordered pair that has an input, or x-coordinate, of 2.

$(2, 1)$ is the only relevant point. Since the output is 1 when the input is 2, $f(2) = 1$.

Example 9: Use the graph of the function h to find x when $h(x) = 1$.

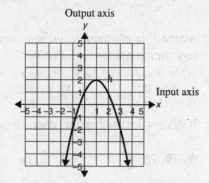

Since 1 is an output, find all ordered pairs that have an output, or y-coordinate, of 1. An easy way to do this is to draw a horizontal line at $y = 1$ and see where this line intersects the graph of the given function.

Two points have an output, or y-value, of 1. These points are $(0, 1)$ and $(2, 1)$, so $h(x) = 1$ for two different values, $x = 0$ and $x = 2$.

Practice

1. If $f(x) = 2x - 1$, find $f(-2)$.

A. $-\dfrac{3}{2}$ B. $-\dfrac{1}{2}$ C. -3 D. 1

2. Using the function machine in the diagram and the fact that $f(x) = 10$, solve for x.

A. 10 B. 3

C. 0 D. $-\dfrac{1}{3}$

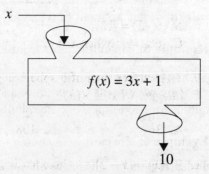

3. Use the graph of $f(x)$ to determine $f(1)$.

A. 0 B. 4
C. -2 D. 2

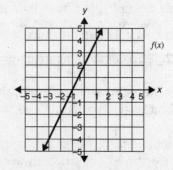

4. Sally works part-time at a video store and is paid according to the function

$$P(t) = 60 + \sqrt{t + 48}$$

where P is payment in dollars, and t is time in hours. If Sally works for 16 hours, how much money will she earn?

   A. $64.00   **B.** $68.00   **C.** $188.00   **D.** $124.00

5. If $h(2) = 3$, which point must lie on the graph of h?

   A. (3, 2)   **B.** (2, 3)   **C.** (2, $h(3)$)   **D.** (3, $h(2)$)

6. For which function is $f(3) = 1$?

   A. $f(x) = 3x + 1$ **B.** $f(x) = x + 2$ **C.** $f(x) = x - 2$ **D.** $f(x) = 3 - 2x$

7. Given $f(x) = 2x - 3$, for what value of x is $f(x) = 13$?

   A. 5   **B.** 8   **C.** 13   **D.** 23

8. The function G is defined as follows: $G = \{(1, 2), (3, -6), (4, 3), (7, 3)\}$. What is $G(3)$?

   A. 4   **B.** 7   **C.** 4 and 7   **D.** −6

9. Given the table below of values for some function f, which statement about f is *not* true?

x	−2	−1	0	1	2
$f(x)$	4	1	0	1	4

   A. $f(-2) = f(2)$ **B.** $f(0) = 0$
   C. $f(x) = x^2$ when $x = -2$ **D.** $f(-1) + f(1) = 0$

10. The surface area of a sphere is given by the formula $A(r) = 4\pi r^2$. To the *nearest integer*, what is $A(3)$?

   A. 36   **B.** 108   **C.** 113   **D.** 1421

11. If $f(x) = (x - 2)(x + 3)$, what is $f(1)$?

   A. −6   **B.** −4   **C.** 0   **D.** 6

12. According to the graph of f, if $f(x) = -2$, what is x?

   A. −2   **B.** 1
   C. −1   **D.** 4

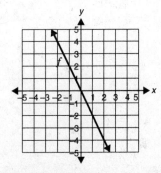

13. Use the function machine to determine which is *not* a possible rule for $f(x)$?

A. $f(x) = x^2$
B. $f(x) = x + 20$
C. $f(x) = 5x$
D. $f(x) = 5x + 20$

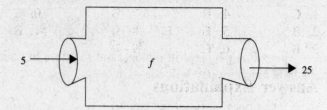

Answers

1. **C**		4. **B**		7. **B**		10. **C**		12. **B**
2. **B**		5. **B**		8. **D**		11. **B**		13. **D**
3. **B**		6. **C**		9. **D**				

Answer Explanations

1. **C**   The input (x-value) is given as -2. Then, $f(-2) = 2(-2) + 1 = -4 + 1 = -3$.

2. **B**   Since $f(x) = 10$ tells you that the output is 10, set $3x + 1 = 10$ and solve for x. Thus, $x = 3$.

   Alternative solution: With your graphing calculator, graph $y = 10$ and $y = 3x + 1$ and find their intersection point, $(3, 10)$.

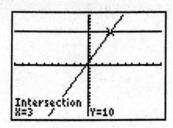

3. **B**   When asked to find $f(1)$, you must find the value of y when $x = 1$. On the graph, the point $(1, 4)$ tells you that, when $x = 1$, $y = 4$.

4. **B**   Since $t = 16$,

$$P(16) = 60 + \sqrt{16 + 48} = 60 + \sqrt{64} = 60 + 8 + 68$$

   Thus, Sally will earns $68.00 if she works for 16 hours.

5. **B**   In the statement $h(2) = 3$, 2 is the input and 3 is the output. Thus, the point $(2, 3)$ lies on the graph of h.

6. **C**   Using the function from choice C, you see that $f(3) = 3 - 2 = 1$, that is, $f(3) = 1$.

7. **B**   Since $f(x) = 13$ tells you that the output is 13, set $2x - 3 = 13$ and solve for x. Thus, $x = 8$.

   Alternative solution: With your graphing calculator, graph $y = 13$ and $y = 2x - 3$ and find their intersection point, $(8, 13)$.

8. **D** $G(3)$ means that the input (first coordinate) must be 3. Use this information to determine the output. The point $(3, -6)$ has an output value of -6.

9. **D**   Since $f(-1) = 1$ and $f(1) = 1$, $f(-1) + f(1) = 2$, not 0.

10. **C** $A(3)$ asks you to find the surface area when the radius is 3:

$$A(3) = 4\pi(3)^2 = 36\pi \approx 113$$

11. **B**   Since $f(x) = (x - 2)(x + 3)$, substituting 1 for x gives

$$f(1) = (1 - 2)(1 + 3) = (-1)(4) = -4$$

12. **B**   When $f(x) = -2$, the output (y-value) must be -2. $(1, -2)$ is the point on the graph having a y-value of -2. The x-coordinate of this point is 1.

13. **D**   When the input is 5, equation D yields

$$f(5) = 5(5) + 20 = 25 + 20 = 45$$

This is not the required output of 25, so $f(x) = 5x + 20$ is *not* a possible rule for $f(x)$.

3.3 Domain and Range

Now that you know how to identify a function, it's time to take a closer look at input and output. For example, examine the birthday function below. This function takes someone's name as the input and returns his or her birthday as the output.

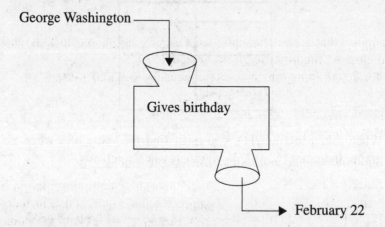

What other inputs could you use? You could input the names of other persons. The set of all possible inputs (in this case, all persons' names) is the **domain** of a function.

What are the possible outputs? The outputs are all of the 365 days that make up the year (366 in a leap year). The set of all possible outputs is the **range** of a function.

In this section you will be asked to find the domain and range of various functions from a table, graph, equation, or verbal description.

Example 1: Find the domain and range of $f(x)$.

x	-4	-2	0	2	4	6	8
$f(x)$	7	-3	5	-1	3	1	-5

The domain is the set of all the x-values: $\{-4, -2, 0, 2, 4, 6, 8\}$.

The range is the set of all the $f(x)$ values, usually rearranged in increasing order: $\{-5, -3, -1, 1, 3, 5, 7\}$.

Example 2: Find the domain and range of the following function:

$$\{(0, 3), (2, 5), (4, 3), (-2, -1), (6, 5)\}$$

When ordered pairs are listed, they are always in the form (input, output). The domain is the set of all inputs: $\{-2, 0, 2, 4, 6\}$.

The range is the set of all outputs: {−1, 3, 5}. Notice that, if an output such as 3, appears twice, it is listed only once in the range.

Finding the domain and range from the graph of a function can be tricky, especially when the graph has endpoints. Examples 3–7 illustrate how to determine domain and range for different types of graphs.

Example 3: Find the domain and range of the given graph.

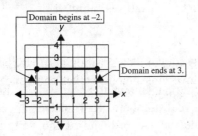

When determining the domain and range of a function from a graph, it can be helpful to draw dotted lines from the endpoints to the axes (see figure).

Domain: $-2 \leq x \leq 3$
Range: $y = 2$

Notice in Example 3 that ≤, *not* <, symbols were used in writing the domain. That's because the graph had closed (filled-in) circles at the endpoints.

The rule for determining which correct inequality symbols to use is:

- for "closed" endpoints (●), use ≤ or ≥ symbols.
- for "open" endpoints (○), use < or > symbols.

Example 4: Find the domain and range of the given graph.

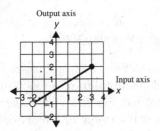

Since the right endpoint is filled in but the left endpoint is not, this function includes the point (3,2) and does *not* include the point (−2, −1). The domain extends horizontally from −2 to 3 (excluding −2). The range extends vertically from −1 to 2 (excluding −1).

Domain: $-2 < x \leq 3$
Range: $-1 < y \leq 2$

Example 5: Find the domain and range of the given graph.

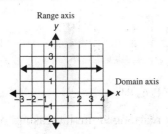

This function does not have endpoints. It continues to the right and left forever. Its domain covers all values of x. Since the line is horizontal, this function has only one range value, $y = 2$.

Domain: all real numbers
Range: $y = 2$

Example 6: Find the domain and range of the given graph.

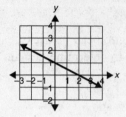

As in Example 5, this function does not have endpoints. It goes both right and left forever, as well as up and down forever. For this line and all diagonal lines without endpoints, both the domain and the range are all real numbers.

Domain: all real numbers
Range: all real numbers

Example 7: Find the domain and range of the parabola below.

Quadratic functions have U-shaped graphs called parabolas. The domain of every quadratic function is all real numbers because any real number can be used as an input.

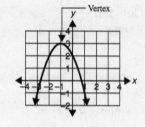

Since this function is known to be a parabola, its domain is all real numbers. To find the range, first determine the y-coordinate of the vertex. The vertex of this parabola has a y-value of 3. Since the graph opens downward, all other y-coordinates of this parabola are less than 3. Therefore, the range is all numbers less than or equal to 3.

Domain: all real numbers
Range: $y \leq 3$

When asked to find the domain and range of a function given its *equation*, consider the function's *graph*, and then apply the techniques shown in Examples 3–7.

Example 8: Find the domain and range of $f(x) = 3x + 4$.

This is an equation of a linear function in the familiar $y = mx + b$ form. It has a slope of 3 and a y-intercept of 4. Since the function graphs as a diagonal line, both its domain and range are all real numbers (refer to Example 6).

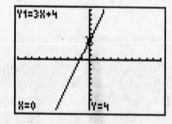

Domain: all real numbers
Range: all real numbers

Example 9: Find the domain and range of $f(x) = x^2 - 6x + 7$.

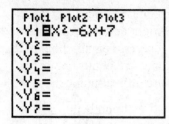

This is an equation of a quadratic function. It has the form $y = ax^2 + bx + c$. Like all quadratic functions, its domain is all real numbers. To find the range, graph the function on your calculator and use the techniques in Example 7. The range is $y \geq -2$.

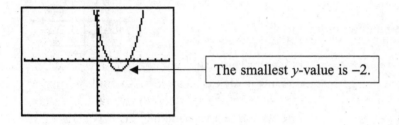

The smallest y-value is -2.

Example 10: What is the range of the function $f(x) = 3x - 7$ when the domain is $\{-1, 2, 4, 5\}$?

Here the domain is *restricted* to just four elements. Substitute the four values into the function for x. The set of outputs will be the range.

Sometimes a chart helps in keeping organized.

Domain	$f(x) = 3x - 7$	Outputs ($f(x)$), the Range
−1	$f(-1) = 3(-1) - 7$	−10
2	$f(2) = 3(2) - 7$	−1
4	$f(4) = 3(4) - 7$	5
5	$f(5) = 3(5) - 7$	8

The range of $f(x) = 3x - 7$ is $\{-10, -1, 5, 8\}$.

Here are four important facts to remember about finding domain and range:

- Domain elements are the first components in ordered pairs; range elements are the second components. Remember the form: (input, output).
- On a graph, the horizontal axis is the "input," or domain, axis and the vertical axis is the "output," or "range," axis.
- When given an equation of a function, you can graph it on your calculator. Use the graph to help you find the domain and range.
- Both linear and quadratic functions have domains of **all real numbers**.

Practice

Use the graph of the parabola at the right for questions 1 and 2.

1. Find the domain of the function in the graph.

   A. $x \geq 0$
   B. $y \leq 4$
   C. $-2 \leq x \leq 2$
   D. All real numbers

2. Find the range of the function in the graph.

   A. $y \leq 4$
   B. $0 \leq y \leq 4$
   C. $-2 \leq y \leq 2$
   D. All real numbers

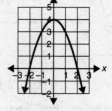

Use the graph at the right for questions 3 and 4.

3. Find the domain of the relation in the graph.

   A. $x = 2$
   B. $y = 2$
   C. $x = -2$
   D. All real numbers

4. Find the range of the relation in the graph.

   A. $x = 2$
   B. $y = 2$
   C. $-1 \leq y \leq 4$
   D. All real numbers

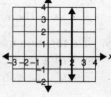

Use the graph at the right for questions 5 and 6.

5. Which statement about the graph is *not* true?

   A. Its domain is all real numbers.
   B. Its range is $\{-1\}$.
   C. It is a function.
   D. The equation of this graph is $x = -1$.

6. Which of the following statements is TRUE about the graph?

   A. The input is a constant.
   B. The output is a constant.
   C. Every ordered pair has the form (k, k).
   D. The graph does not represent a function.

7. Which graph has domain $x \geq 2$?

A.

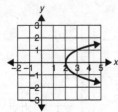

B.

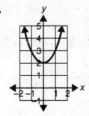

C.

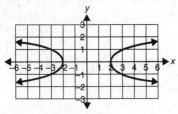

D.

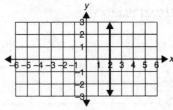

8. Which graph has a range of all real numbers?

A.

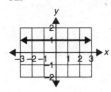

B.

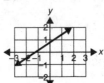

C.

D.

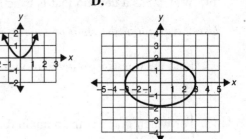

9. The function machine in the diagram produces the area of a circle when given a value for the radius. What is the domain of this function?

A. All real numbers
B. All positive numbers and 0
C. $\{1, 2, 3, 4, 5, \ldots\}$
D. $\{\pi, 2\pi, 3\pi, 4\pi, \ldots\}$

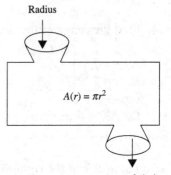

10. What is the domain of the following set of ordered pairs?
$\{(0, 3), (1, -1), (2, 4), (3, 3)\}$

A. All real numbers
B. $x \geq 0$
C. $\{-1, 3, 4\}$
D. $\{0, 1, 2, 3\}$

11. What is the range of $f(x) = 2x - 5$ when the domain is $\{1, 3, 5\}$?

A. $\{3, 4, 5\}$
B. All real numbers
C. $\{-3, 1, 5\}$
D. $\{1, 3, 5\}$

12. What is the range of $y = x^2$?

A. All real numbers
B. $\{0, 1, 4, 9, 16, 25, \ldots\}$
C. All integers
D. $y \geq 0$

13. Which function has domain {0, 1, 2, 3}?

A.

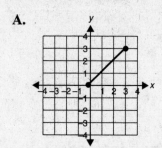

B.

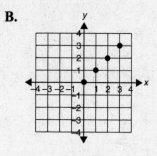

C.

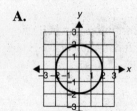

x	2	1	−1	−2
y	0	1	2	3

D. {(1, −1), (2, −1), (−3, 3), (−1, 0)}

14. Which has a domain that is exactly the same as its range?

A. $f(x) = x^2$
B. $f(x) = x - 1$
C. $x = 2$
D. $f(x) = 2$

15. For which graph is the domain different from the range?

A.

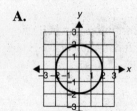

B.

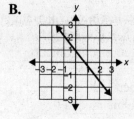

C.

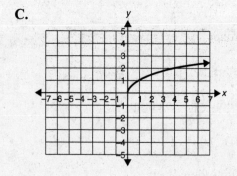

D.

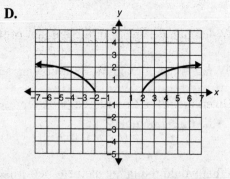

16. Which number is <u>not</u> an element of the domain?

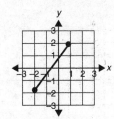

    A. 0   **B.** $\dfrac{1}{2}$

    C. 1   **D.** 2

17. What is the range of the graph?

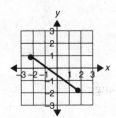

    A. $-2 \le y \le 2$ **B.** $y \ge -2$

    C. $-2 \le y \le 1$ **D.** All real numbers

18. Which number is in the range of the given function, but <u>not</u> in the domain? {(0, 1), (1, 2), (2, 3), (3, 4)}

    A. 0   **B.** 1   **C.** 3   **D.** 4

19. Assume that the pattern of ordered pairs shown in the table continues for 100 entries. What number would have to be in the domain of the function?

x	0	1	3	6	10	15	. . .
y	0	5	10	15	20	25	. . .

    A. 30   **B.** 34   **C.** 35   **D.** 36

20. Which number is <u>not</u> in the domain of the function $f(x) = \sqrt{x-1}$?

    A. 1   **B.** 2   **C.** 3   **D.** 0

21. Given the set of 26 ordered pairs represented by this function:

$$\{(a, a^2), (b, b^3), (c, c^4), (d, d^5), \ldots, (z, z^{27})\}$$

What would the <u>range</u> element be for the fifth ordered pair?

    A. d^5 **B.** e^5 **C.** (e, e^6) **D.** e^6

22. Which choice is <u>reasonable</u> as an element of the range of the function machine shown?

A. Your teacher's name

B. $\dfrac{1}{2}$

C. 4

D. 50

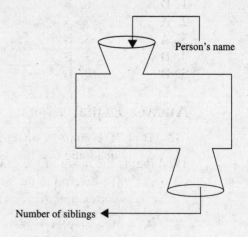

Person's name

Number of siblings

Answers

1. **D**	6. **B**	11. **C**	16. **D**	21. **D**
2. **A**	7. **A**	12. **D**	17. **C**	22. **C**
3. **A**	8. **B**	13. **B**	18. **D**	
4. **D**	9. **B**	14. **B**	19. **D**	
5. **D**	10. **D**	15. **D**	20. **D**	

Answer Explanations

1. **D** The graph is a parabola; therefore, the function is quadratic. The domain of a quadratic function is all real numbers.

2. **A** To determine the range, you need the y-coordinate of the vertex. Since the vertex point is (0, 4), and the graph lies *below* this vertex, the range is $y \le 4$.

3. **A** The graph is a vertical line. All points lying on this graph will be of the form $(2, k)$, where k is any number. The only input value is 2; thus the domain is $x = 2$.

4. **D** Since the graph is a vertical line and goes upward and downward forever, all numbers are possible outputs. The range, therefore, is all real numbers.

5. **D** Since the graph is a horizontal line, the equation will be of the form $y =$ some number. Thus, the equation could not be $x = -1$ since this produces a vertical line.

6. **B** The equation of the horizontal line is $y = -1$. Since the y-values are the outputs and are always equal to -1, the output is a constant.

7. **A** The vertex of sideways parabola A is (2, 0). The graph continues to the right forever; thus the domain (all possible x-values) is all values greater than or equal to 2.

8. **B** A diagonal line has both domain and range of all real numbers.

9. **B** Since the radius of a circle cannot be a negative quantity, the possible inputs (domain) are all positive numbers and 0.

10. **D** In a listing of ordered pairs, the domain is the set of first coordinates. For the given list, the first coordinates, written in order, are {0, 1, 2, 3}.

11. **C** The given domain (set of inputs) is {1, 3, 5}. Calculate $f(1) = -3, f(3) = 1$, and $f(5) = 5$; then the range is {−3, 1, 5}.

12. **D** Using your graphing calculator, examine the graph of $y = x^2$. The vertex point is (0, 0), and the graph is *above* this point. Therefore the range is $y \ge 0$.

13. **B** The graph of function B is the set of ordered pairs {(0, 1), (1, 2), (2, 3), (3, 4)}. The domain is the first coordinate of each of the ordered pairs: {0, 1, 2, 3}.

14. **B** Since $f(x) = x - 1$ is a linear function, both its domain and range are all real numbers.

15. **D** The domain of graph D is $x \le -2$ or $x \ge 2$. The range is $y \ge 0$ since all the values are on or above the x-axis.

16. **D** Since the domain is the set of possible inputs (x-values) and the highest value of x on the graph is 1, 2 is not in the domain.

17. **C** The range is the set of possible outputs (*y*-values). The graph extends vertically from the lowest *y*-value, −2, to the highest *y*-value, 1. Since both endpoints are closed (have filled-in circles), use the ≤ symbol. Thus, the range is $-2 \leq y \leq 1$.

18. **D** The domain is the set of first coordinates of the ordered pairs: {0, 1, 2, 3}. The range is the set of second coordinates: {1, 2, 3, 4}. The only range value not in the domain is 4.

19. **D** The domain (possible *x*-values) would be as follows if the pattern continues: {0, 1, 3, 6, 10, 15, 21, 28, 36, . . .}. Notice that the difference between consecutive terms increases by 1 each time.

20. **D** If 0 is substituted into the function for *x*, you will need to evaluate $f(0) = \sqrt{0-1} = \sqrt{-1}$. This is not possible because $\sqrt{-1}$ yields a nonreal result.

21. **D** The fifth ordered pair would be (e, e^6). The second coordinate, e^6, would be the range element.

22. **C** This function machine takes someone's name as an input and returns the number of siblings he or she has as the output. Of the given choices, only 4 is reasonable as a number of siblings.

3.4 Zeros of a Function

A number that is an *input* of a function and produces an output equal to 0 is called a *zero* of that function.

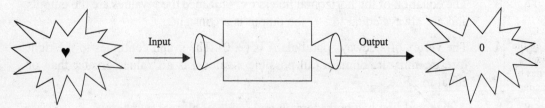

♥ is the **zero** of this function.

When ♥ is a zero of a function, $f(♥) = 0$. The point (♥, 0) will lie on the graph of the function.

As shown in Examples 1–3, the zeros of a function can often be determined simply by reading a graph, a table, or a listing that represents the function.

<u>**Example 1:**</u> On the graph of a function, the **x-intercepts** of the graphs are zeros of the function.

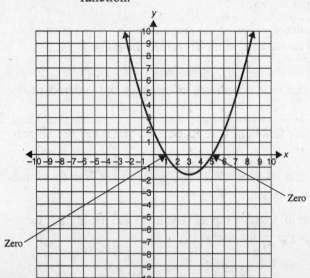

1 and 5 are the zeros of this function.

Example 2: In a table, zeros are the **x-values** that have y-values equal to 0.

x	y
-3	4
-2	0
-1	2
0	6
1	0
2	8

zero ⟶ (-2, 0)

zero ⟶ (1, 0)

Zeros of a function are always x-values (inputs), *not* y-values (outputs).

-2 and 1 are the zeros of this function. (NOTE: 6 is *not* a zero of the function).

Example 3: In a list of ordered pairs (x, y), the zeros are the **x-values** that are paired with y-values of 0.

$$\left\{ (5,-5), \left(\frac{1}{2},0\right), (0,-2), \left(\frac{3}{4},\frac{1}{4}\right) \right\}$$

$\frac{1}{2}$ is the zero of this function.

(NOTE: -2 is *not* a zero of the function).

If you are shown a "complete" graph of a function, you can tell how many real zeros that function has. Just count the number of x-intercepts!

Example 4: Determine the number of real zeros for each function graphed below.

Note: A *complete* graph of a function is one that shows all the important properties of the function.

<u>Linear functions can have:</u>

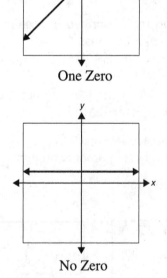

One Zero

No Zero

<u>Quadratic functions can have:</u>

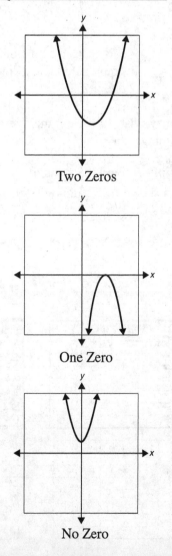

Two Zeros

One Zero

No Zero

Finding zeros when given the equation of a function is one of the most important skills you must learn in algebra. The technique is simple: To find zeros from an equation, set y equal to zero and solve for x. Examples 5–10 illustrate the technique for linear and quadratic functions.

Example 5: Find the zeros of $y = 2x - 1$.

$$0 = 2x - 1 \qquad \text{Set } y = 0.$$
$$1 = 2x \qquad \text{Solve for } x.$$
$$\boxed{x = \frac{1}{2}}$$

$\frac{1}{2}$ is the only zero of $y = 2x - 1$.

Example 6: Find the zeros of $2x + 3y = 6$.

$$2x + 3(0) = 6 \qquad \text{Set } y = 0.$$
$$2x + 0 = 6$$
$$2x = 6 \qquad \text{Solve for } x.$$
$$\boxed{x = 3}$$

3 is the only zero of $2x + 3y = 6$. The functions in Examples 5 and 6 both graph as diagonal lines. Each has only one x-intercept and therefore, only one zero.

You may wish to review the "zero product property" described in section 2.13 before continuing.

Example 7: Find the zeros of $f(x) = (x - 5)(x + 2)$.

$f(x)$ is the same as y.

$$y = (x - 5)(x + 2)$$
$$0 = (x - 5)(x + 2) \qquad \text{Set } y = 0.$$
$$x - 5 = 0 \quad \text{or} \quad x + 2 = 0 \qquad \text{Set each factor} = 0.$$
$$\text{(Apply zero product property).}$$
$$\boxed{x = 5} \quad \text{or} \quad \boxed{x = -2} \qquad \text{Solve for } x.$$

Step 1

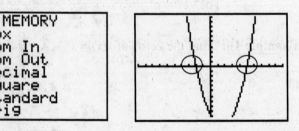

Step 2   Step 3

Notice in Example 7 that the zeros of the function are 5 and −2 and the factors were $(x − 5)$ and $(x + 2)$.

By working backward, you can use the x-intercepts (the zeros) of a function to help you factor polynomials as illustrated in Example 8.

Example 8: Factor $y = x^2 + 5x − 6$ by finding the zeros.

The **factor theorem** states:

If a is a zero of $f(x)$, then $(x − a)$ is a factor of $f(x)$.

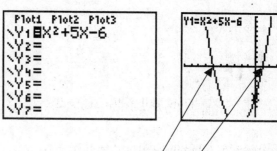

Step 1: Graph $y = x^2 + 5x − 6$.

Step 2: Find the zeros.   The zeros are −6 and 1.

Step 3: Convert the zeros to   If −6 is a zero, then one of the factors
          factors. (Apply the   must be $(x + 6)$.
          Factor Theorem)   If 1 is a zero, then one of the factors must
                                        be $(x − 1)$.

Step 4: Write in factored $y = (x + 6)(x − 1)$
          form and check. $y = x^2 − 1x + 6x − 6$ FOIL
                                       $y = x^2 + 5x − 6$ ✔

The equation $y = x^2 + 5x − 6$ in factored form is $y = (x + 6)(x − 1)$.

Example 9: Find the zeros of $y = x^2 − 4$.

$$0 = x^2 − 4$$ Set $y = 0$.
$$0 = (x − 2)(x + 2)$$ Factor.
$$x − 2 = 0 \quad \text{or} \quad x + 2 = 0$$ Set each factor = 0.

$$\boxed{x = 2} \quad \text{or} \quad \boxed{x = −2}$$ Solve for x.

The zeros of $y = x^2 − 4$ are 2 and −2.

Example 10: Find the zeros of $f(x) = x^2 + 2$.

$$0 = x^2 + 2$$
$$x^2 = −2$$
$$x = ±\sqrt{−2}$$

The function f has no real zeros.

Practice

1. Which of the following linear functions has no zeros?

   A. $y = 2x$ **B.** $y = 2$ **C.** $y = 2x - 2$ **D.** $x + y = 0$

2. How many real zeros does this function have?

   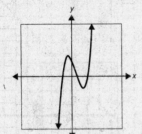

   A. 0   **B.** 1

   C. 3   **D.** 4

3. Which number is the zero of the function $f(x) = 3x - 6$?

   A. 0   **B.** 2   **C.** 3   **D.** −6

4. Which quadratic function has exactly one zero?

   A. $y = (x - 1)^2$ **B.** $y = x^2 - 1$ **C.** $y = x^2 + 1$ **D.** $y = -x^2 + 1$

5. Which number is a zero of the function $y = x^2 + x - 2$?

   A. 0   **B.** −1   **C.** 2   **D.** −2

6. Identify the zero from the given table of values:

x	y
−3	−5
0	3
1	−1
2	0

   A. 0   **B.** 3

   C. 2   **D.** −3

7. Which function has −3 as a zero?

   A. $y = x + 3$ **B.** $y = (x - 3)(x + 2)$

   C. $f(x) = 3$ **D.** $f(x) = x^2 + 9$

8. Which graph has −2 as a zero?

A.

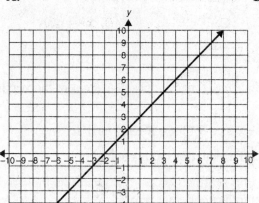

B.

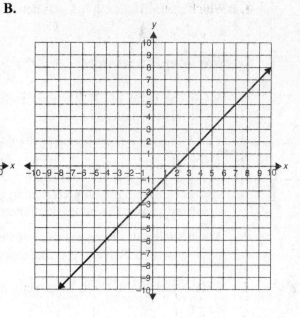

C.

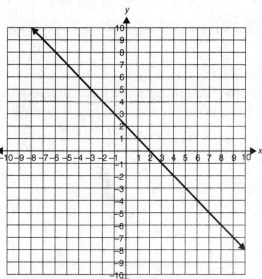

D.

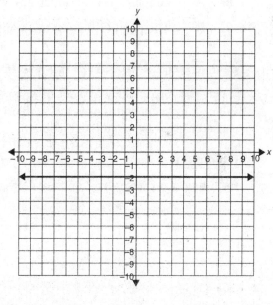

9. If 3 is a zero of some function f, which statement about the function is *not* true?

    A. $f(3) = 0$
    B. The point (0, 3) lies on the graph of function f.
    C. The graph of function f crosses the x-axis at $x = 3$.
    D. If f is a linear function, $f(x) = 2x - 6$ could be its equation.

Answers

1. **B**   3. **B**   5. **D**   7. **A**   9. **B**
2. **C**   4. **A**   6. **C**   8. **A**

Answer Explanations

1. **B**   The graph of $y = 2$ is a horizontal line. Since it does not intersect the x-axis, this function has no zeros.

2. **C**   Since this function intersects the x-axis 3 times, it has 3 real zeros.

3. **B**   Setting $f(x) = 0$ gives $0 = 3x - 6$. The solution of this equation is $x = 2$.

4. **A**   Using the graphing calculator, you see that $y = (x - 1)^2$ intersects the x-axis only once. Therefore, this function has only one zero.

5. **D**   Setting $y = 0$ and factoring gives $0 = (x + 2)(x - 1)$. Then, either $x + 2 = 0$ or $x - 1 = 0$. Solving, you find that $x = -2$ and $x = 1$ are the zeros of this function.

   Alternate solution: Graph $y = x^2 + x - 2$ on a calculator and count the number of x intercepts.

6. **C**   2 is the input (x-value) that has an output (y-value) of zero.

7. **A**   Setting $y = 0$ gives $0 = x + 3$. The solution of this equation is $x = -3$.

8. **A**   Graph A has an x-intercept of -2, which is the zero of the function.

9. **B**   The point $(3, 0)$, *not* the point $(0, 3)$, lies on the graph of f.

3.5 From Patterns to Rules

When you look closely at a set of ordered pairs, you can often uncover a pattern in the values. Linear functions have the simplest pattern: whenever x changes by a fixed amount, y also changes by some fixed amount.

Example 1: Examine the given set of ordered pairs for a pattern.

Each time x increases by 2 units, y decreases by 5 units.

The symbol Δ means "change in."

$\Delta x = 2$

x	y
-2	15
0	10
2	5
4	0
6	-5

$\Delta y = -5$

Since a **constant change in** x produces a **constant change in** y, this function is **linear.**

Example 2: Write an equation for the linear function that contains the ordered pairs in the table for Example 1.

Examples of slopes:

$$m = \frac{4}{3}$$

As x increases by 3, y **increases** by 4.

$$m = \frac{-4}{3}$$

As x increases by 3, y **decreases** by 4.

Slope: $\qquad\qquad\qquad\qquad m = \dfrac{\Delta y}{\Delta x} = \dfrac{-5}{2}$

y-Intercept: $\qquad\qquad\qquad b = 10$ (The point $(0, 10)$ is in the table.)

Slope-intercept form: $\qquad y = mx + b$

$$y = \frac{-5}{2}x + 10$$

Example 3: Plot the points in the table from Example 1 to determine whether they follow a linear pattern.

You can see from the graph that a straight line would connect all of the given points. Therefore, the ordered pairs in the table follow a linear pattern.

Notice that the line has a y-intercept of 10 and a slope of $-\dfrac{5}{2}$, which is consistent with the result of Example 2.

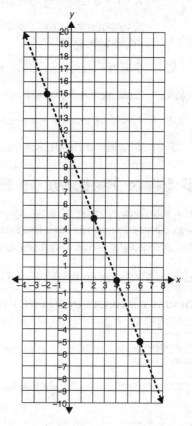

Of course, not all patterns are linear. Only linear functions exhibit a linear pattern. Consider the following table of values:

x	−2	−1	0	1	2	3
y	4	1	0	1	4	9

The pattern exhibited in the table is *not* linear because the y-values change by varying amounts as the x-values increase by a constant amount. This table reflects a quadratic pattern. Each y-value is the square of the corresponding x-value. The pattern follows the rule $y = x^2$.

In Algebra I, we are principally concerned with linear and quadratic patterns, but as you continue in your study of mathematics, you will see that many other patterns exist.

Practice

1. If the table at the right represents ordered pairs from a linear function, what is the value of A?

   A. 9.2   **B.** 9.8
   C. 9.9   **D.** 9.1

x	y
2	9.5
2.4	A
2.8	8.9
3.2	8.6

2. Given the linear function $y = 2x - 3$. Each time x increases by 5 units, how does y change?

   A. y increases by 5 units.
   B. y decreases by 5 units.
   C. y increases by 10 units.
   D. y decreases by 10 units.

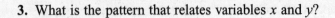

Use the graph at the right to answer questions 3 and 4.

3. What is the pattern that relates variables x and y?

   A. x increases three times as fast as y.
   B. y increases three times as fast as x.
   C. When x increases by 3 units, y decreases by 1 unit.
   D. When x increases by 1 unit, y decreases by 3 units.

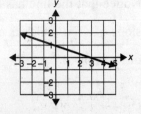

4. Suppose the point (a, b) lies on this graph. Which of the following ordered pairs must also lie on the graph?

   A. (b, a) **B.** $(a + 1, b + 1)$ **C.** $(a + 3, b - 1)$ **D.** $(a + 1, b - 1)$

5. Suppose the point $(100, 45)$ lies on the graph of a linear function whose slope is $\frac{2}{3}$. If the point $(103, y)$ also lies on this graph, what is the value of y?

   A. 48   **B.** 47   **C.** 43   **D.** 42

Use the following information to answer questions 6 and 7.

Mark's chemistry teacher gave the following table on a recent test:

Degrees Celsius:	5	10	15	20	25
Degrees Fahrenheit:	41	50	59	68	77

The table compares Celsius temperatures with equivalent Fahrenheit temperatures.

6. From the table, it is apparent that the relationship between Celsius and Fahrenheit temperatures is linear because

   A. Celsius temperature increases by a constant 5°.
   B. Fahrenheit temperature increases by a constant 9°.
   C. Each time Celsius temperature increases by 5°, Fahrenheit temperature increases by 9°.
   D. Fahrenheit temperature is consistently higher than Celsius temperature.

7. Which of the following equations describes the relationship between Celsius temperature (C) and Fahrenheit temperature (F)?

   A. $C = \dfrac{9}{5}F + 32$ **B.** $F = \dfrac{9}{5}C + 32$ **C.** $F = \dfrac{9}{5}(C + 32)$ **D.** $F = \dfrac{5}{9}(C - 32)$

---

8. Which table represents a linear pattern?

   A.

-2	-1	0	1	2
5	3	1	-1	-3

   B.

-2	-1	0	1	2
5	-5	5	-5	5

   C.

-2	-1	0	1	2
2	1	0	1	2

   D.

-2	-1	0	1	2
1	10	100	1000	10,000

Use the following information to answer questions 9 and 10.

Anna rode her stationary bike at a constant rate of speed for 1 hour. The table below shows the distance readings displayed on the odometer of the bike every 10 minutes.

Time (min):	0	10	20	30	40	50	60
Distance (mi)	5	7	9	11	13	15	17

9. What was Anna's speed?

   A. 2 mi/hr   **B.** 0.2 mi/min   **C.** 2 mi/min   **D.** 0.2 mi/hr

10. Which equation represents Anna's distance, d, as a function of time, t?

   A. $d = 0.2t$ **B.** $d = 5t + 5$ **C.** $d = 0.2t + 5$ **D.** $d = 0.2t + 2$

Use the following table of values to answer questions 11 and 12:

x	1	2	3	4	5
y	70	60	50	40	30

11. If the above table were expanded to include other points belonging to the same linear function, which point could *not* belong?

   A. (0, 80)   **B.** (10, −20)   **C.** (6.5, 15)   **D.** (50, 300)

12. Which equation contains *all* of the ordered pairs in the table?

   A. $y = 10x + 60$ **B.** $y = -10x + 70$ **C.** $y = -10x + 80$ **D.** $y = 10x + 80$

13. The ordered pairs in the given table follow a quadratic pattern. What is the value of A?

x	−6	−3	0	3	6	9
y	36	9	0	9	36	A

   A. −9   **B.** 0   **C.** 45   **D.** 81

Answers

1. **A**	4. **C**	7. **B**	10. **C**	13. **D**
2. **C**	5. **B**	8. **A**	11. **D**	
3. **C**	6. **C**	9. **B**	12. **C**	

Answer Explanations

1. **A**   Since the pattern is linear, when x changes by a fixed amount, y also changes by a fixed amount. The x's increase by 0.4 as the y's decrease by 0.3. The amount 0.3 can be found by noticing that the y-value of 8.9 decreases to 8.6. Therefore, 9.5 would decrease to 9.2, the value of A.

2. **C**   Since the slope of the line $y = 2x - 3$ is $\frac{\Delta y}{\Delta x} = \frac{2}{1}$, you know that, as the x-values increase by 1, the y-values increase by 2. Therefore, if the x-values increase by 5, the y-values will increase by twice as much, 10.

3. **C**   The line has a slope of $\frac{-1}{3}$. Therefore, as the x-values increase by 3, the y-values decrease by 1.

4. **C**   Since, from question 3, as the x-values increase by 3, the y-values decrease by 1, the point (a, b) would become $(a + 3, b - 1)$.

5. **B**   A slope of $\frac{2}{3}$ means that, as the x-values increase by 3, the y-values increase by 2. The point $(100, 45)$ becomes $(103, 47)$ using this pattern.

6. **C**   Each time the Celsius values increase by 5°, the Fahrenheit values increase by 9°. Although choices A through D all correctly describe the table, only choice C explains why the relationship between Celsius and Fahrenheit temperatures is linear.

7. **B**   The slope is the change in F over the change in C, $\frac{\Delta F}{\Delta C} = \frac{9}{5}$. On the table, locate the value $(5, 41)$. The preceding point must have been $(0, 32)$ since C increases by 5 as F increases by 9. The point $(0, 32)$ is the y-intercept. The equation, therefore, is $F = \frac{9}{5}C + 32$.

8. **A**   In table A, the values in the first row increase by a constant 1 while the values in the second row decrease by a constant 2.

9. **B**   Since distance = rate · time, $d = rt$, solve for r: $r = \frac{d}{t}$. You can find the rate, therefore, by dividing distance by time. Anna traveled 12 miles over the 60-minute time interval. Therefore, her speed, or rate, is

$$\frac{12 \, \text{mi}}{60 \, \text{min}} = 0.2 \, \text{mi/min}$$

10. **C**   Anna's rate (or slope) is 0.2 (see question 9). The point $(0, 5)$ is the y-intercept. Using $y = mx + b$ yields the equation $d = 0.2t + 5$.

11. **D** The pattern shows that, as x-values increase by 1, y-values *decrease* by 10. The point (50, 300) is not possible because both the x- and y-values have increased.

12. **C** The pattern shows that, as x-values increase by 1, y-values *decrease* by 10. This translates to a slope of

$$\frac{\Delta y}{\Delta x} = \frac{-10}{1} = -10$$

The point (1, 70) indicates that the previous point (the y-intercept) must have been (0, 80). Using $y = mx + b$ yields $y = -10x + 80$.

13. **D** The pattern is quadratic with $y = x^2$. Since $x = 9$, $y = 9^2 = 81$, so $A = 81$.

3.6 Direct Variation

When two variable quantities have a constant ratio, their relationship is called a *direct variation*. In this section you will learn how to recognize direct variations from tables and graphs and how to write equations for direct variations.

A. Identifying Direct Variation from a Table

For a direct variation, the ratio of y to x, also written as $\frac{y}{x}$, will be the same for *all* ordered pairs in a table.

Direct Variation	Not Direct Variation

Example 1:

x	y	Divide: y/x
1	3	3/1 = 3
2	6	6/2 = 3
3	9	9/3 = 3
4	12	12/4 = 3

This table of values represents a direct variation because the ratio $\frac{y}{x}$ has a constant value, 3.

x	y	Divide: y/x
1	6	6/1 = 6
2	9	9/2 = 4.5
3	12	12/3 = 4
4	15	15/4 = 3.75

The relationship shown in this table of values is *not* a direct variation because you get different numbers when you divide $\frac{y}{x}$.

Example 2:

x	6	5	4	3
y	12	10	8	6

$$\frac{12}{6} = \frac{10}{5} = \frac{8}{4} = \frac{6}{3} = 2$$

This table represents a direct variation because, when you divide y by x, you get a constant ratio of 2.

x	4	3	2	1
y	12	10	8	6

$$\frac{12}{4} \neq \frac{10}{3} \neq \frac{8}{2} \neq \frac{6}{1}$$

The relationship shown in this table is *not* a direct variation because the ratios of y to x are different for different ordered pairs.

B. Identifying Direct Variation from a Graph

A direct (linear) variation will always graph as a *line* through the *origin*.

| Direct Variation | Not Direct Variation |

Example 3:

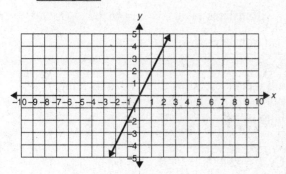

This graph represents a direct variation since the line passes through the origin.

Because the line does *not* contain the origin, this graph does *not* represent a direct variation.

C. Writing an Equation for Direct Variation

A direct (linear) variation can always be represented by an equation of the form $y = kx$, where k is called the *constant of variation*.

Example 4: Write an equation for the direct variation represented in the table below.

Step 1: Write the direct variation equation:

$$y = kx$$

Step 2: Substitute any pair of values from the table, and solve for k:

$$10 = k(5)$$
$$2 = k$$

x	y
5	10
7	14
9	18
11	22

Step 3: Rewrite the direct variation equation, replacing k with its value, found in step 2:

$$\boxed{y = 2x}$$

Example 5 illustrates how to use a direct variation relationship to find the value for an unknown.

Example 5: If A varies directly as B and $A = 6$ when $B = 18$, find B when $A = 4$.

Step 1: Write the direct variation equation:

$$A = kB$$

Step 2: Substitute the given pair of values, and solve for k:

$$6 = k(18)$$
$$\frac{1}{3} = k$$

Step 3: Rewrite the direct variation equation, replacing k with its value, found in step 2:

$$A = \frac{1}{3}B$$

Step 4: Finally, substitute the given value for A and solve for B:

$$4 = \frac{1}{3}B \longrightarrow \boxed{B = 12}$$

Many real-world problems involve direct variation. In such cases, you will have to translate words into symbols. Some common translations follow:

Common Translations into Equations		
"y varies directly as x"	translates to	$y = kx$
"a and b vary directly"	translates to	$a = kb$
"y is directly proportional to x"	translates to	$y = kx$

Example 6: The volume (V) of a gas in a certain container varies directly as its temperature (T). When the volume is 42 cubic centimeters, the temperature is 7°C. Which equation represents this relationship?

A. $V = \dfrac{7}{T}$ **B.** $V = 7T$ **C.** $V = 294T$ **D.** $V = 6T$

Find the constant of variation, k, by substituting 42 for V and 7 for T into the equation $V = kT$.

$$42 = k(7)$$
$$6 = k$$

Rewrite the equation substituting 6 for k. $V = 6T$

Practice

1. Which table represents a direct variation?

A.

x	2	4	6	8
y	2	3	4	5

B.

x	2	4	6	8
y	8	7	6	5

C.

x	2	4	6	8
y	8	6	4	2

D.

x	2	4	6	8
y	4	8	12	16

2. Which could *not* be a graph of a direct variation relationship?

A.

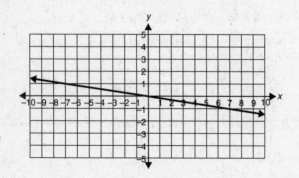

B.

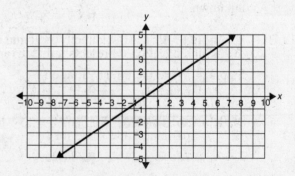

C.

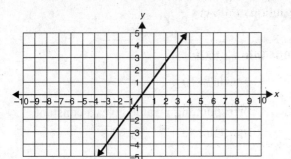

D.

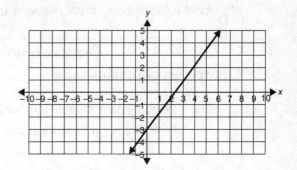

3. In the table shown, if x and y vary directly, which *must* be the value of a?

    A. 12   B. 10
    C. 15   D. 14

x	y
6	2
a	5
18	6

4. If y varies directly as x and $x = 8$ when $y = 32$, which equation correctly relates x and y?

    A. $y = 8x$ B. $y = \dfrac{1}{4}x$ C. $y = 4x$ D. $y = 32x$

5. If Jerry works for 3 hours, he earns \$13.50. If he works for 5 hours, he earns \$22.50. How much money will he earn if he works for 8 hours? (Assume his hourly wage is constant.)

    A. \$32.50   B. \$36.00   C. \$32.00   D. \$34.50

6. There are 120 calories in a 10-ounce can of cola. If Brandon drank 4 ounces and there is a direct variation between ounces and calories, how many calories did Brandon consume?

    A. 30   B. 40   C. 12   D. 48

7. The resistance (R) of a copper wire varies directly as its length (L). Which equation represents this relationship?

    A. $R = kL$ B. $R = \dfrac{k}{L}$ C. $L = \dfrac{k}{R}$ D. $R = k + L$

8. Which equation represents a direct variation relationship?

    A. $y = 3x + 1$ B. $6 = 4x + y$ C. $y = -2x$ D. $xy = 4$

9. If a varies directly as b, and $a = 15$ when $b = 20$, what is a when $b = 36$?

    A. 0.75   B. 11.25   C. 27   D. 48

Answers

1. **D**   3. **C**   5. **B**   7. **A**   9. **C**
2. **D**   4. **C**   6. **D**   8. **C**

Answer Explanations

1. **D**   Dividing each y-value in table D by its corresponding x-value gives a constant ratio of 2:

$$\frac{y}{x} = \frac{4}{2} = \frac{8}{4} = \frac{12}{6} = \frac{16}{8} = 2$$

2. **D**   The graphs of a direct variation equation *must* go through the origin.

3. **C**   In the table, the ratio of y to x is

$$\frac{y}{x} = \frac{2}{6} = \frac{5}{a} = \frac{6}{18}$$

which simplifies to $\frac{1}{3}$. Since $\frac{5}{15}$ simplifies to $\frac{1}{3}$, the value of a must be 15.

4. **C**   Since y varies directly as x, $y = kx$. Substitute 32 for y and 8 for x:

$$32 = k(8) \rightarrow k = 4$$

Substituting 4 for k into $y = kx$ gives the equation $y = 4x$.

5. **B**   If Jerry works for 3 hrs and earns \$13.50, his hourly rate is $\frac{13.50}{3} = \$4.25\,\text{hr}$. If he works 8 hr, he will be paid $\$4.25(8) = \$36.00$.

6. **D**   If there are 120 cal in 10 oz of soda, there are $\frac{120}{10} = 12\,\text{cal/oz}$. If Brandon drinks 4 oz, he will have consumed $12(4) = 48$ cals.

7. **A**   "R varies directly as L" translates into $R = kL$.

8. **C**   The equation $y = -2x$ is the only choice of the form $y = kx$.

9. **C**   Substitute 15 for a and 20 for b into $a = kb$:

$$15 = k(20) \rightarrow k = \frac{3}{4}$$

Therefore, $a = \frac{3}{4}b$.

Substitute 36 for b: $a = \frac{3}{4}(36) = 27$.

Chapter 4

Statistics and Data Analysis

4.1 What Are Statistics and Data Analysis?

The field of statistics is about collecting and organizing data, analyzing the data, and using the data to draw conclusions and make predictions. In Algebra I, we use *matrices* to organize and work with data. *Box-and-whisker plots* are also used to present the data in a way that makes them easy to analyze. We make *scatterplots* to visualize patterns in the data and to fit the data points as closely as possible with a *line of best fit*.

This chapter covers how to create and use matrices, box-and-whisker plots (also known as box plots), scatterplots, and lines of best fit. We discuss the meaning of the term *range* and remind you how to find the measures of central tendency referred to as *mean*, *median*, and *mode*.

4.2 Using Matrices

What is a matrix?

A **matrix** is just an arrangement of data into neat rows and columns enclosed by big brackets [   ]. Once the data are organized in this way, it's easy to analyze and manipulate them.

Just as a rectangle has length and width, so a matrix has dimensions. The *dimensions* of a matrix are written as "number of rows" by "number of columns," or ROWS × COLUMNS. For example:

$$[B] = \begin{bmatrix} 7 & 6 & -9 & -1 \\ 5 & 0 & 7 & 2 \end{bmatrix} \left.\vphantom{\begin{matrix}7\\5\end{matrix}}\right\} \text{ROWS} = 2$$

COLUMNS = 4

2 × 4 Matrix

$$[G] = \begin{bmatrix} 3 \\ 4 \\ -1 \end{bmatrix} \left.\vphantom{\begin{matrix}3\\4\\-1\end{matrix}}\right\} \text{ROWS} = 3$$

COLUMNS = 1

3 × 1 Matrix

A. Addition and Subtraction

Two matrices can be added or subtracted only if their dimensions are the *same*.

Consider matrix *A* and matrix *B* shown below. These matrices *can* be added because they have exactly the same dimensions; each one is 3 × 2. To *add* matrices, just add the entries that are in corresponding positions.

$$[A] = \begin{bmatrix} 1 & 2 \\ 3 & 4 \\ 5 & 6 \end{bmatrix} \qquad [B] = \begin{bmatrix} 3 & 0 \\ -1 & 4 \\ 5 & 7 \end{bmatrix}$$

3 × 2 matrix   3 × 2 matrix

$$[A]+[B] = \begin{bmatrix} 1 & 2 \\ 3 & 4 \\ 5 & 6 \end{bmatrix} + \begin{bmatrix} 3 & 0 \\ -1 & 4 \\ 5 & 7 \end{bmatrix} = \begin{bmatrix} 1+3 & 2+0 \\ 3+-1 & 4+4 \\ 5+5 & 6+7 \end{bmatrix} = \begin{bmatrix} 4 & 2 \\ 2 & 8 \\ 10 & 13 \end{bmatrix}$$

You can also *subtract* matrices when they have the same dimensions.

$$[B]-[A] = \begin{bmatrix} 3 & 0 \\ -1 & 4 \\ 5 & 7 \end{bmatrix} - \begin{bmatrix} 1 & 2 \\ 3 & 4 \\ 5 & 6 \end{bmatrix} = \begin{bmatrix} 3-1 & 0-2 \\ -1-3 & 4-4 \\ 5-5 & 7-6 \end{bmatrix} = \begin{bmatrix} 2 & -2 \\ -4 & 0 \\ 0 & 1 \end{bmatrix}$$

> *Common Error Alert!*
> $[B] - [A]$ and $[A] - [B]$ are not the same!

Now, suppose that matrix C, a 3×1 matrix, is given as $[C] = \begin{bmatrix} 2 \\ 7 \\ 1 \end{bmatrix}$.

Is it possible to add matrix C and matrix A? **NO!**

$\begin{bmatrix} 1 & 2 \\ 3 & 4 \\ 5 & 6 \end{bmatrix} + \begin{bmatrix} 2 \\ 7 \\ 1 \end{bmatrix}$ is impossible because matrix A and matrix C have different dimensions.

Matrix C has no second column to combine with the second column of matrix A.

B. Scalar Multiplication

You can *multiply* any matrix by a constant (called the *scalar multiplier*). Just multiply every entry in the matrix by the *scalar*. Here's an example:

Find: $\quad 4\begin{bmatrix} 3 & 0 & -2 \\ 5 & -2 & 1 \end{bmatrix}$ ——the scalar multiplier

Answer: $\quad 4\begin{bmatrix} 3 & 0 & -2 \\ 5 & -2 & 1 \end{bmatrix} = \begin{bmatrix} 4\cdot3 & 4\cdot0 & 4\cdot-2 \\ 4\cdot5 & 4\cdot-2 & 4\cdot1 \end{bmatrix} = \begin{bmatrix} 12 & 0 & -8 \\ 20 & -8 & 4 \end{bmatrix}$

C. Applications

Matrices are very helpful in answering real-world questions. Consider Example 1.

Example 1: The counselors at Garfield High School wanted to analyze the distribution of students in the various math classes during the current school year. In order to organize the data, they arranged them into the matrices shown below:

[A] Girls

	Alg I	Geo	Alg II
Freshmen	69	60	10
Sophomores	34	105	106
Juniors	13	25	132
Seniors	10	14	60

[B] Boys

	Alg I	Geo	Alg II
Freshmen	85	68	5
Sophomores	30	83	123
Juniors	5	43	115
Seniors	3	17	54

- Find the total enrollment, by class, in each of the three math courses. To do this, ADD the matrices:

$$[A]+[B] = \begin{bmatrix} 69+85 & 60+68 & 10+5 \\ 34+30 & 105+83 & 106+123 \\ 13+5 & 25+43 & 132+115 \\ 10+3 & 14+17 & 60+54 \end{bmatrix} = \begin{bmatrix} 154 & 128 & 15 \\ 64 & 188 & 229 \\ 18 & 68 & 247 \\ 13 & 31 & 114 \end{bmatrix}$$

- Compare the number of girls to the number of boys, by class, in each course. To do this, SUBTRACT the matrices:

$$[A]-[B] = \begin{bmatrix} 69-85 & 60-68 & 10-5 \\ 34-30 & 105-83 & 106-123 \\ 13-5 & 25-43 & 132-115 \\ 10-3 & 14-17 & 60-54 \end{bmatrix} = \begin{bmatrix} -16 & -8 & 5 \\ 4 & 22 & -17 \\ 8 & -18 & 17 \\ 7 & -3 & 6 \end{bmatrix}$$

Notice that some of the entries in the answer matrix are negative! Does that seem odd? Here's an explanation. Since you subtracted the matrices in the order $[A] - [B]$, each entry in the answer matrix represents **how many more girls than boys** were in each class. Therefore, positive entries indicate more girls than boys; negative entries mean more boys than girls. For example, the entry −16 in the first row of the answer matrix tells you that 16 more freshman boys than freshman girls were taking Algebra I.

D. Using Your Calculator for Matrices

Example 2: Find $[A] + [B]$, where

$$[A] = \begin{bmatrix} 1 & 2 \\ 3 & 4 \\ 5 & 6 \end{bmatrix} \quad \text{and} \quad [B] = \begin{bmatrix} 3 & 0 \\ -1 & 4 \\ 5 & 7 \end{bmatrix}.$$

> Although your calculator can do operations on matrices, there are many opportunities to make input errors.
>
> Sometimes, it is easier to do the operations by hand!

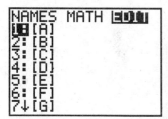

1. Press **MATRX**. Go to **EDIT**. **ENTER**.

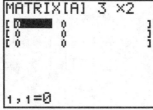

2. Enter dimensions 3 × 2.

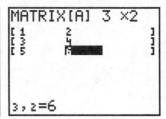

3. Input data for matrix $[A]$: Be sure to press **ENTER** after each entry, especially the last.

4. Repeat the process for matrix $[B]$.

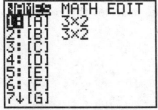

5. Press **QUIT. MATRX. ENTER**.

6. $[A]$ is on the home screen. Press +.

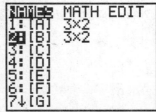

7. Press **MATRX. ENTER** to put $[B]$ on the home screen also.

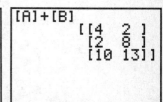

8. Press **ENTER** for the answer.

$$\text{Read from the screen: } [A]+[B] = \begin{bmatrix} 4 & 2 \\ 2 & 8 \\ 10 & 13 \end{bmatrix}.$$

Practice

1. What are the dimensions of the following matrix?

$$\begin{bmatrix} 1 & -1 & 0 & 5 \\ -6 & 2 & -3 & 1 \end{bmatrix}$$

A. 4×2 **B.** 3×2 **C.** 2×4 **D.** 2×2

2. Which of the three matrices are equal?

$$[U] = \begin{bmatrix} 3 & -4 & 3(5) \\ 0 & 1 & 2 \end{bmatrix} \quad [V] = \begin{bmatrix} 3 & -4 & 15 \\ 0 & 1 & 6 \end{bmatrix} \quad [W] = \begin{bmatrix} 2+1 & -4 & 2(7)+1 \\ 1-1 & 1+0 & 4+2 \end{bmatrix}$$

A. [U] = [V] **B.** [V] = [W] **C.** [U] = [W] **D.** [U] = [V] = [W]

3. $[A] = \begin{bmatrix} 2 & 1 \\ 4 & -2 \\ 5 & 7 \\ 0 & -1 \end{bmatrix}$ $[B] = \begin{bmatrix} 3 & 6 \\ 1 & 2 \\ -1 & 0 \\ 9 & 1 \end{bmatrix}$

$[A] + [B] = ?$

A. $\begin{bmatrix} 5 & 7 \\ 5 & 0 \\ 4 & 7 \\ 9 & -2 \end{bmatrix}$ **B.** $\begin{bmatrix} 5 & 7 \\ 5 & 0 \\ 6 & 7 \\ 9 & -2 \end{bmatrix}$ **C.** $\begin{bmatrix} -1 & -5 \\ 3 & -4 \\ 6 & 7 \\ -9 & -2 \end{bmatrix}$ **D.** $\begin{bmatrix} 5 & 7 \\ 5 & 0 \\ 4 & 7 \\ 9 & 0 \end{bmatrix}$

4. Which operation would result in the matrix $\begin{bmatrix} 5 & 0 \\ -6 & 4 \end{bmatrix}$?

A. $\begin{bmatrix} 3 & -1 \\ -3 & 1 \end{bmatrix} + \begin{bmatrix} 2 & 1 \\ 2 & 3 \end{bmatrix}$ **B.** $\begin{bmatrix} 4 & 2 \\ -1 & 1 \end{bmatrix} - \begin{bmatrix} -1 & 2 \\ 5 & -3 \end{bmatrix}$

C. $\frac{1}{2}\begin{bmatrix} 10 & 0 \\ -3 & 8 \end{bmatrix}$ **D.** $\begin{bmatrix} -1 & 2 \\ 5 & -3 \end{bmatrix} - \begin{bmatrix} 4 & 2 \\ -1 & 1 \end{bmatrix}$

5. The matrix $2\begin{bmatrix} 3 & 6 & 9 \\ 6 & 3 & 0 \\ -6 & 12 & -3 \end{bmatrix}$ is equivalent to—

A. $\frac{1}{3}\begin{bmatrix} 2 & 4 & 6 \\ 4 & 2 & 0 \\ -4 & 8 & -2 \end{bmatrix}$ **B.** $3\begin{bmatrix} 2 & 4 & 6 \\ 4 & 2 & 0 \\ -4 & 8 & -2 \end{bmatrix}$

C. $\begin{bmatrix} 6 & 12 & 18 \\ 12 & 6 & 2 \\ -12 & 24 & -6 \end{bmatrix}$ **D.** $\frac{1}{2}\begin{bmatrix} 6 & 12 & 18 \\ 12 & 6 & 0 \\ -12 & 24 & -6 \end{bmatrix}$

6. Which matrix is equal to $\begin{bmatrix} 1 & 1 \\ 1 & 1 \end{bmatrix}$?

A. $\begin{bmatrix} 1 & 1 & 1 \\ 1 & 1 & 1 \\ 1 & 1 & 1 \end{bmatrix}$

B. $\begin{bmatrix} 2 & 2 \\ 2 & 2 \end{bmatrix}$

C. $\begin{bmatrix} 1 & 1 \\ 1 & 1 \end{bmatrix}$

D. A, B, and C are all equal to $\begin{bmatrix} 1 & 1 \\ 1 & 1 \end{bmatrix}$.

Given

$$[A] = \begin{bmatrix} a & b & e \\ c & d & f \end{bmatrix} \quad [B] = \begin{bmatrix} g & h & i \\ j & k & l \end{bmatrix} \quad [C] = \begin{bmatrix} m & n \\ o & p \\ q & r \end{bmatrix}$$

where all the letters within these matrices represent numbers.

Use these matrices to answer questions 7 and 8.

7. Which operation *cannot* be performed on the above matrices?

A. $[A] + [B]$　　　**B.** $[B] - [A]$　　　**C.** $[B] + [C]$　　　**D.** $\frac{1}{2}[C]$

8. Which statement is true?

A. $[A] - [B] = [B] - [A]$
B. $[A] + [B] = [B] + [A]$
C. $2[A] = [B]$
D. $[A] + [B] = [C]$

---

9. Matrix Q below is a "magic" matrix because the sum of the numbers along any row, column, or diagonal is exactly the same. (Try it!) Matrix R is a magic matrix, too!

$$[Q] = \begin{bmatrix} 8 & 1 & 6 \\ 3 & 5 & 7 \\ 4 & 9 & 2 \end{bmatrix} \qquad [R] = \begin{bmatrix} 7 & 2 & 9 \\ 8 & 6 & 4 \\ 3 & 10 & 5 \end{bmatrix}$$

Which of the following would *not* turn out to be a magic matrix?

A. $2[Q]$

B. $[R] = \begin{bmatrix} 1 & 1 & 1 \\ 1 & 1 & 1 \\ 1 & 1 & 1 \end{bmatrix}$

C. $[Q] + [R]$
D. A, B, and C all produce magic matrices.

Use the following information and matrices to answer questions 10–12.

Simon and Cosmo do volunteer work to earn the service hours they need for graduation (besides, they're nice people). Matrix S shows how many hours Simon spent during the month of April volunteering at the animal shelter and the local hospital. Matrix C provides the same kind of data for Cosmo.

$$[S] = \begin{array}{c} \\ Week\ 1 \\ Week\ 2 \\ Week\ 3 \\ Week\ 4 \end{array} \begin{array}{cc} Shelter & Hospital \\ \left[\begin{array}{cc} 1 & 1 \\ 3 & 0 \\ 2.5 & 1 \\ 0 & 4 \end{array}\right] \end{array} \qquad [C] = \begin{array}{c} \\ Week\ 1 \\ Week\ 2 \\ Week\ 3 \\ Week\ 4 \end{array} \begin{array}{cc} Shelter & Hospital \\ \left[\begin{array}{cc} 2 & 1 \\ 0 & 3 \\ 1.5 & 1.5 \\ 2.5 & 0 \end{array}\right] \end{array}$$

10. Which matrix operation would indicate the total combined hours that Cosmo and Simon served at the shelter and the hospital during the month of April?

    A. $[C] + [S]$ **B.** $[C] \times [S]$ **C.** $[C] - [S]$

11. $[C] - [S]$ is equal to—

    A. $\begin{bmatrix} 1 & 0 \\ -3 & 3 \\ -1 & 0.5 \\ 2.5 & -4 \end{bmatrix}$ **B.** $\begin{bmatrix} -1 & 0 \\ 3 & -3 \\ 1 & -0.5 \\ -2.5 & 4 \end{bmatrix}$ **C.** $\begin{bmatrix} 3 & 2 \\ 3 & 3 \\ 4 & 2.5 \\ 2.5 & 4 \end{bmatrix}$ **D.** $\begin{bmatrix} 1 & 0 \\ -1 & 2 \\ 0.5 & 0.5 \\ 1.5 & -1 \end{bmatrix}$

12. A negative entry in the *second* column of the $[C] - [S]$ matrix can be interpreted to mean that, during that week in April—

    A. Cosmo worked more hours at the hospital than Simon did
    B. Cosmo worked more hours at the animal shelter than Simon did
    C. Simon worked more hours at the animal shelter than Cosmo did
    D. Simon worked more hours at the hospital than Cosmo did

Answers

1. **C**	4. **B**	7. **C**	10. **A**
2. **B**	5. **B**	8. **B**	11. **A**
3. **D**	6. **C**	9. **D**	12. **D**

Answer Explanations

1. **C**   The dimensions of a matrix are given in the form *row × column*. This matrix has 2 horizontal rows and 4 vertical columns.

2. **B**   Matrix $[W]$ can be simplified to $\begin{bmatrix} 2+1=3 & -4 & 2(7)+1=15 \\ 1-1=0 & 1+0=1 & 4+2=7 \end{bmatrix}$, which is equivalent to matrix $[V]$.

3. **D**   Adding matrices A and B:

$$\begin{bmatrix} 2 & 1 \\ 4 & -2 \\ 5 & 7 \\ 0 & -1 \end{bmatrix} + \begin{bmatrix} 3 & 6 \\ 1 & 2 \\ -1 & 0 \\ 9 & 1 \end{bmatrix} = \begin{bmatrix} 2+3=5 & 1+6=7 \\ 4+1=5 & -2+2=0 \\ 5+-1=4 & 7+0=7 \\ 0+9=9 & -1+1=0 \end{bmatrix} = \begin{bmatrix} 5 & 7 \\ 5 & 0 \\ 4 & 7 \\ 0 & 0 \end{bmatrix}$$

4. **B**   Performing the subtraction in choice B yields:

$$\begin{bmatrix} 4 & 2 \\ -1 & 1 \end{bmatrix} - \begin{bmatrix} -1 & 2 \\ 5 & -3 \end{bmatrix} = \begin{bmatrix} 4-(-1) & 2-2 \\ -1-5 & 1-(-3) \end{bmatrix} = \begin{bmatrix} 5 & 0 \\ -6 & 4 \end{bmatrix}$$

5. **B**   Simplifying the given matrix yields:

$$2\begin{bmatrix} 3 & 6 & 9 \\ 6 & 3 & 0 \\ -6 & 12 & -3 \end{bmatrix} = \begin{bmatrix} 6 & 12 & 18 \\ 12 & 6 & 0 \\ -12 & 24 & -6 \end{bmatrix}$$

Simplifying choice B yields:

$$3\begin{bmatrix} 2 & 4 & 6 \\ 4 & 2 & 0 \\ -4 & 8 & -2 \end{bmatrix} = \begin{bmatrix} 6 & 12 & 18 \\ 12 & 6 & 0 \\ -12 & 24 & -6 \end{bmatrix}$$

6. **C**   Equivalent matrices must be **exactly** the same.

7. **C**   Matrices can be added only if they have the same dimensions. Matrix $[B]$ is a 2×3 and matrix $[C]$ is a 3×2. Therefore, they cannot be added.

8. **B**   Addition of matrices is commutative.

9. **D**   All three choices produce a new "magic" matrix. Choice A produces a "magic" matrix where the sum of the numbers along any row or column is 30. Choice B produces a "magic" matrix where the sum of the number along any row or column is 15. Choice C produces a matrix where the sum of the numbers along any row or column is 33.

10. **A**   The total combined hours would be the sum $[C] + [S]$ of the two matrices.

11. **A** Subtracting:

$$
\begin{array}{cc} & \textit{Shelter} \quad \textit{Hospital} \\ \begin{array}{c} \textit{Week 1} \\ \textit{Week 2} \\ \textit{Week 3} \\ \textit{Week 4} \end{array} & \begin{bmatrix} 2 & 1 \\ 0 & 3 \\ 1.5 & 1.5 \\ 2.5 & 0 \end{bmatrix} \end{array} - \begin{array}{cc} & \textit{Shelter} \quad \textit{Hospital} \\ \begin{array}{c} \textit{Week 1} \\ \textit{Week 2} \\ \textit{Week 3} \\ \textit{Week 4} \end{array} & \begin{bmatrix} 1 & 1 \\ 3 & 0 \\ 2.5 & 1 \\ 0 & 4 \end{bmatrix} \end{array}
$$

$$
= \begin{bmatrix} 2-1 & 1-1 \\ 0-3 & 3-0 \\ 1.5-2.5 & 1.5-1 \\ 2.5-0 & 0-4 \end{bmatrix} = \begin{bmatrix} 1 & 0 \\ -3 & 3 \\ -1 & 0.5 \\ 2.5 & -4 \end{bmatrix}
$$

12. **D** The entry of –4 into the second column of $[C] - [S]$ results from subtracting the 4 hours that Simon worked at the hospital from the 0 hours Cosmo worked during Week 4. Thus, Simon worked more hours than Cosmo at the hospital.

4.3 Mean, Median, and Mode

Mean, **median**, and **mode** are three different measures of *central tendency*. Each one is a number that gives you a sense of how data balance out or cluster around a particular "central" value.

A. Finding the Mean

> Finding a mean is exactly the same as "averaging" a set of numbers.

Add all the elements in the data set. Then divide by the number of elements you added.

Example 1: Find the mean of this set of values: {6, 20, 10, 0, 10, 30, 15}.

Input → Mean machine → Output $\dfrac{6 + 20 + 10 + 0 + 10 + 30 + 15}{7} = 13$

6, 20, 10, 0, 10, 30, 15

The mean is 13.

B. Finding the Median

List all the data elements in order from smallest to largest. The median is the number that lands exactly in the middle of the list.

- If there is an *odd* number of data elements, the median will actually be one of the data elements in the set. (See Example 2.)

- If there is an *even* number of data elements, no single element can be exactly in the middle. Then, to find the median, you must average the two data elements that share the middle position. (See Example 3.)

Example 2:

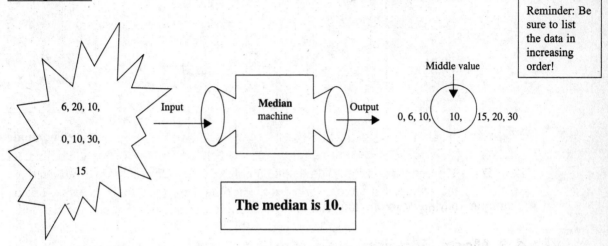

Reminder: Be sure to list the data in increasing order!

The median is 10.

For these data, the mean (calculated in Example 1) and the median (calculated in Example 2) turn out to have different values. The mean is 13; the median is 10. The mean and the median of a data set may or may not have the same value.

You should always have exactly the same number of data elements listed before the median and after it.

Example 3:

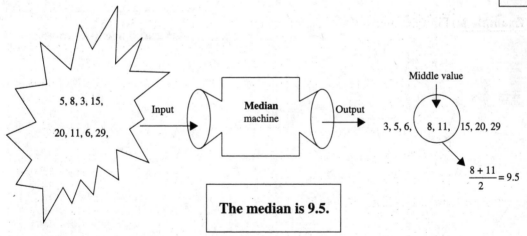

The median is 9.5.

C. *Finding the Mode*

Arrange the elements in order from smallest to largest. Then choose the data value that appears most frequently in the list. A data set can have more than one mode, exactly one mode, or no mode at all.

Example 4: Exactly one mode

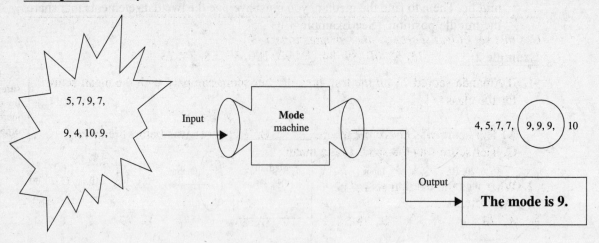

5, 7, 9, 7,
9, 4, 10, 9,

Input → Mode machine

4, 5, 7, 7, (9, 9, 9,) 10

Output → **The mode is 9.**

Example 5: More than one mode

We call this data set *bimodal*.

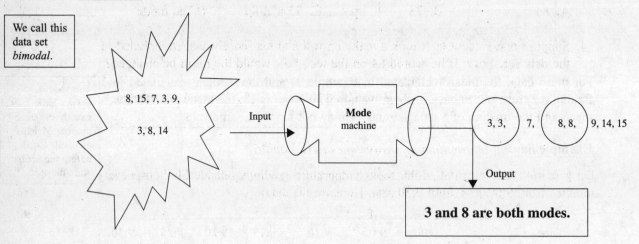

8, 15, 7, 3, 9,
3, 8, 14

Input → Mode machine

(3, 3,) 7, (8, 8,) 9, 14, 15

Output → **3 and 8 are both modes.**

Example 6: No mode

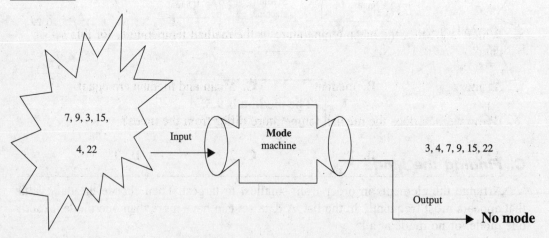

7, 9, 3, 15,
4, 22

Input → Mode machine

3, 4, 7, 9, 15, 22

Output → **No mode**

Here's an easy way to remember all three measures of central tendency:

| MEAN = AVERAGE | MEDIAN = MIDDLE | MODE = MOST OFTEN |

Practice

Use this set of test scores to answer questions 1–4:
73, 55, 70, 89, 84, 73, 98, 100, 87, 65, 84, 73

1. If Amanda scored 73 on the test, how did her score compare with the mean score for the class?

   A. Her score was above the mean.   **B.** Her score was below the mean.
   C. Her score was the same as the mean.

2. What was the median score?

   A. 73   **B.** 78.5   **C.** 84   **D.** 79

3. Find the mode(s).

   A. 84   **B.** 73   **C.** 73 and 84   **D.** no mode

4. Suppose one student later took a make-up test and his score was then included in the data set above. If he scored 84 on the test, how would the mean be changed?

   A. It would be raised.   **B.** It would be lower.   **C.** It would not change.

Use the following information to answer questions 5 and 6.

On a cold winter morning, John took temperature readings outside his house every 5 minutes from 9:00 A.M. until 9:30 A.M. Here are his data:

Time:	9:00	9:05	9:10	9:15	9:20	9:25	9:30
Temperature (°F):	32	33	34	36	35	36	38

5. Which is greater, the mean temperature or the median temperature, for this set of data?

   A. mean   **B.** median   **C.** Mean and median are equal.

6. By how much does the median temperature differ from the mode?

   A. 0°   **B.** 1°   **C.** 2°   **D.** 3°

Use the following information to answer questions 7–9:

During spring break, Daniel and Andres spent many hours playing video games at home. Their mothers were so worried that they kept daily records of the total amounts of time the boys spent each day on their video game systems. Here are the records:

	Mon.	Tues.	Wed.	Thurs.	Fri.	Sat.	Sun.
Daniel's times (hr):	4.5	3	5	5	2	4.5	0
Andres' times (hr):	5	4	4	6	3.5	1	6

7. On average, which boy spent more time per day playing video games?

   A. Daniel
   B. Andres
   C. Daniel and Andres spent the same amount of time per day, on average.

8. Which boy had the greater median playing time per day?

   A. Daniel
   B. Andres
   C. Daniel and Andres had the same median playing time per day.

9. Which boy's median playing time was greater than his mean playing time?

   A. Daniel's
   B. Andres'
   C. Each boy's median was greater than his mean.
   D. Each boy's mean was greater than his median.

10. In which of the following data sets are the mean, the median, and the mode all equal to one another?

    A. {15, 20, 25, 25, 30, 35}
    B. {15, 20, 25, 30, 35, 40}
    C. {15, 20, 30, 30, 40}
    D. {15, 20, 20, 25, 25, 30}

11. Susan is trying out for the golf team at her school. In four try-out rounds, she made the following scores on a par-72 golf course: 78, 80, 75, 72.

    To make the team, Susan must have an average score of 75 or lower after five rounds. What is the highest score she can get on the fifth round and still make the team?

    A. 68   B. 70   C. 72   D. 75

Answers

1. **B**	4. **A**	6. **B**	8. **A**	10. **A**
2. **B**	5. **B**	7. **B**	9. **A**	11. **B**
3. **B**				

Answer Explanations

1. **B**   Add the scores, and divide by 12. The mean is 79.25, so 73 is below the mean.

2. **B**   Put the numbers in order from smallest to largest. Since there is an even number of data values, the median is the average of the two values that share the middle position. The average of 73 and 84 is 78.5.

3. **B**   73 is the number that occurs most frequently.

4. **A**   Since 84 is above the mean, this added score would raise the mean.

5. **B**   The median temperature is 35°. The mean temperature is 34.857°. The median is larger.

6. **B**   The mode is 36°. The median is 35°. These values differ by 1°.

7. **B**   You can answer this question just by scanning the data. Andres spent more time on 5 days out of 7. Andres had a mean playing time of 4.2 hr/day, while Daniel's mean was only about 3.4 hr/day.

8. **A**   Daniel's median was 4.5. Andres' median was 4.

9. **A**   Daniel had a median of 4.5 and a mean of 3.4. Andres had a median of 4 and a mean of 4.2. Daniel's median was greater than his mean.

10. **A**   In set A, the mean, median, and mode are all 25.

11. **B**   Probably the easiest approach to this problem is to try the choices one at a time. Choice A gives Susan an average score below 75. Choice B, 70, puts her average score right at 75, so 70 is the maximum she can get and still make the team.

4.4 Box-and-Whisker Graphs

Box-and-whisker graphs are a way to show data with emphasis on the median and range. Example 1 illustrates how to create and interpret a box-and-whisker graph. Creating such a graph involves finding five key numbers and then using them to draw the "box" and the "whiskers."

A. Creating a Box-and-Whisker Graph

Example 1: Consider the following temperatures, which were recorded during a winter day in Richmond.

Time of day	8 A.M.	9 A.M.	10 A.M.	11 A.M.	12 noon	1 P.M.	2 P.M.	3 P.M.	4 P.M.	5 P.M.	6 P.M.	7 P.M.	8 P.M.
Temp. (°F)	27	29	38	40	40	42	43	43	40	28	27	22	20

Summarize the data by creating a box-and-whisker plot.

Step	Example
1. Order the data from smallest to largest.	20, 22, 27, 27, 28, 29, 38, 40, 40, 40, 42, 43, 43
2. Draw a number line.	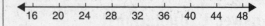
3. Plot the smallest value and the largest value.	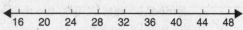
4. A. Find the median of the data set.	
B. Draw a vertical line on the graph to mark the median.	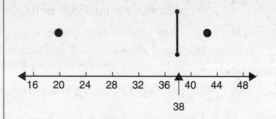
5. A. Find the *median* of the *lower half* of the data. This value is called the *lower quartile*. B. Find the *median* of the *upper half* of the data. This value is called the *upper quartile*. C. Draw vertical lines on the graph to mark the upper and lower quartiles.	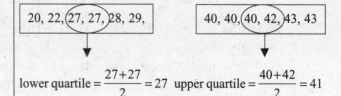 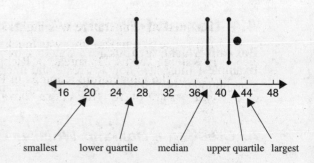
6. Draw "the box" connecting the lower and upper quartiles, 27 and 41. Make the "whiskers" by connecting the ends of the box to the extreme data values, 20 and 43.	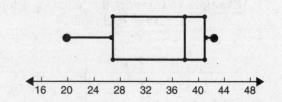

B. Interpreting a Box-and-Whisker Graph

The **range** of a data set indicates the spread of the data values. It is represented on the box-and-whisker plot by the distance between the ends of the two whiskers.

Example 2: Using the box-and-whisker plot from Example 1, determine the range of temperatures and interpret your answer.

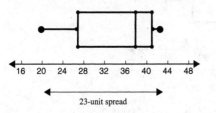

The range is $43 - 20 = \boxed{23}$.

The temperatures that day in Richmond had a 23° spread.

Box-and-whisker plots make it easy to compare different data sets. Suppose the temperatures were also recorded in Raleigh, NC, on the same winter day that they were recorded in Richmond.

Example 3: Compare the box-and-whisker plots for the temperatures that were recorded on the same winter day in Richmond, VA, and Raleigh, NC.

Raleigh:

Richmond:

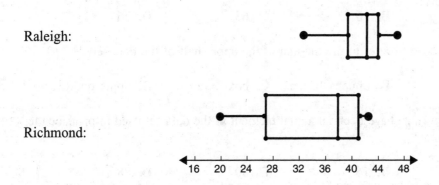

By comparing the two statistical plots, you can see that:

- The median temperature was higher (by 4°F) in Raleigh than in Richmond.
- The range of temperatures was much less in Raleigh than in Richmond (14° spread in Raleigh versus 23° spread in Richmond).
- 75% of the temperature readings in Raleigh were higher than Richmond's median temperature of 38° (the entire "box" and upper "whisker" for Raleigh are above 38°).

Practice

Use the box-and-whisker graph shown below to answer questions 1–8.

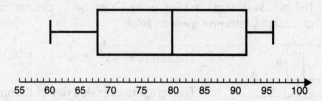

1. What is the range of the data?

   A. 12   B. 16   C. 36   D. 80

2. What is the median of the data?

   A. 36   B. 76   C. 80   D. 88

3. Which of the following numbers represents the lower quartile?

   A. 4   B. 16   C. 68   D. 76

4. What term is used to refer to the median of the upper half of the data set?

   A. range   B. upper whisker   C. box   D. upper quartile

5. Which number must have been an actual element in the data set used to produce the given "box" plot?

   A. 60   B. 76   C. 80   D. 88

6. Of all the data used to produce the plot, what percent is represented by one "whisker"?

   A. 8%   B. 16%   C. 25%   D. 50%

Now let's put the above box-and-whisker graph into context. Suppose the graph represents the scores that Mr. Herring's Algebra I students made on a recent test.

Use this information and the given box to answer questions 7 and 8.

7. From the graph, you can tell that about half of the class scored between—

   A. 80 and 92 points   B. 60 and 68 points
   C. 68 and 92 points   D. 60 and 96 points

8. Which statement is *not* correct based on the box plot?

   A. The highest score in the class was 96.
   B. The worst score in the class was farther from the median than was the best score.
   C. More students scored below 80 than above 80.
   D. A student who scored 65 on the test was in the bottom 25% of the class.

Now suppose that Mrs. Cohen's class took the same test. The box-and-whisker plot for her class looked like this:

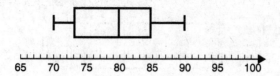

Compare the two box plots (for Mr. Herring's and Mrs. Cohen's classes) to answer questions 9 and 10.

9. The two graphs have the same—

A. median
C. right-hand whisker length
B. lower quartile
D. all of the above

10. Because the plot for Mrs. Cohen's class covers a shorter distance than the plot for Mr. Herring's class, you can conclude that—

A. Mrs. Cohen's students are smarter
B. there was less variability in the scores in Mrs. Cohen's class
C. Mrs. Cohen had fewer students than Mr. Herring had
D. Mr. Herring needs to shave his whiskers

Answers

1. **C**	3. **C**	5. **A**	7. **C**	9. **A**
2. **C**	4. **D**	6. **C**	8. **D**	10. **B**

Answer Explanations

1. **C**   The data values span from 60 to 96. The range is the "spread" of the data: $96 - 60 = 36$.

2. **C**   The median is indicated by the vertical line inside the box.

3. **C**   The lower quartile is indicated by the vertical line at the left side of the box.

4. **D**   This is the definition of "upper quartile."

5. **A**   The lowest and highest values on the box plot are actual data elements. Since 60 is the lowest value on the box plot, it is an actual data element.

6. **C**   Each whisker represents 25% of the data. Also, each of the two parts of the box represents 25% of the data.

7. **C**   The box, which spans from 68 to 92, contains half of the data.

8. **D**   The lower whisker represents 25% of the data, and 65 is in this whisker.

9. **A**   Each graph has a median of 80.

10. **B**   The range for Mrs. Cohen's class is 20. The range for Mr. Herring's class is 36. A smaller range means less variability (spread) in the data.

4.5 Lines of Best Fit

What is a scatterplot?

When we want to show how two different quantities (or variables) are related to one another, we can plot them as ordered pairs on a graph. Such a display of data is called a **scatterplot**.

Example 1: Mrs. Cohen ran an experiment to see whether the amounts of sleep her students got the night before a test had any connection with how well they scored on the test.

All of her students recorded how much sleep they got the preceding night, and Mrs. Cohen recorded their corresponding test scores. Shown on the right is a table of the data for her 15 students.

Student's Name	Hours of sleep	Test Score
Vyomika	7.5	79
Rebecca	8.25	85
Chris	7.5	92
Jigmey	7.25	82
Nathaniel	4	60
Carmen	6	70
Jackson	5.25	67
Crissie	6.5	85
David	4.75	72
Gerald	6	75
Craig	4.5	73
Hannah	6.5	80
Arielle	7	69
Jae-Hyung	7.25	82
Susie	7.5	94

The graph below is a scatterplot of the data shown in the table. Each point on the graph corresponds to a particular student. For example, the point (8.25, 85), marked on the graph with an *A*, corresponds to the student named Rebecca (see table). This point reflects the fact that Rebecca slept for 8.25 hours the night before the test and then scored 85% on the test.

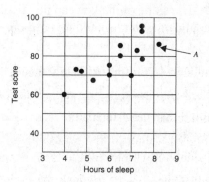

What is the purpose of a scatterplot? What is a "line of best fit"?
A scatterplot provides a nice way to visualize data. It shows whether the data points show a general trend or pattern. Sometimes the data will seem to slant in an upward direction; sometimes, in a downward direction. Sometimes the data show no particular pattern at all, indicating that the two variables represented in the graph have no particular relationship to one another.

When the data do seem to follow a basic linear pattern, we try to "fit a line" to the data. We want to draw the line so that it follows the same upward, or downward, trend as the data points. The line need not pass through any of the data points *exactly*, but it should roughly balance out the points that lie above the line with the points that lie below it. A line whose purpose is to model the data in this way is referred to as a **line of best fit**.

Example 2: Which graph shows the most reasonable line of best fit for the data from Example 1?

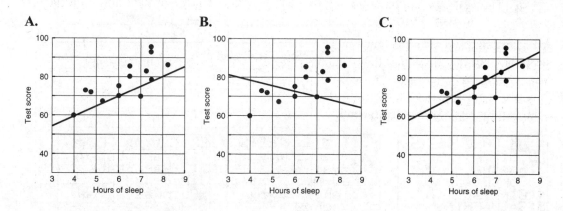

A. **B.** **C.**

Answer: C is the best choice.

- B cannot be the right choice because it slants downward while the trend of the data is upward.
- Although the line in choice A actually hits about four of the data points, choice C does a better job of balancing out the points that lie above the line with the ones that lie below.

Once we have drawn a reasonable line of best fit, we often try to write an equation to describe it.

Example 3: Write an equation, in $y = mx + b$ form, for the line of best fit graphed as choice C above.

Step 1: Find the slope, m. The slope of the line can be calculated using any two points on the line. (Actual data points should be used *only* if they happen to fall on the line of best fit.) Choosing the points (8, 86) and (5, 69), calculate the slope to be $\dfrac{86-69}{8-5} = \dfrac{17}{3}$, or approximately 6.

Step 2: Find the y-intercept, b. Don't be tricked here. The y-intercept is not 60 or even close to 60. (Notice that the "sleep axis" started at 3, not 0.) Use a ruler to extend the line of best fit backward until you find the point on the line where x equals 0. This seems to be about where $y = 40$.

Step 3: Find the equation of the line. Since the y-intercept is about 40 ($b = 40$) and the slope is about 6 ($m = 6$), write the equation of the line of best fit in $y = mx + b$ form as:

$$y = 6x + 40$$

Example 4: Use your calculator to find the line of best fit.

Using your calculator to find the line of best fit is often easier and certainly more accurate than trying to find the line by hand. The steps involved in using your calculator to determine the line of best fit for a given set of data are outlined below.

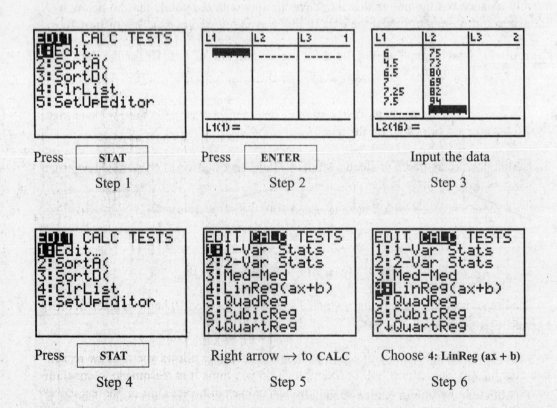

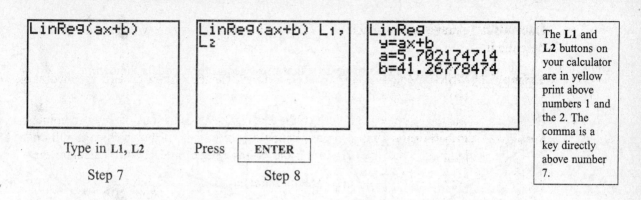

Type in **L1, L2**

Step 7

Press [**ENTER**]

Step 8

The **L1** and **L2** buttons on your calculator are in yellow print above numbers 1 and the 2. The comma is a key directly above number 7.

As you can see, the calculator found the slope, a, to be 5.702 ... and the y-intercept, b, to be 41.2677.... The equation, therefore, would be approximately:

$$y = 5.7x + 41.3$$

Notice that the line of best fit found by the calculator and the line of best fit determined by hand in Example 3 are very similar.

You may be wondering why you would ever need to find the line of best fit. Remember that having an equation for a line allows you to find *many* points that lie on the line. In particular, you might use points on the line of best fit to make inferences or predictions, as illustrated in Example 5.

Example 5: Use the estimated line of best fit, $y = 6x + 40$, to:

A. Predict the score that a student who had had no sleep at all the previous night would achieve on Mrs. Cohen's test.

If the student had no sleep at all, x would equal 0.

Let $x = 0$, and solve for y:

$$y = 6(0) + 40 \longrightarrow y = 40$$

The line of best fit suggests that a student who had had no sleep the previous night would have a score of 40 on the test.

B. Predict how many hours of sleep a student would have needed in order to get a perfect score on Mrs. Cohen's test.

For a perfect score, y would have to equal 100.

Let $y = 100$, and solve for x:

$$100 = 6x + 40 \longrightarrow x = 10$$

The line of best fit suggests that a student would have needed 10 hours of sleep in order to get a perfect score.

As you can see from Example 5, a line of best fit sometimes allows you to draw reasonable conclusions, sometimes not. In Example 5, do you think it is reasonable to conclude that the amount of sleep a person gets determines, or even influences, his or her test score? Lines of best fit allow you to make interesting conjectures, but you have to be careful about drawing conclusions.

Practice

1. Which graph shows a line of best fit that most accurately models the data?

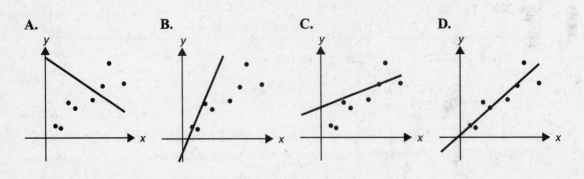

A.   B.   C.   D.

Use the scatterplot below to answer questions 2–4.

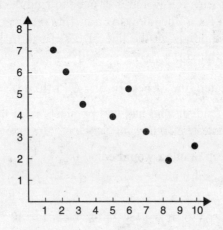

2. The line of best fit for these data would have a slope that is—

   A. positive   **B.** negative   **C.** zero   **D.** undefined

3. Which real-life situation could most reasonably be reflected by the scatterplot?

   A. Growth of a child over time: (age, height)
   B. Teacher's salary over time: (years on the job, dollars)
   C. Shoe size versus IQ
   D. Speed of a car approaching a stop sign: (time, speed)

4. If the scale on each axis is 1 unit, which would be the most reasonable equation for a line of best fit?

   A. $y = \dfrac{-2}{3}x + 8$ **B.** $y = -x + 8$ **C.** $y = x + 7$ **D.** $y = -3x + 10$

Use the scatterplot below to answer questions 5 and 6.

The scatterplot illustrates the percentage of students at Smartyville High that used graphing calculators in school on a daily basis over the time period from the year 1990 to the year 2000.

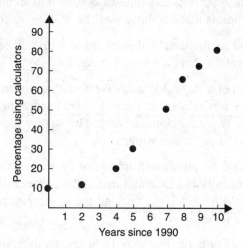

5. For the year 1996, the most reasonable estimate for the percentage of students using graphing calculators on a daily basis at Smartyville High is—

A. 30%   **B.** 45%   **C.** 52%   **D.** 60%

6. What is the most reasonable estimate for the slope of a line of best fit for the data in the scatterplot?

A. −1   **B.** $\frac{1}{3}$ **C.** 1   **D.** 8

Answers

1. **D**   2. **B**   3. **D**   4. **A**   5. **B**   6. **D**

Explanations

1. **D**   Graph D is the only one that follows the upward trend of the data and balances out the points that lie above the line with those that lie below.

2. **B**   Since the trend of the data is downward, the line of best fit must also slant down and, therefore, have a negative slope.

3. **D**   Since the speed of a car would decrease as the car approached a stop sign, this would correspond to data that show a downward trend. The scatterplots for choices A and B would slant upward. The scatter plot for choice C would logically show no particular pattern.

4. **A**   Choice C should be eliminated immediately since its slope is positive. The slopes for choices B and D would make these lines fall too fast for the data. You should actually sketch the lines on the scatterplot to see for yourself that the best choice is A.

5. **B**   Draw the line of best fit. The year 1996 corresponds to an x-value of 6. The corresponding y-value on your line of best fit would be somewhere around 45. Therefore, choice B, 45%, gives the most reasonable estimate.

6. **D**   This one is tricky because the y-axis is scaled in units of 10 while the x-axis is scaled in units of 1. Therefore, even though the slope of the best-fit line seems close to 1, it's really more like 10. Choice D is the closest answer.

Practice Tests

Answer Sheet: Practice Test 1

1. Ⓐ Ⓑ Ⓒ Ⓓ	18. Ⓕ Ⓖ Ⓗ Ⓙ	35. Ⓐ Ⓑ Ⓒ Ⓓ
2. Ⓕ Ⓖ Ⓗ Ⓙ	19. Ⓐ Ⓑ Ⓒ Ⓓ	36. Ⓕ Ⓖ Ⓗ Ⓙ
3. Ⓐ Ⓑ Ⓒ Ⓓ	20. Ⓕ Ⓖ Ⓗ Ⓙ	37. Ⓐ Ⓑ Ⓒ Ⓓ
4. Ⓕ Ⓖ Ⓗ Ⓙ	21. Ⓐ Ⓑ Ⓒ Ⓓ	38. Ⓕ Ⓖ Ⓗ Ⓙ
5. Ⓐ Ⓑ Ⓒ Ⓓ	22. Ⓕ Ⓖ Ⓗ Ⓙ	39. Ⓐ Ⓑ Ⓒ Ⓓ
6. Ⓕ Ⓖ Ⓗ Ⓙ	23. Ⓐ Ⓑ Ⓒ Ⓓ	40. Ⓕ Ⓖ Ⓗ Ⓙ
7. Ⓐ Ⓑ Ⓒ Ⓓ	24. Ⓕ Ⓖ Ⓗ Ⓙ	41. Ⓐ Ⓑ Ⓒ Ⓓ
8. Ⓕ Ⓖ Ⓗ Ⓙ	25. Ⓐ Ⓑ Ⓒ Ⓓ	42. Ⓕ Ⓖ Ⓗ Ⓙ
9. Ⓐ Ⓑ Ⓒ Ⓓ	26. Ⓕ Ⓖ Ⓗ Ⓙ	43. Ⓐ Ⓑ Ⓒ Ⓓ
10. Ⓕ Ⓖ Ⓗ Ⓙ	27. Ⓐ Ⓑ Ⓒ Ⓓ	44. Ⓕ Ⓖ Ⓗ Ⓙ
11. Ⓐ Ⓑ Ⓒ Ⓓ	28. Ⓕ Ⓖ Ⓗ Ⓙ	45. Ⓐ Ⓑ Ⓒ Ⓓ
12. Ⓕ Ⓖ Ⓗ Ⓙ	29. Ⓐ Ⓑ Ⓒ Ⓓ	46. Ⓕ Ⓖ Ⓗ Ⓙ
13. Ⓐ Ⓑ Ⓒ Ⓓ	30. Ⓕ Ⓖ Ⓗ Ⓙ	47. Ⓐ Ⓑ Ⓒ Ⓓ
14. Ⓕ Ⓖ Ⓗ Ⓙ	31. Ⓐ Ⓑ Ⓒ Ⓓ	48. Ⓕ Ⓖ Ⓗ Ⓙ
15. Ⓐ Ⓑ Ⓒ Ⓓ	32. Ⓕ Ⓖ Ⓗ Ⓙ	49. Ⓐ Ⓑ Ⓒ Ⓓ
16. Ⓕ Ⓖ Ⓗ Ⓙ	33. Ⓐ Ⓑ Ⓒ Ⓓ	50. Ⓕ Ⓖ Ⓗ Ⓙ
17. Ⓐ Ⓑ Ⓒ Ⓓ	34. Ⓕ Ⓖ Ⓗ Ⓙ	

DIRECTIONS

Read and solve each question. Then mark the space on the answer sheet for the best answer.

---

1 Which is an example of the associative property of addition?

A $(4 + 3a) + b = 4 + 4a$
B $(4 + 3a) + b = (4 + 3)a + b$
C $(4 + 3a) + b = 4 + (3a + b)$
D $(4 + 3a) + b = 4 + 3(a + b)$

---

2 A can of soup is a cylinder and holds 45π cubic inches of soup. The can has a radius of 3 inches.

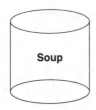

Soup

What is the height of the soup can?

F 4 in.
G 5 in.
H 9 in.
J 15 in.

---

3 Which property of real numbers justifies the following statement?

$5m(2n + 6) - 4n$ is equivalent to $5m(2n) + 5m(6) - 4n$.

A The associative property of addition
B The commutative property of multiplication
C The distributive property of multiplication over addition
D Multiplicative identity property

---

4 What is the solution to $3x - 3 < 5x - 11$?

F $x > 4$
G $x < 4$
H $x < -7$
J $x < -4$

---

5 The graph of $y = \dfrac{-2}{3}x - 1$ is shown.

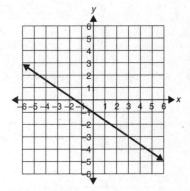

If the line in the graph is shifted up 3 units, which is the equation of the new line?

A $y = \dfrac{2}{3}x - 1$

B $y = \dfrac{2}{3}x + 2$

C $y = \dfrac{-2}{3}x + 3$

D $y = \dfrac{-2}{3}x + 2$

6 Which is the graph of a line that appears to have a slope of −3 and an x-intercept of 2?

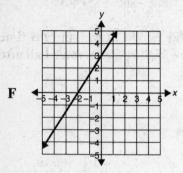

F

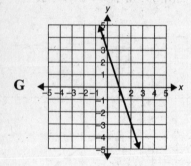

G

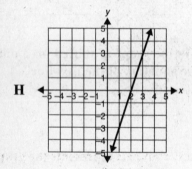

H

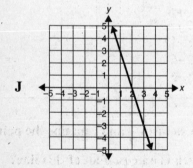

J

7 What is the slope of the line that contains the points (5, 4) and (−1, 16)?

A $\dfrac{-1}{2}$

B −2

C 3

D $\dfrac{-11}{5}$

8

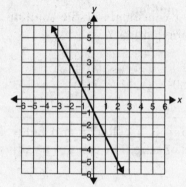

Which best represents the equation of the line shown?

F $y = 2x - 1$

G $y = -2x + 1$

H $y = \dfrac{-1}{2}x - 1$

J $y = -2x - 1$

9

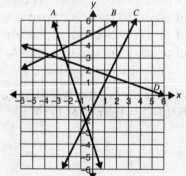

Which line on the graph appears to have a slope of $\dfrac{-1}{3}$?

A A

B B

C C

D D

10 What is the slope of the line represented by the equation $3x - 6y = 12$?

F 3

G -2

H $\dfrac{-1}{2}$

J $\dfrac{1}{2}$

---

11 What is the x-coordinate of the solution to this system of equations?

$$\begin{cases} 6x + 4y = -4 \\ 6x - 9y = -30 \end{cases}$$

A $x = 2$

B $x = -2$

C $x = \dfrac{34}{5}$

D $x = -1$

---

12 The Athletic Booster Club sells slices of pizza and buckets of popcorn at basketball games. Last Saturday, the members sold a total of 39 items and took in $94.00. If they charge $2.00 for a slice of pizza and $3.00 for a bucket of popcorn, how many slices of pizza and buckets of popcorn did they sell?

F 29 slices of pizza, 12 buckets of popcorn

G 23 slices of pizza, 16 buckets of popcorn

H 20 slices of pizza, 19 buckets of popcorn

J 30 slices of pizza, 9 buckets of popcorn

---

13 Which is an equation for the line that contains the points $(-2, -3)$ and $(6, 1)$?

A $y = \dfrac{1}{2}x - 3$

B $y = \dfrac{-1}{2} - 4$

C $y = 2x - 11$

D $y = \dfrac{1}{2}x - 2$

---

14 The height that a lacrosse ball reaches can be described by the equation

$$h = -16t^2 + 35t + 5$$

where h is the height in feet and t is time in seconds. How high is the lacrosse ball after 2 seconds?

F 6.5 ft

G 11 ft

H 23 ft

J 47 ft

---

15 Which is a solution to $2(x + 2)^2 = 32$?

A -10

B -6

C -4

D 6

16

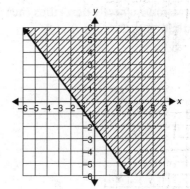

The inequality that best represents the graph is—

F $2x - 3y \leq 6$

G $4x - 2y \geq -12$

H $4x + 3y \leq -6$

J $4x + 3y \geq -6$

---

17 A line has a slope of $\dfrac{1}{3}$ and contains the point $(-3, 4)$. Which is an equation of this line?

A $3x - y = -13$

B $x - 3y = -5$

C $x - 3y = -15$

D $2x - 3y = -12$

18 Mario earns money on Saturday nights by parking cars at a local restaurant. He gets paid $20.00 a night plus $7.00 per hour in tips. If P equals the amount of money he makes and x represents the number of hours he works, which equation could be used to determine his earnings?

F $P = 20.00x + 7.00$
G $P = 27.00x$
H $P = 7.00(20.00 + x)$
J $P = 20.00 + 7.00x$

19 What is the value of $a - 2(b + 3c)$ if $a = 3$, $b = -1$, and $c = 4$?

A -19
B 11
C 17
D 29

20 Which expression correctly describes the sum of x and 4 divided by 2 more than y?

F $\dfrac{x+4}{2} + y$

G $x + \dfrac{4}{y+2}$

H $\dfrac{x+4}{y+2}$

J $\dfrac{x}{4} + \dfrac{2}{y}$

21 Which is equivalent to $\dfrac{(2x^2)^4}{x^2}$?

A $8x^4$
B $16x^6$
C $2x^6$
D $8x^6$

22 At the end of 1994 the Department of Energy's (DOE) inventory of high-level radioactive waste was approximately 378,400 cubic meters. In scientific notation it is—

F $3.784 \times 10^{-5}\,\text{m}^3$
G $378.4 \times 10^3\,\text{m}^3$
H $3784.00 \times 10^2\,\text{m}^3$
J $3.784 \times 10^5\,\text{m}^3$

23 Consider the following models:

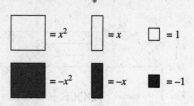

What polynomial is represented by this diagram?

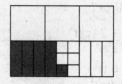

A $3x^2 - 7x + 5$
B $3x^2 - x + 5$
C $3x^2 + x + 4$
D $3x^2 - x + 4$

24 Which is closest to the value of w if $w = 6\sqrt{7} - 3\sqrt{7}$?

F 5.6
G 7.9
H 21
J 147

25 $\dfrac{8x^4y - 4x^6y^2 + 24x^9y^5}{4x^3y}$ is equivalent to—

A $2x - x^3y + 6x^6y^4$
B $2xy - x^3y + 6x^6y^4$
C $2x - x^2y + 20x^3y^4$
D $2xy - x^2y + 6x^3y^4$

26 One factor of $2x^2 - 5x - 3$ is—

F $2x - 1$
G $x + 3$
H $x - 3$
J $2x + 3$

27 A rectangular toolbox has a width of 2 feet, a height of $3x$ feet, and a length of $2x + 4$ feet.

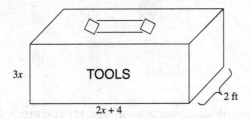

Which expression represents the volume of the toolbox?

A $12x^2 + 24x$ ft^3
B $8x + 4$ ft^3
C $5x + 6$ ft^3
D $6x^2 + 8$ ft^3

28 What is the <u>complete</u> factorization of $3x^3 - 75x$?

F $3x(x^2 - 25)$
G $3(x^3 - 25x)$
H $3x(x - 5)(x + 5)$
J $(3x^2 - 15)(x + 5)$

29 The length of the hypotenuse of a right triangle can be determined by evaluating the expression $\sqrt{a^2 + b^2}$, where a and b are the lengths of the legs. To the *nearest tenth* of an inch, what is the length of the hypotenuse of a triangle with legs that have lengths $a = 5.5$ inches and $b = 3.3$ inches?

A 2.9 in.
B 6.4 in.
C 8.8 in.
D 41.1 in.

30 Bhavana went to dinner at a nice restaurant. The price of her meal was $16.50, and she left a 15% tip. There was also a tax of 5% on the price of her meal. If C represents the total cost for her meal, including tax and tip, which equation represents how much Bhavana spent for dinner?

F $C = 16.50 + 0.15(16.50) + 0.05(16.50)$
G $C = 0.85(16.50) + 0.05(16.50)$
H $C = 1.20(16.50)$
J $C = 16.50 + 0.15(16.50 + 0.05(16.50))$

31

x	−4	2	8
y	7	4	1

Which equation is satisfied by all the points in the table?

A $2x - y = -15$
B $x - 2y = 10$
C $x + 2y = 10$
D $-2x + y = 15$

32 Which of the following tables does *not* represent a function?

F

x	y
6	8
7	11
9	15
11	20

G

x	y
3	4
6	3
9	4
12	3

H

x	y
1	7
2	7
3	7
4	7

J

x	y
16	4
64	8
16	−4
−8	−8

33

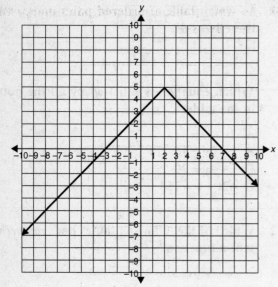

What is the range of the function shown?

A All real numbers
B All real numbers greater than 0
C All real numbers greater than or equal to 5
D All real numbers less than or equal to 5

34 If *a* varies directly as *b* and *a* = 6 when *b* = 24, what is the value of *a* when *b* = 9?

F 0.25
G 2.25
H 4.25
J 36

35

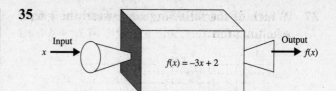

Input x → $f(x) = -3x + 2$ → Output $f(x)$

According to the function machine in the diagram, what is $f(-3)$?

A −7
B $\dfrac{5}{3}$
C 2
D 11

36 The manager of a skateboard warehouse has determined that the function $s = -3t^2 + 28t + 20$ models the number of skateboards left in inventory, where *s* is the number of skateboards remaining after *t* days from the last resupply. After how many days will the inventory of skateboards equal 0?

F 3
G 8
H 10
J 20

37 Which of the following represents the graph of a function?

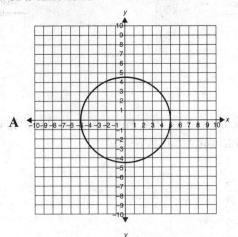

A

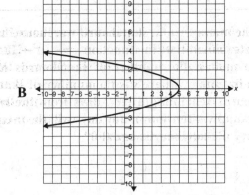

B

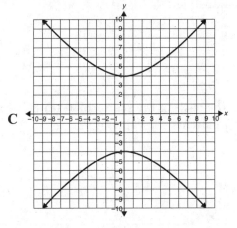

C

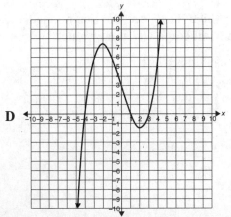

D

38 In which table of ordered pairs does *q* vary directly as *p*?

F
p	3	−2.5	−1
q	6	5	−2

G
p	7	8	3
q	3.5	−4	6

H
p	3	−2.5	1
q	−6	5	−2

J
p	−2	−4	3
q	2	8	14

39 What is the zero of the function $f(x) = 15 - 3x$?

A −5
B 0
C 5
D 15

40

x	–6	3	9
y	5	2	0

Which graph appears to contain all the points in the table?

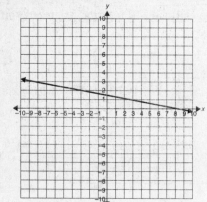

F

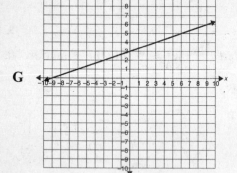

G

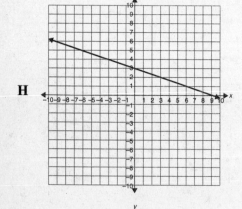

H

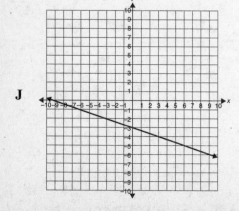

J

41 What is the range of the function $f(x) = x^2 + 3x$ when the domain is $\{-2, 2, 4\}$?

A $\{-2, 2, 4\}$
B $\{-2, -2, 4\}$
C $\{-10, 10, 28\}$
D $\{-2, 10, 28\}$

42 The ordered pairs in the table follow a quadratic pattern.

–2	0	3	7	x
4	0	9	49	81

What is the value of x?

F 4
G 9
H 12
J 14

43

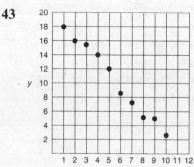

On the basis of the scatterplot, which x-value best matches a y value of 9?

A 5
B 6
C 9
D 11

44 In which data set do mean, median, and mode all equal the same value?

F $\{5, 8, 8, 8, 10\}$
G $\{5, 7, 9, 9, 15\}$
H $\{3, 5, 6, 7, 8\}$
J $\{33, 33, 33, 40, 42\}$

45 $[M] = \begin{bmatrix} 3 & 7 \\ -1 & 5 \\ 8 & 2 \end{bmatrix}$ $[N] = \begin{bmatrix} -2 & 7 \\ 2 & 0 \\ 7 & -1 \end{bmatrix}$

$2[M] + [N] = ?$

A $\begin{bmatrix} 2 & 28 \\ 2 & 10 \\ 30 & 2 \end{bmatrix}$

B $\begin{bmatrix} 4 & 21 \\ 0 & 10 \\ 23 & 3 \end{bmatrix}$

C $\begin{bmatrix} 4 & 21 \\ 0 & 10 \\ 23 & 0 \end{bmatrix}$

D $\begin{bmatrix} 2 & 28 \\ 2 & 10 \\ 30 & 0 \end{bmatrix}$

46 Manny collects baseball cards. He has 220 cards of Yankee players, 137 cards of Orioles players, 85 cards of Mets players, 277 cards of Rockies players, and 331 cards of Dodgers players. What is the median number of baseball cards that Manny has for the five teams?

F 85
G 210
H 220
J 331

47 Christine has been keeping track of her algebra grades this year and made the box-and-whisker graph shown below.

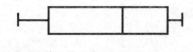

80 81 82 83 84 85 86 87 88 89 90 91 92 93 94 95
Grades

What is the range of the grades Christine has received this year?

A 3
B 8
C 11
D 15

48 Joel planted squash, peppers, and watermelon in a garden. Matrix A shows the number of each crop he picked one weekend in July.

	Squash	Peppers	Watermelon	
Saturday	3	2	1	$= A$
Sunday	1	5	0	

Matrix B shows the numbers he picked one weekend in August.

	Squash	Peppers	Watermelon	
Saturday	9	10	2	$= B$
Sunday	12	14	5	

Which matrix correctly shows the difference, $[B] - [A]$, in the amounts he picked in July and August?

F $\begin{bmatrix} 6 & 8 & 1 \\ 11 & 9 & 3 \end{bmatrix}$

G $\begin{bmatrix} 12 & 12 & 3 \\ 13 & 19 & 5 \end{bmatrix}$

H $\begin{bmatrix} 6 & 8 & 1 \\ 11 & 9 & 5 \end{bmatrix}$

J $\begin{bmatrix} -6 & -8 & -1 \\ -11 & -9 & -5 \end{bmatrix}$

49

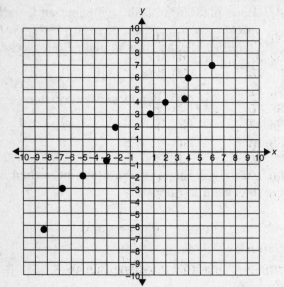

Which equation best represents the data shown on the scatterplot?

A $y = x$

B $y = 2(x - 1)$

C $x - y = -2$

D $y = 2 - x$

50 Which of the following matrices *cannot* be added?

F $\begin{bmatrix} 6 & 8 & 1 \\ 11 & 9 & 3 \end{bmatrix} + \begin{bmatrix} -2 & 7 & 8 \\ 0 & 1 & 8 \end{bmatrix}$

G $\begin{bmatrix} 3 \\ 4 \\ 6 \end{bmatrix} + \begin{bmatrix} 9 & 8 \\ 4 & 3 \\ 2 & 3 \end{bmatrix}$

H $\begin{bmatrix} 2 & -1 \\ 3 & 2 \end{bmatrix} + \begin{bmatrix} 1 & 0 \\ 0 & 1 \end{bmatrix}$

J $\begin{bmatrix} 3 \\ 5 \end{bmatrix} + \begin{bmatrix} 4 \\ 7 \end{bmatrix}$

Answer Key for Practice Test 1

1. C	11. B	21. B	31. C	41. D
2. G	12. G	22. J	32. J	42. G
3. C	13. D	23. D	33. D	43. B
4. F	14. G	24. G	34. G	44. G
5. D	15. B	25. A	35. D	45. B
6. J	16. J	26. H	36. H	46. H
7. B	17. C	27. A	37. D	47. C
8. J	18. J	28. H	38. H	48. H
9. D	19. A	29. B	39. C	49. C
10. J	20. H	30. F	40. H	50. G

Answer Explanations

1. **C**   The associative property of addition strictly changes the grouping, not the order, of the terms: $(4 + 3a) + b = 4 + (3a + b)$.

2. **G**   Use the formula for the volume of a cylinder, $V = \pi r^2 h$, and substitute 45π for V and 3 for r. Solve: $45\pi = \pi(3)^2 h$ yields $h = 5$.

3. **C**   Both of the quantities $2n$ and 6 have been multiplied by $5m$. This is the distributive property: $a(b + c) = ab + ac$.

4. **F**   Solve $3x - 3 < 5x - 11$:
$$3x < 5x - 11 + 3$$
$$3x < 5x - 8$$
$$3x - 5x < -8$$
$$-2x < -8$$
$$x > 4$$

(Remember to switch the $<$ sign in the last step.)

5. **D**   Shifting the graph up 3 units will cause the y-intercept to increase by 3: $-1 + 3 = 2$. The new equation is $y = \dfrac{2}{3}x + 2$.

6. **J**   Graphs H and J have x-intercepts of 2. Of these two, only graph J has a negative slope of -3.

7. **B**   Use the slope formula:
$$m = \frac{y_2 - y_1}{x_2 - x_1} = \frac{16 - 4}{-1 - 5} = \frac{12}{-6} = -2.$$

8. **J**   The graph has a y-intercept of -1 and a slope of -2. The equation, in $y = mx + b$ form, is $y = -2x - 1$.

9. **D**   Lines B and C can be eliminated because they have positive slopes. The slope of line A is -3. The slope of line D is $\dfrac{-1}{3}$.

10. **J**   Rewrite the equation $3x - 6y = 12$ in $y = mx + b$ form:
$$-6y = -3x + 12$$
$$y = \frac{1}{2}x - 2$$

The slope, m, is $\dfrac{1}{2}$.

11. **B** This system can be solved by elimination. Multiply the second equation by -1, and then add it to the first equation to eliminate the x-term.

$$6x + 4y = -4$$
$$(+) \quad -6x + 9y = 30$$
$$\overline{}$$
$$13y = 26 \longrightarrow y = 2$$

Substitute the value $y = 2$ back into the first equation to obtain the value of x:

$$6x + 4(2) = -4$$
$$6x + 8 = -4$$
$$6x = -12$$
$$x = -2$$

12. **G** Let $x =$ the number of slices of pizza sold, and $y =$ the number of buckets of popcorn sold. The following system of equations can be written and solved:

$$\begin{cases} x + y = 39 \\ 2.00x + 3.00y = 94.00 \end{cases}$$

Solve the first equation for y:

$$x + y = 39$$
$$y = 39 - x$$

Substitute $39 - x$ for y into the second equation, and solve:

$$2.00x + 3.00(39 - x) = 94$$
$$2x + 117 - 3x = 94$$
$$-x + 117 = 94$$
$$-x = -23 \longrightarrow x = 23$$

Substitute $x = 23$ into the first equation, $x + y = 39$:

$$23 + y = 39 \longrightarrow y = 16$$

Therefore, 23 slices of pizza and 16 buckets of popcorn were sold.

13. **D** Use the slope formula:

$$m = \frac{y_2 - y_1}{x_2 - x_1} = \frac{1 - (-3)}{6 - (-2)} = \frac{4}{8} = \frac{1}{2}.$$

Use the point $(6, 1)$, the slope $\frac{1}{2}$, and the equation $y = mx + b$ to find the y-intercept.

$$1 = \frac{1}{2}(6) + b$$
$$1 = 3 + b \longrightarrow b = -2$$

Write the equation using the form $y = mx + b$, where $m = \dfrac{1}{2}$ and $b = -2$:

$$y = \frac{1}{2}x - 2$$

14. **G** Substitute 2 for t into $h = -16t^2 + 35t + 5$
$$h = -16(2)^2 + 35(2) + 5 \rightarrow h = 11 \text{ ft}$$

15. **B** Solve the equation $2(x+2)^2 = 32$ by isolating the square:

$$(x+2)^2 = 16$$
$$\sqrt{(x+2)^2} = \pm\sqrt{16}$$
$$x + 2 = \pm 4 \quad \text{This is a solution also, but is not listed in the choices.}$$
$$x = -6 \text{ or } x = 2$$

A solution is -6.

16. **J** The boundary line has a y-intercept of -2 and a slope of $\dfrac{-4}{3}$.

Use the $y = mx + b$ form: $\qquad y = \dfrac{-4}{3}x - 2$

Rewrite in standard form: $\qquad 3y = -4x - 6$
$$4x + 3y = -6$$

Since the point $(0, 0)$ lies inside the shaded region, use it to determine whether the inequality sign is $\leq$ or $\geq$:

$$4(0) + 3(0) = -6$$
$$0 = -6$$

Since $0 \geq -6$, insert the symbol $\geq$ into your equation to make it a correct inequality: $4x + 3y \geq -6$.

17. **C** Use the point $(-3, 4)$, the slope $\dfrac{1}{3}$, and the equation $y = mx + b$ to find the y-intercept:

$$4 = \frac{1}{3}(-3) + b$$
$$4 = -1 + b \longrightarrow b = 5$$

Write the equation using $y = mx + b$,

where $m = \dfrac{1}{3}$ and $b = 5$: $\qquad y = \dfrac{1}{3}x + 5$

Rewrite in standard form: $3y = x + 15 \longrightarrow x - 3y = -15$

18. **J** Total amount = fixed amount + (amount per item) · (number of items)

$$P = 20.00 + 7.00x$$

19. **A**   Substitute 3 for a, -1 for b, and 4 for c in the given expression:

$$3 - 2(-1 + 3(4))$$

Use the correct order of operations:

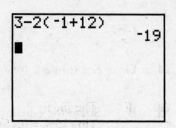

$$3 - 2(-1 + 12)$$
$$3 - 2(11)$$
$$3 - 22$$
$$-19$$

20. **H**   The "sum of x and 4" means $x + 4$, and "2 more than y" means $y + 2$. Division yields $\dfrac{x+4}{y+2}$.

> To learn how to use scientific notation mode on your calculator, refer to Section 1.8.

21. **B** $\dfrac{(2x^2)^4}{x^2} = \dfrac{2^4 x^8}{x^2}\dfrac{16x^8}{x^2} = 16x^6$

22. **J**   Moving the decimal point 5 places to the left gives 3.78400. Therefore, 3.784 must be multiplied by 10^5: 3.784×10^5.

23. **D**

     $= 3x^2$ $= -4x$ $= 3x$

     $= 5$ $= -1$

Therefore, $3x^2 - 4x + 3x + 5 - 1 = 3x^2 - x + 4$.

24. **G**   Evaluate with your calculator:

```
6√(7)-3√(7)
         7.937253933
```

The answer is about 7.9.

25. **A** $\dfrac{8x^4 y - 4x^6 y^2 + 24x^9 y^5}{4x^3 y} = \dfrac{8x^4 y}{4x^3 y} - \dfrac{4x^6 y^2}{4x^3 y} + \dfrac{24x^9 y^5}{4x^3 y} = 2x - x^3 y + 6x^6 y^4$

26. **H**   The factors of $2x^2 - 5x - 3$ are $(2x + 1)(x - 3)$.

27. **A**   The volume of a rectangular prism can be found by multiplying length $\times$ width $\times$ height:

$$V = (2x + 4) \times 2 \times 3x = 6x(2x + 4) = 12x^2 + 24x$$

28. **H**   First factor out a GCF of $3x$: $3x(x^2 - 25)$

Then, factor the binomial as a difference of perfect squares: $3x(x - 5)(x + 5)$

29. **B**   Substitute 5.5 for *a* and 3.3 for *b* and use your calculator: $\sqrt{(5.5)^2 + (3.3)^2} = 6.414\ldots$, or 6.4 to the nearest tenth.

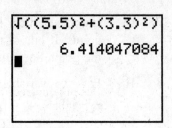

```
√((5.5)²+(3.3)²)
          6.414047084
■
```

30. **F**   The meal: $16.50
   Tip (15% = 0.15)   15% of $16.50 = 0.15(16.50)
   Tax (5% = 0.05)   5% of $16.50   = 0.05(16.50)

$$C = 16.50 + 0.15(16.50) + 0.05(16.50)$$

31. **C**   Substitute the points in the tables into the equation $x + 2y = 10$ for *x* and *y*:

   (−4, 7)   (2, 4)   (8, 1)
   −4 + 2(7) = 10   2 + 2(4) = 10   8 + 2(1) = 10
   −4 + 14 = 10✓   2 + 8   = 10✓   8 + 2   = 10✓

32. **J**   No function can have two different *x*-values for the same *y*-value. In table J, the *x*-value of 16 is paired with 4 *and* −4.

33. **D**   The range gives all possible outputs (*y*-values). The highest *y*-value on the graph occurs at the vertex point, (2, 5). The rest of the graph lies below this point. Therefore, the *y*-values are all real numbers less than or equal to 5.

34. **G**   Use the direct variation equation: $a = k \cdot b$

   Substitute 6 for *a* and 24 for *b*: $6 = k(24)$

$$\frac{6}{24} = k \longrightarrow \frac{1}{4} = k$$

   Substitute $\frac{1}{4}$ for *k*: $a = \frac{1}{4}b$

   Substitute 9 for *b*: $= \frac{1}{4}(9) = 2.25$

   When $b = 9$, $a = 2.25$.

35. **D**   If $f(x) = -3x + 2$, then $f(-3) = -3(-3) + 2 = 9 + 2 = 11$.

36. **H**   Set $s = -3t^2 + 28t + 20$ equal to 0, factor, and solve.

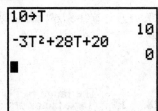

$$-3t^2 + 28t + 20 = 0$$
$$(-3t - 2)(t - 10) = 0$$
$$-3t - 2 = 0 \text{ or } t - 10 = 0$$
$$t = -\frac{2}{3} \qquad t = 10$$

```
10→T
               10
-3T²+28T+20
                0
■
```

The inventory will equal 0 after 10 days.

Alternative approach: Test each choice by substituting into the given equation and evaluating on your calculator. Choice H, 10, produces the desired value of 0 for the number of skateboards.

$$s = -3(10)^2 + 28(10) + 20 = -300 + 280 + 20 = 0$$

37. **D**   Use the vertical line test. Pass vertical lines through each graph at various points. If one of the vertical lines intersects a graph at more than one place, the graph does *not* represent a function. Only graph D passes the test.

38. **H**   For two variables to vary directly, the quotient of all values must be a constant.

Table H:

p	3	−2.5	1
q	−6	5	−2

$$\frac{-6}{3} = \frac{5}{-2.5} = \frac{-2}{1} = -2$$

39. **C**   The zero of a function is the value of x that produces an output of 0. Graphically, zeros appear as x-intercepts.

Algebraic solution:

$$15 - 3x = 0$$
$$15 = 3x$$
$$x = 5$$

The zero, or x-intercept, is 5.

Graphical solution:

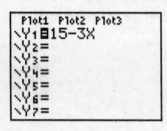

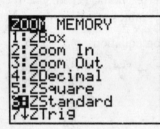

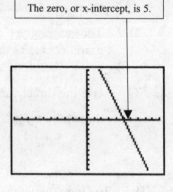

Step 1   Step 2   Step 3

40. **H**   The table indicates an x-intercept at $(9, 0)$. This eliminates choices G and J. Additionally, graph H contains the point $(3, 2)$ while graph J does not. The correct choice is H.

41. **D**   The domain is a listing of inputs (x-values). Substitute −2 for x, 2 for x, and 4 for x in the given function:

$$f(-2) = (-2)^2 + 3(-2)$$
$$= 4 - 6$$
$$= -2$$

$$f(-2) = (2)^2 + 3(2)$$
$$= 4 + 6$$
$$= 10$$

$$f(4) = (4)^2 + 3(4)$$
$$= 16 + 12$$
$$= 28$$

The range (set of outputs) is $\{-2, 10, 28\}$.

42. **G** The values in the bottom row of the table are obtained by squaring the elements in the top row:

$$(-2)^2 = 4, 0^2 = 0, 3^2 = 9, 7^2 = 49, x^2 = 81$$

Since $9^2 = 81$, choice G is correct.

43. **B** Draw the horizontal line $y = 9$ on the graph. This line intersects the grid at approximately $x = 6$.

44. **G** For data set G, {5, 7, 9, 9, 15}:

The mean (average) $= \dfrac{5+7+9+9+15}{5} = 9$.

The mode (most frequent value) = 9.
The median (middle value) = 9.

For detailed instructions on using your calculator for matrices, see Section 4.2.

45. **B** $[M] = \begin{bmatrix} 3 & 7 \\ -1 & 5 \\ 8 & 2 \end{bmatrix} \qquad [N] = \begin{bmatrix} -2 & 7 \\ 2 & 0 \\ 7 & -1 \end{bmatrix}$

$2[M] = 2\begin{bmatrix} 3 & 7 \\ -1 & 5 \\ 8 & 2 \end{bmatrix} = \begin{bmatrix} 6 & 14 \\ -2 & 10 \\ 16 & 4 \end{bmatrix}$

$2[M] + [N] = \begin{bmatrix} 6 & 14 \\ -2 & 10 \\ 16 & 4 \end{bmatrix} + \begin{bmatrix} -2 & 7 \\ 2 & 0 \\ 7 & -1 \end{bmatrix} = \begin{bmatrix} 6+-2 & 14+7 \\ -2+2 & 10+0 \\ 16+7 & 4+-1 \end{bmatrix}$

$= \begin{bmatrix} 4 & 21 \\ 0 & 10 \\ 23 & 3 \end{bmatrix}$

46. **H** To find the median, order the data {220, 137, 85, 277, 331} from smallest to largest:

$$85, 137, 220, 277, 331$$

The median is the middle value, 220.

47. **C** To find the range of a box-and-whisker graph, find the value at the end of each "whisker." These values are 83 and 94. Then, subtract: $94 - 83 = 11$.

48. **H** $[A] = \begin{bmatrix} 3 & 2 & 1 \\ 1 & 5 & 0 \end{bmatrix} \qquad [B] = \begin{bmatrix} 9 & 10 & 2 \\ 12 & 14 & 5 \end{bmatrix}$

$[B] - [A] = \begin{bmatrix} 9-3 & 10-2 & 2-1 \\ 12-1 & 14-5 & 5-0 \end{bmatrix} = \begin{bmatrix} 6 & 8 & 1 \\ 11 & 9 & 5 \end{bmatrix}$

49. **C**   Draw a line that goes through as many points as possible and keeps as many points above the line as below. Find the equation of this line. It appears to have slope 1 and y-intercept 2.

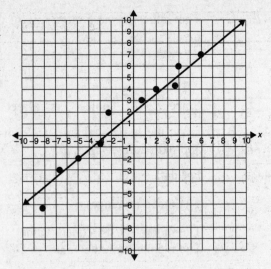

Write the equation in $y = mx + b$ form: $y = x + 2$ ⟶

Rewrite in standard form: $-x + y = 2$ $x - y = -2$

50. **G**   Matrices can be added only if they have *exactly* the same dimensions. In choice G, the first matrix is 3×1 while the second is 3×2.

Answer Sheet: Practice Test 2

1. Ⓐ Ⓑ Ⓒ Ⓓ	18. Ⓕ Ⓖ Ⓗ Ⓙ	35. Ⓐ Ⓑ Ⓒ Ⓓ
2. Ⓕ Ⓖ Ⓗ Ⓙ	19. Ⓐ Ⓑ Ⓒ Ⓓ	36. Ⓕ Ⓖ Ⓗ Ⓙ
3. Ⓐ Ⓑ Ⓒ Ⓓ	20. Ⓕ Ⓖ Ⓗ Ⓙ	37. Ⓐ Ⓑ Ⓒ Ⓓ
4. Ⓕ Ⓖ Ⓗ Ⓙ	21. Ⓐ Ⓑ Ⓒ Ⓓ	38. Ⓕ Ⓖ Ⓗ Ⓙ
5. Ⓐ Ⓑ Ⓒ Ⓓ	22. Ⓕ Ⓖ Ⓗ Ⓙ	39. Ⓐ Ⓑ Ⓒ Ⓓ
6. Ⓕ Ⓖ Ⓗ Ⓙ	23. Ⓐ Ⓑ Ⓒ Ⓓ	40. Ⓕ Ⓖ Ⓗ Ⓙ
7. Ⓐ Ⓑ Ⓒ Ⓓ	24. Ⓕ Ⓖ Ⓗ Ⓙ	41. Ⓐ Ⓑ Ⓒ Ⓓ
8. Ⓕ Ⓖ Ⓗ Ⓙ	25. Ⓐ Ⓑ Ⓒ Ⓓ	42. Ⓕ Ⓖ Ⓗ Ⓙ
9. Ⓐ Ⓑ Ⓒ Ⓓ	26. Ⓕ Ⓖ Ⓗ Ⓙ	43. Ⓐ Ⓑ Ⓒ Ⓓ
10. Ⓕ Ⓖ Ⓗ Ⓙ	27. Ⓐ Ⓑ Ⓒ Ⓓ	44. Ⓕ Ⓖ Ⓗ Ⓙ
11. Ⓐ Ⓑ Ⓒ Ⓓ	28. Ⓕ Ⓖ Ⓗ Ⓙ	45. Ⓐ Ⓑ Ⓒ Ⓓ
12. Ⓕ Ⓖ Ⓗ Ⓙ	29. Ⓐ Ⓑ Ⓒ Ⓓ	46. Ⓕ Ⓖ Ⓗ Ⓙ
13. Ⓐ Ⓑ Ⓒ Ⓓ	30. Ⓕ Ⓖ Ⓗ Ⓙ	47. Ⓐ Ⓑ Ⓒ Ⓓ
14. Ⓕ Ⓖ Ⓗ Ⓙ	31. Ⓐ Ⓑ Ⓒ Ⓓ	48. Ⓕ Ⓖ Ⓗ Ⓙ
15. Ⓐ Ⓑ Ⓒ Ⓓ	32. Ⓕ Ⓖ Ⓗ Ⓙ	49. Ⓐ Ⓑ Ⓒ Ⓓ
16. Ⓕ Ⓖ Ⓗ Ⓙ	33. Ⓐ Ⓑ Ⓒ Ⓓ	50. Ⓕ Ⓖ Ⓗ Ⓙ
17. Ⓐ Ⓑ Ⓒ Ⓓ	34. Ⓕ Ⓖ Ⓗ Ⓙ	

DIRECTIONS

Read and solve each question. Then mark the space on the answer sheet for the best answer.

---

1 Which equation illustrates the property of multiplication inverses?

   A $5 \cdot \dfrac{1}{5} = 1$

   B $0 \cdot 5 = 0$

   C $5(a + 3) = 5a + 15$

   D $5 + (-5) = 0$

---

2 A soccer ball is a sphere with a volume of about 288π cubic inches.

What is the approximate radius of the ball?

   F 4 in.
   G 6 in.
   H 9 in.
   J 15 in.

---

3 What is the solution to $\dfrac{1}{3}x - 3 \geq 2x + 2$?

   A $x \geq -3$

   B $x \geq \dfrac{1}{3}$

   C $x \leq \dfrac{-1}{3}$

   D $x \leq -3$

---

4 The transitive property is applied in which statement?

   F If $a = 4$ and $b = 4$, then $a = b$.
   G If $a = b$, then $b = a$.
   H $4(a + b) = 4a + 4b$
   J If $a = 7$, then $a + b = 7 + b$.

---

5 The graph of $y = \dfrac{1}{2}x + 1$ is shown.

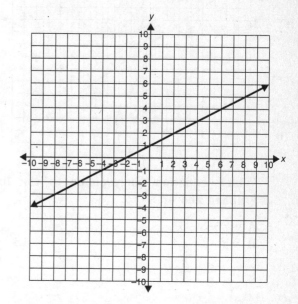

If the line is reflected across the y-axis and shifted down 3 units, what is the equation of the new line?

   A $y = \dfrac{1}{2}x - 3$

   B $y = 2x - 3$

   C $y = -2x - 2$

   D $y = \dfrac{-1}{2}x - 2$

---

6 What is the slope of the line that contains the points $(3, -1)$ and $(-1, -5)$?

   F -3
   G -2
   H 1

   J $\dfrac{3}{2}$

7

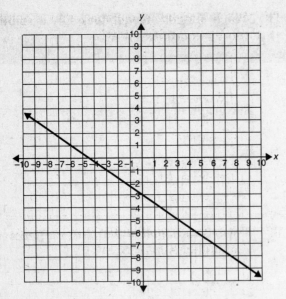

Which equation corresponds to the line graphed above?

A $y = -x - 3$

B $y = -3x - 4$

C $y = \dfrac{2}{3}x - 4$

D $y = \dfrac{-2}{3}x - 3$

8 What is the slope of the line represented by the equation $3x - 6y + 12$?

F 3

G −2

H $\dfrac{-1}{2}$

J $\dfrac{1}{2}$

9

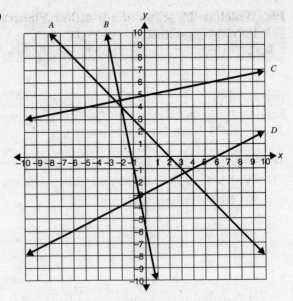

Which line on the graph appears to have a slope of −5?

A A

B B

C C

D D

10 Which is the graph of a line that appears to have the equation $2x - 4y = 8$?

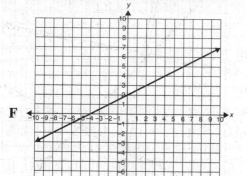

F

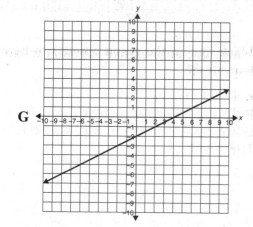

G

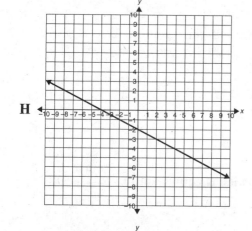

H

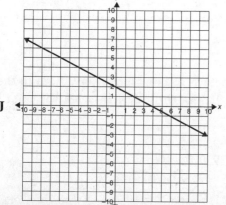

J

11 Which system of equations has a solution whose *y*-coordinate is 3?

A $\begin{cases} 5x + 2y = 4 \\ -3x - 2y = 3 \end{cases}$

B $\begin{cases} 3x - y = 3 \\ x + 3y = 11 \end{cases}$

C $\begin{cases} x + 3 = y \\ -6x + 3y = 9 \end{cases}$

D $\begin{cases} x - 3y = -3 \\ 2x - y = 4 \end{cases}$

12 Which is an equation for a line that does *not* contain the point $(-3, -4)$?

F $y = \dfrac{4}{3}x$

G $y = \dfrac{4}{5}x + \dfrac{1}{5}$

H $y = 2x + 2$

J $y = \dfrac{-3}{4}x - \dfrac{25}{4}$

13 A rectangular photograph has a length that is 4 inches greater than twice its width. If the photograph has an area of 70 square inches, what is its perimeter?

A 34 in.
B 35 in.
C 38 in.
D 74 in.

14 When Lynnette's team won the championship softball game, Lynnette threw her glove straight up in the air. The height that the glove reached can be described by the equation

$$h = -16t^2 + 20t + 7$$

where *h* is the height in feet, and *t* is time in seconds. Approximate how long a period elapsed from the time she threw the glove until it struck grounds?

F 0.5 sec
G 1.5 sec
H 2 sec
J 3 sec

15 What is the solution to $3(x - 3)^2 + 1 = 76$?

A -2
B $-2, 8$
C $1 \pm \dfrac{\sqrt{77}}{3}$
D 8

16 Which is the graph of the inequality $x + 2y > 6$?

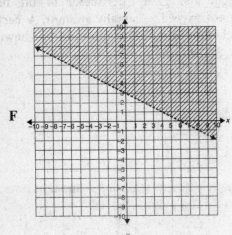

F

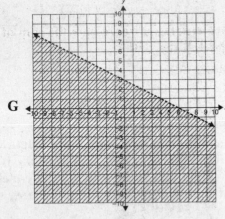

G

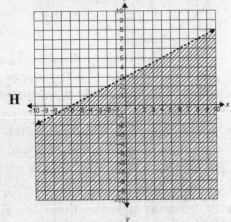

H

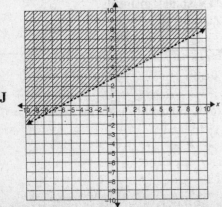

J

17 A line has a slope of 4 and contains the point $\left(2, \dfrac{-1}{2}\right)$. Which is an equation of this line?

A $8x - 2y = 1$
B $x + 2y = 8$
C $8x - 2y = 17$
D $x + 2y = 1$

18 The Rent-A-Heap rental car company charges a fixed amount of $30.00 plus $0.25 per mile for a 1-day rental. If P = the amount the company charges, and x = the number of miles driven, which equation can be used to find the total rental charges?

F $P = 30.00x + 0.25$
G $P = 30.00 + 0.25x$
H $P = 0.25(30.00 + x)$
J $P = 30.25x$

19 Twice the difference between x and 3 can be represented by which mathematical expression?

A $2x - 3$
B $2(x - 3)$
C $3 - 2x$
D $2 - x \cdot 3$

20 What is the value of $2x - 3(y + z) + 3$ if $x = 1, y = -2$, and $z = 4$?

F -4
G -1
H 0
J 23

21 Which is equivalent to $\dfrac{2(2a^2)^3}{4a^3}$?

A a^2
B a^3
C $4a^2$
D $4a^3$

22 The average distance from Earth to the Sun is 92,950,000 miles. In scientific notation it is—

F 9.295×10^{-7} mi
G 929.5×10^5 mi
H 9295.00×10^{-4} mi
J 9.295×10^7 mi

23 Consider the following models:

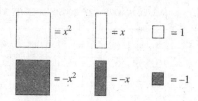

What polynomial is represented by this diagram?

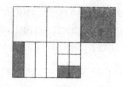

A $3x^2 + 4x + 6$
B $x^2 + 2x + 2$
C $2x^2 + 3x + 4$
D $x^2 - x + 2$

---

24 $(3x + 1)$ is a factor of which expression?

F $3x^2 + 4x - 4$
G $3x^2 - 13x + 4$
H $3x^2 + 13x + 4$
J $3x^2 + 11x - 4$

---

25 $\dfrac{2x^4y - 4x^6y^2 + 36x^3y^5}{4x^2y}$ is equivalent to—

A $2x^2 - x^4y + 9xy^4$
B $-2x^2y - x^4y + 32xy^4$
C $\dfrac{1}{2}x^2 - x^4y + 9xy^4$
D $\dfrac{1}{2}x^2 - x^3y + 9xy^5$

---

26 Which is closest to the value of $4\sqrt{3}$?

F 3.5
G 6.9
H 12
J 48

---

27 A shipping company sets a limit on the size of package that it will ship. The sum of the height and girth (perimeter of the base) cannot exceed a certain amount. A certain package is the rectangular prism shown in the diagram.

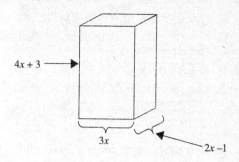

Which expression represents the sum of the height and the girth?

A $9x + 2$
B $6x^2 + x + 3$
C $14x + 1$
D $24x^3 - 3$

---

28 What is the *complete* factorization of $18x - 8x^3$?

F $2(9x - 4x^3)$
G $(2x - 2)(9 + 4x^2)$
H $2x(9 - 4x^2)$
J $2x(3 - 2x)(3 + 2x)$

---

29 The area of a regular polygon can be determined by evaluating the expression $\dfrac{1}{2}a \cdot p$, where a stands for the apothem (the distance from the center to a side), and p is the perimeter of the polygon. To the *nearest tenth*, what is the area of a polygon that has $a = 7.2$ centimeters and $p = 64$ centimeters?

A 115.2 cm^2
B 210 cm^2
C 230.4 cm^2
D 460.8 cm^2

30 Kelly goes on a shopping spree at a department store and chooses a pair of shoes priced at $85.50 and two shirts priced at $35.95 each. At the register when she goes to pay, the cashier tells her that everything is 20% off. Which expression correctly represents what Kelly should pay?

F $C = 0.20(85.50 + 2(35.95))$

G $C = (85.50 + 2(35.95)) - 0.20(85.50 + 2(35.95))$

H $C = 1.20(85.50 + 2(35.95))$

J $C = (85.50 + 2(35.95)) - 0.80(85.50 + 2(35.95))$

---

31 Which table represents a function?

A

x	y
8	8
9	11
10	8
11	11

B

x	y
8	8
11	9
8	10
11	11

C

x	y
8	8
8	11
8	8
8	11

D

x	y
11	8
8	11
11	8
8	11

32 Which function has a range of all real numbers less than or equal to 0?

F
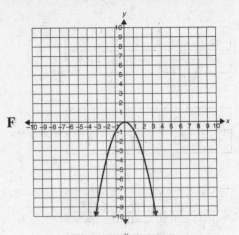

G
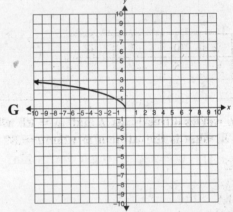

H
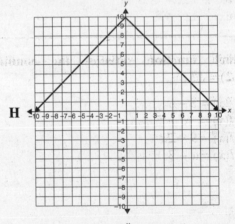

J
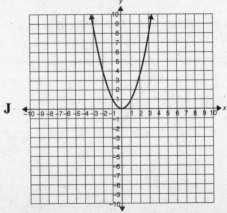

33 Which table represents points that lie on the graph of $2x - 3y = 15$?

A
x	0	5	10
y	−5	−10	−15

B
x	3	6	9
y	−3	−1	1

C
x	−3	−6	−9
y	−7	−10	13

D
x	0	2	4
y	−5	−1	3

34 If a varies directly as b and $a = 18$ when $b = 9$, what is the value of b when $a = 3$?

F $\dfrac{2}{3}$

G 1.5

H 2

J 6

35 Which function satisfies the condition $f(-2) = 1$?

A $f(x) = 5 - x^2$

B $f(x) = -x^2 - 5$

C $f(x) = 9 + 2x^2$

D $f(x) = x - 3$

36 Which graph represents a direct variation?

F
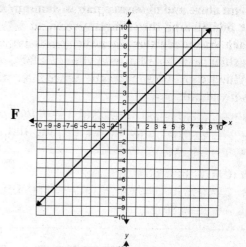

G
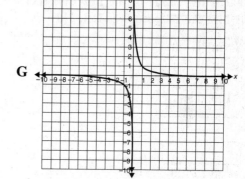

H
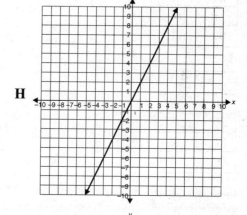

J
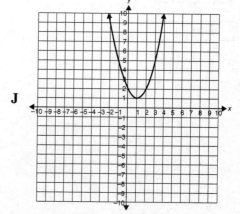

37 The temperature in degrees Celsius from noon until midnight on a day in January can be modeled by the function

$$T = \frac{-1}{4}x^2 + \frac{11}{4}x - \frac{9}{2},$$

where T = temperature and x = *hours past noon*. At what time in the evening did the temperature drop to 0°C?

A 5:30 P.M.
B 7:00 P.M.
C 9:00 P.M.
D Midnight

38 What is the range of the function $f(x) = 5 - 2x$ when the domain is $\{-1, 3, 7\}$?

F $\{-9, -1, 7\}$
G $\{-1, 3, 7\}$
H $\{-1, 1, 3\}$
J $\{1, 3, 7\}$

39 Which of the following does *not* represent the graph of a function?

A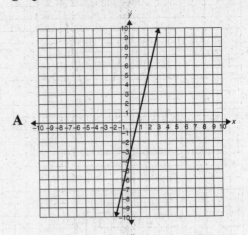

B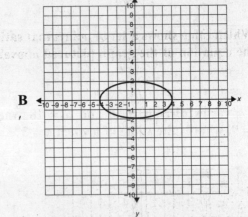

C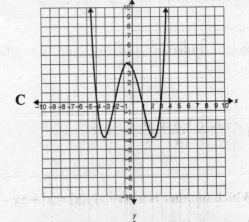

D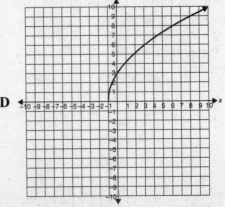

40

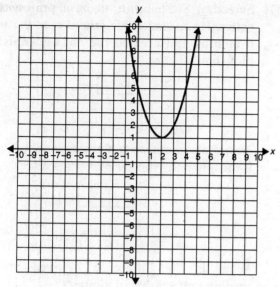

Which table shows a set of points that satisfy the equation of the graph pictured above?

F

x	0	2	4
y	5	1	5

G

x	5	1	5
y	0	2	4

H

x	2	4	8
y	4	6	8

J

x	−2	0	2
y	10	5	10

41 Which number is a zero of $f(x) = x^2 + 5x - 6$?

A −6
B −3
C 2
D 6

42 Which function represents the data shown in the table?

x	−4	−3	−2	−1
f(x)	9	8.5	8	7.5

F $f(x) = \dfrac{1}{2}x - 9$

G $f(x) = 7 + \dfrac{1}{2}x$

H $f(x) = 9 - \dfrac{1}{2}x$

J $f(x) = 7 - \dfrac{1}{2}x$

43

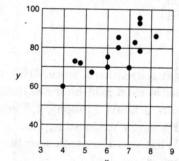

According to the scatterplot, which x-value would best match a y value of 85?

A 4.5
B 5.5
C 6.5
D 7.5

44 {3, 14, 16, 3, 14, 7, 14, 16}

What is the *product* of the mode and the median in the given set of data?

F 48
G 119
H 196
J 224

45 $A = \begin{bmatrix} -1 & 0 \\ 8 & 6 \\ -2 & 5 \end{bmatrix}$ $B = \begin{bmatrix} 1 & -1 \\ 3 & 4 \\ 2 & 0 \end{bmatrix}$

$$-0.5[A] + [B] = ?$$

A $\begin{bmatrix} 1.5 & -1 \\ -1 & 1 \\ 3 & 0 \end{bmatrix}$

B $\begin{bmatrix} 0 & -1 \\ 11 & 10 \\ 0 & 5 \end{bmatrix}$

C $\begin{bmatrix} 1.5 & -1 \\ -1 & 1 \\ 3 & -2.5 \end{bmatrix}$

D $\begin{bmatrix} 6 & -1 \\ -37 & -26 \\ 12 & -25 \end{bmatrix}$

46 Molly works at a used book store. Over the past week, she worked 5.75 hours Saturday, 8 hours Sunday, 3 hours Monday, 4.5 hours Tuesday, and 4 hours Wednesday, Thursday, and Friday. What was the mean number of hours she worked per day?

F 4.5
G 4.75
H 5.25
J 26.5

47 Someday, Steve wants to be a professional golfer. He recorded his scores over the past 6 months and created the box-and-whisker plot shown below.

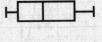

66 68 70 72 74 76 78 80 82 84

Jimmy also wants to golf professionally. There is the box-and-whisker plot of his scores.

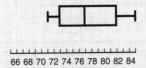

66 68 70 72 74 76 78 80 82 84

What is the difference between Steve's median golf score and Jimmy's?

A 0
B 2
C 3
D 14

48 Sun Jian works in a candy store. Each month he must take inventory. Matrix A shows the number of each item he had in stock for the first 2 weeks of August.

	Runts	Nerds	Skittles
Week 1	43	17	29
Week 2	13	66	0

$= [A]$

Matrix B shows the number of each item he had in stock for the first 2 weeks in December.

	Runts	Nerds	Skittles
Week 1	15	50	45
Week 2	19	36	21

$= [B]$

Which matrix correctly shows the difference, $[B]-[A]$, in the amounts he had in stock in August and December?

F $\begin{bmatrix} 28 & -33 & -16 \\ -6 & 30 & -21 \end{bmatrix}$

G $\begin{bmatrix} -28 & 33 & 16 \\ 6 & -30 & 21 \end{bmatrix}$

H $\begin{bmatrix} 58 & 67 & 74 \\ 32 & 102 & 21 \end{bmatrix}$

J $\begin{bmatrix} 28 & 33 & 16 \\ 6 & 30 & 21 \end{bmatrix}$

49 Which scatterplot would *most* likely have the equation $y = -x - 1$ as its line of best fit?

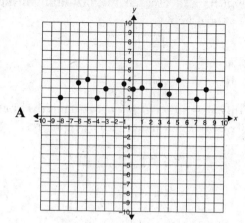

A

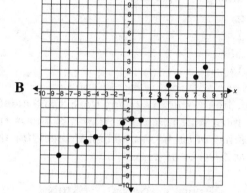

B

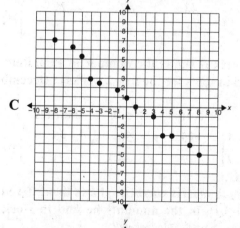

C

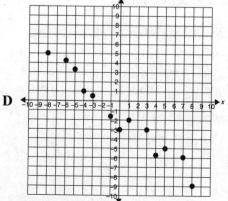

D

50 Ms. Quarry gave her class a practice SAT. She took their scores and created the box-and-whisker plot shown below.

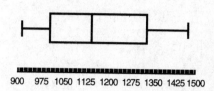

What is the approximate range of SAT scores in Ms. Quarry's class?

F 575
G 900
H 1150
J 1475

Answer Key for Practice Test 2

1. A	11. C	21. D	31. A	41. A
2. G	12. G	22. J	32. F	42. J
3. D	13. C	23. B	33. B	43. D
4. F	14. G	24. H	34. G	44. H
5. D	15. B	25. C	35. A	45. C
6. H	16. F	26. G	36. H	46. G
7. D	17. C	27. C	37. C	47. C
8. J	18. G	28. J	38. F	48. G
9. B	19. B	29. C	39. B	49. D
10. F	20. G	30. G	40. F	50. F

Answer Explanations

1. **A**   5 and $\frac{1}{5}$ are multiplicative inverses because their product equals 1, the identity for multiplication.

2. **G**   The volume formula for a sphere is $V = \frac{4}{3}\pi r^3$

     Substitute: $288\pi = \frac{4}{3}\pi r^3$

$$288 = \frac{4}{3}r^3$$

$$r^3 = \frac{3}{4}(288)$$

$$= 216$$

     Therefore, $r = 6$ because $6^3 = 216$.

3. **D** $\frac{1}{3}x - 3 \geq 2x + 2$

$$\frac{1}{3}x - 2x \geq 2 + 3$$

$$\frac{-5}{3}x \geq 5$$

$$x \leq \frac{-3}{5} \cdot 5 \text{ Reverse the inequality symbol!}$$

$$\leq -3$$

     The solution is $x \leq -3$.

4. **F**   The transitive property states: If $a = b$ and $b = c$, then $a = c$. In choice F, both a and b equal 4, so they equal each other.

5. **D**   Reflection over the y-axis changes the slope to $\frac{-1}{2}$. Shifting down 3 units changes the y-intercept to -2. Therefore, the equation of the new line is $y = \frac{-1}{2}x - 2$.

6. **H** Use the slope formula, $m = \dfrac{y_2 - y_1}{x_2 - x_1}$, and substitute:

$$m = \frac{-5-(-1)}{-1-3} = \frac{-4}{-4} = 1$$

7. **D** The graphed line has a slope of $\dfrac{-2}{3}$ and a y-intercept of -3. Therefore, its

equation is $y = \dfrac{-2}{3}x - 3$.

8. **J** Rewrite the equation in $y = mx + b$ form to find the slope of the line:

$$3x - 6y = 12$$
$$-6y = -3x + 12$$
$$y = \frac{1}{2}x - 2$$

The slope of the line is $\dfrac{1}{2}$.

9. **B** Only choices A and B have negative slopes. Line B rises 5 units for each unit it runs to the left, so it has a slope of -5.

10. **F** Rewrite the equation $2x - 4y = 8$ in $y = mx + b$ form:

$$2x - 4y = 8$$
$$-4y = -2x + 8$$
$$y = \frac{1}{2}x - 2$$

This form indicates that the line has a slope of $\dfrac{1}{2}$ and a y-intercept of -2. This is true for choice F.

11. **C** In choice C, $\begin{cases} x+3 = y \\ -6x+3y = 9 \end{cases}$.

Solve by substituting $(x + 3)$ for y into the second equation:

$$-6x + 3(x+3) = 9$$
$$-6x + 3x + 9 = 9$$
$$-3x = 0$$
$$x = 0$$

Substitute 0 for x into the first equation: $y = 3$.

12. **G** Substitute $(-3, -4)$ into $y = \dfrac{4}{5}x + \dfrac{1}{5}$:

$$-4 = \frac{4}{5}(-3) + \frac{1}{5}$$
$$-4 = \frac{-11}{5}$$

Since $4 \neq \dfrac{-11}{5}$, choice G does *not* contain the given point.

13. **C** The formula for area of a rectangle is width × length. Then:

$$70 = x(2x + 4)$$
$$70 = 2x^2 + 4x$$
$$2x^2 + 4x - 70 = 0$$
$$x^2 + 2x - 35 = 0$$
$$(x + 7)(x - 5) = 0$$
$$x + 7 = 0 \text{ or } x - 5 = 0$$
$$x \cancel{=} -7 \qquad x = 5$$

The width of a rectangle cannot be negative, so width = 5.
Length = $2x + 4 = 2(5) + 4 = 14$

Perimeter = $P = 2L + 2W$
$$= 2(14) + 2(5) = 38 \text{ in.}$$

14. **G** Use the calculator to graph $y = -16x^2 + 20x + 7$; then find the positive x-intercept of the graph. (Refer to A Calculator Tutorial on page 3.)

15. **B** Solve by "isolating the square":

$$3(x - 3)^2 + 1 = 76$$
$$3(x - 3)^2 = 75$$
$$(x - 3)^2 = 25$$
$$x - 3 = \pm 5$$
$$x - 3 = 5 \text{ or } x - 3 = -5$$
$$x = 8 \qquad x = -2$$

16. **F** Rewrite the given inequality:

$$x + 2y > 6$$
$$2y > -x + 6$$
$$y > \frac{-1}{2}x + 3$$

From this form, you see that the boundary line has a slope of $\frac{-1}{2}$ and a y-intercept of 3. This is true for choices F and G. Testing the point $(0, 0)$ in $x + 2y > 6$ gives $0 > 6$, which is false. Therefore, choice F correctly shades *away* from the test point and is the graph of the given inequality.

17. **C** Substitute $m = 4$, $x = 2$, and $y = \frac{-1}{2}$ into the $y = mx + b$ form:

$$\frac{-1}{2} = 4(2) + b$$

$$\frac{-1}{2} = 8 + b$$

$$b = \frac{-17}{2}$$

An equation of the line is $y = 4x - \frac{17}{2}$.

Change to standard form: $-4x + y = \frac{-17}{2}$

Multiply by -2: $\qquad 8x - 2y = 17$, which is choice C.

18. **G**   \$30.00 is the fixed charge. $0.25x$ is the additional cost for driving x miles. The total cost, P, of the rental car is the sum of these quantities: $P = 30.00 + 0.25x$.

19. **B**   The difference between x and $3 \rightarrow x - 3$.

       Twice this difference $\rightarrow 2(x - 3)$.

20. **G**   Substitute: $2(1) - 3(-2 + 4) + 3$

$$2 - 3(2) + 3 = -1$$

21. **D** $\dfrac{2\left(2a^2\right)^3}{4a^3} = \dfrac{2\left(8a^6\right)}{4a^3} = \dfrac{16a^6}{4a^3} = 4a^3$

22. **J**   The decimal point goes after the first nonzero digit. This eliminates choices G and H. 10^7 will shift the decimal point 7 spaces to the right, so choice J is the correct answer.

23. **B**   2 large white squares $\rightarrow 2x^2$

       1 large shaded square $\rightarrow -x^2$

       3 white rectangles $\rightarrow 3x$

       1 shaded rectangle $\rightarrow -x$

       4 small white squares $\rightarrow 4$

       2 small shaded squares $\rightarrow -2$

       Combining like terms gives a final answer of $x^2 + 2x + 2$.

24. **H**   Choice H factors as $(3x + 1)(x + 4)$.

25. **C**   Split the fraction: $\dfrac{2x^4y}{4x^2y} - \dfrac{4x^6y^2}{4x^2y} + \dfrac{36x^3y^5}{4x^2y}$

       Simplify: $\dfrac{1}{2}x^2 - x^4y + 9xy^4$

26. **G**   Use your calculator; $4\sqrt{3} \approx 6.928$.

27. **C**   The girth is the perimeter of the base, $2L + 2W$. Then:

$$\text{girth} = 2(3x) + 2(2x - 1)$$
$$= 6x + 4x - 2$$
$$= 10x - 2$$

       Since the height is $4x + 3$, the sum of the height and the girth is $14x + 1$.

28. **J**   Factor out the GCF: $18x - 8x^3 = 2x(9 - 4x^2)$. But $9 - 4x^2$ is a difference of perfect squares. Thus, the *complete* factorization of $18x + 8x^3$ is $2x(3 - 2x)(3 + 2x)$.

29. **C**   Substitute: $\dfrac{1}{2} \cdot a \cdot p = 0.5(7.2)(64) = 230.4 \text{ cm}^2$.

30. **G**   The total, C, without a discount would be $85.50 + 2(35.95)$.

       The value of the discount is 20% of that amount, or $0.20(85.50 + 2(35.95))$.

       Subtract: $C = (85.50 + 2(35.95)) - 0.20(85.50 + 2(35.95))$

31. **A** A function must have one and only one y-value for each x-value. This is true only for choice A.

32. **F** Since the range is all numbers less than or equal to zero, the graph of the function cannot lie above the x-axis. This eliminates all choices except F.

33. **B** Be sure to check *every* point in the table. Choice B satisfies $2x - 3y = 15$ for *all three* points:

$$2(3) - 3(-3) = 15$$
$$2(6) - 3(-1) = 15$$
$$2(9) - 3(1) = 15$$

34. **G** Substitute 18 for a and 9 for b in the direct variation equation $a = kb$; then $18 = k(9)$, so $k = 2$.

Substitute this value for k and 3 for a in $a = kb$: $3 = 2b$, so $b = 1.5$.

35. **A** $f(-2) = 1$ means $f(x) = 1$ when $x = -2$. Substitute in choice A:

$$1 = 5 - (-2)^2$$
$$1 = 5 - 4 \quad \text{TRUE}$$

The point $(-2, 1)$ does *not* satisfy the other three answer choices.

36. **H** Graph H is a line passing through the origin and therefore represents a direct variation.

37. **C** Set $T = 0$, and solve $0 = \dfrac{-1}{4}x^2 + \dfrac{11}{4}x - \dfrac{9}{2}$ by graphing on your calculator. (See A Calculator Tutorial, page 3.) The x-intercepts are 2 and 9. Choice C, 9 P.M., is the correct answer since the question asks for the time in the evening.

38. **F** This question asks for *outputs* of the given function. For choice F:

$$f(-1) = 5 - 2(-1) = 7$$
$$f(3) = 5 - 2(3) = -1$$
$$f(7) = 5 - 14 = -9$$

39. **B** Choice B does not pass the vertical line test.

40. **F** The points $(0, 5)$, $(2, 1)$ and $(4, 5)$ from Table F all lie on the graph.

Therefore, they satisfy the equation of the graph.

41. **A** Solve $x^2 + 5x - 6 = 0$ by factoring:

$$(x + 6)(x - 1) = 0$$
$$x + 6 = 0 \text{ or } x - 1 = 0$$
$$x = -6 \qquad x = 1$$

These are the only zeros of $f(x) = x^2 + 5x - 6$.

42. **J** All four points in the table satisfy function J. For example:

$$f(-4) = 7 - \frac{1}{2}(-4) = 7 + 2 = 9$$

$$f(-3) = 7 - \frac{1}{2}(-3) = 7 + 1.5 = 8.5$$

43. **D** A reasonable line of best fit is shown. A horizontal line drawn at $y = 85$ would intersect the line of best fit at about $x = 7.5$.

44. **H** The middle value (median) and the most frequently occurring value (mode) are both 14. The product is $(14)(14) = 196$.

45. **C**
$$-0.5[A] = \begin{bmatrix} 0.5 & 0 \\ -4 & -3 \\ 1 & -2.5 \end{bmatrix} \qquad [B] = \begin{bmatrix} 1 & -1 \\ 3 & 4 \\ 2 & 0 \end{bmatrix}$$

$$-0.5[A] + [B] = \begin{bmatrix} 0.5 & 0 \\ -4 & -3 \\ 1 & -2.5 \end{bmatrix} + \begin{bmatrix} 1 & -1 \\ 3 & 4 \\ 2 & 0 \end{bmatrix} = \begin{bmatrix} 1.5 & -1 \\ -1 & 1 \\ 3 & -2.5 \end{bmatrix}$$

46. **G** Mean number of hours Molly worked $= \dfrac{5.75 + 8 + 3 + 4.5 + 4 + 4 + 4}{7} = 4.75$

47. **C** Steve has a median score of 74. Jimmy has a median score of 77. The difference between 77 and 74 is 3.

48. **G** Subtract each element of matrix A from the corresponding element of matrix B. The correct result is choice G.

49. **D** Since the slope of the line $y = -x - 1$ is -1, the data points must show a downward trend. This is true for choices C and D. The y-intercept of $y = -x - 1$ is -1. A line of best fit through the data in choice D would appear to cross the y-axis at about -1.

50. **F** The scores appear to range from a little more than 900 to a little less than 1500. The difference between these values is 600. Choice F is the best approximation.

Answer Sheet: Practice Test 3

1. Ⓐ Ⓑ Ⓒ Ⓓ	18. Ⓕ Ⓖ Ⓗ Ⓙ	35. Ⓐ Ⓑ Ⓒ Ⓓ
2. Ⓕ Ⓖ Ⓗ Ⓙ	19. Ⓐ Ⓑ Ⓒ Ⓓ	36. Ⓕ Ⓖ Ⓗ Ⓙ
3. Ⓐ Ⓑ Ⓒ Ⓓ	20. Ⓕ Ⓖ Ⓗ Ⓙ	37. Ⓐ Ⓑ Ⓒ Ⓓ
4. Ⓕ Ⓖ Ⓗ Ⓙ	21. Ⓐ Ⓑ Ⓒ Ⓓ	38. Ⓕ Ⓖ Ⓗ Ⓙ
5. Ⓐ Ⓑ Ⓒ Ⓓ	22. Ⓕ Ⓖ Ⓗ Ⓙ	39. Ⓐ Ⓑ Ⓒ Ⓓ
6. Ⓕ Ⓖ Ⓗ Ⓙ	23. Ⓐ Ⓑ Ⓒ Ⓓ	40. Ⓕ Ⓖ Ⓗ Ⓙ
7. Ⓐ Ⓑ Ⓒ Ⓓ	24. Ⓕ Ⓖ Ⓗ Ⓙ	41. Ⓐ Ⓑ Ⓒ Ⓓ
8. Ⓕ Ⓖ Ⓗ Ⓙ	25. Ⓐ Ⓑ Ⓒ Ⓓ	42. Ⓕ Ⓖ Ⓗ Ⓙ
9. Ⓐ Ⓑ Ⓒ Ⓓ	26. Ⓕ Ⓖ Ⓗ Ⓙ	43. Ⓐ Ⓑ Ⓒ Ⓓ
10. Ⓕ Ⓖ Ⓗ Ⓙ	27. Ⓐ Ⓑ Ⓒ Ⓓ	44. Ⓕ Ⓖ Ⓗ Ⓙ
11. Ⓐ Ⓑ Ⓒ Ⓓ	28. Ⓕ Ⓖ Ⓗ Ⓙ	45. Ⓐ Ⓑ Ⓒ Ⓓ
12. Ⓕ Ⓖ Ⓗ Ⓙ	29. Ⓐ Ⓑ Ⓒ Ⓓ	46. Ⓕ Ⓖ Ⓗ Ⓙ
13. Ⓐ Ⓑ Ⓒ Ⓓ	30. Ⓕ Ⓖ Ⓗ Ⓙ	47. Ⓐ Ⓑ Ⓒ Ⓓ
14. Ⓕ Ⓖ Ⓗ Ⓙ	31. Ⓐ Ⓑ Ⓒ Ⓓ	48. Ⓕ Ⓖ Ⓗ Ⓙ
15. Ⓐ Ⓑ Ⓒ Ⓓ	32. Ⓕ Ⓖ Ⓗ Ⓙ	49. Ⓐ Ⓑ Ⓒ Ⓓ
16. Ⓕ Ⓖ Ⓗ Ⓙ	33. Ⓐ Ⓑ Ⓒ Ⓓ	50. Ⓕ Ⓖ Ⓗ Ⓙ
17. Ⓐ Ⓑ Ⓒ Ⓓ	34. Ⓕ Ⓖ Ⓗ Ⓙ	

DIRECTIONS

Read and solve each question. Then mark the space on the answer sheet for the best answer.

---

1   Which statement illustrates the use of the distributive property?

   A $x^2 + 3x = x(x + 3)$
   B $5(3x) = (5 \cdot 3)x$
   C If $x = y$ and $y = z$, then $x = z$,
   D $(x + 3) \cdot 5 = 5(x + 3)$

---

2   Jack had an ice cream cone that was covered on the outside with a layer of chocolate. (The surface area of a cone can be calculated using the formula $A = \pi rl$.) If the surface area covered by chocolate was about 38 square inches and the length l down the side of the cone was 5.5 inches, what was the approximate radius of the cone?

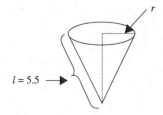

   F 1.5 in.
   G 2 in.
   H 2.2 in.
   J 4 in.

3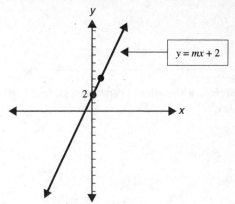

The graph of the line $y = mx + 2$ would shift *up* 1 unit if its equation were changed to—

   A $y = mx + 1$
   B $y = mx + 3$
   C $y = (m + 1)x + 2$
   D $y = (m - 1)x$

---

4   If a and b represent real numbers, which statement is *always* true?

   F If $a > 0$ and $b > 0$, then $a - b > 0$.
   G $a \div 1 = 1 \div a$
   H $(a + b)^2 = a^2 + b^2$
   J $a - b = -1(b - a)$

5 Which equation does not have $x = -2$ as a solution?

A $14 - 3x = 20$

B $6 + 2(x - 1) = 0$

C $\dfrac{1}{2}(x + 4) = x + 3$

D $3(1 - x) = x - 1$

---

6 Which inequality represents the graph shown?

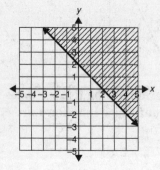

F $y \geq -2x$

G $2y > -x + 2$

H $-y \leq -x + 2$

J $y \geq -x + 2$

7 Which line appears to have slope $\dfrac{1}{3}$ and an x-intercept of -1?

A

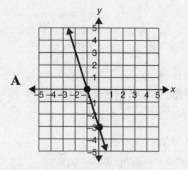

B

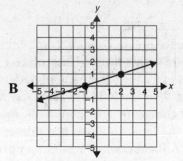

C

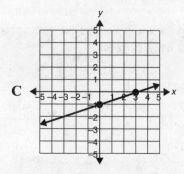

D

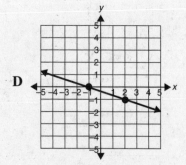

8 What is the slope of a line that contains the points (−2, 5) and (1, −4)?

F 9
G −3
H $\dfrac{1}{3}$
J $-\dfrac{1}{3}$

9 Which line on the grid has a slope of −2?

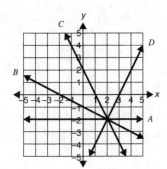

A A
B B
C C
D D

10 Which could be an equation for the vertical line graphed here ($k \neq 0$)?

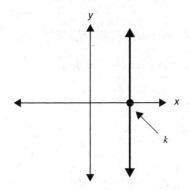

F $x = k$
G $y = k$
H $x + y = k$
J $x - y = k$

11 Which equation represents a line whose slope is $\dfrac{1}{2}$?

A $2y = x$
B $2x + y = 0$
C $y = \dfrac{1}{2}x^2$
D $\dfrac{1}{2}y = x + 2$

12 Which graph represents a system of equations whose solution is (−1, 1)?

F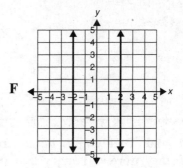

G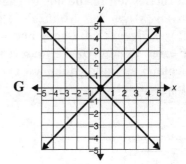

H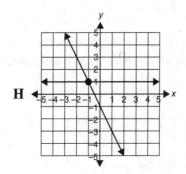

J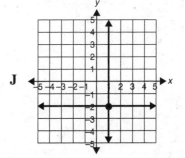

13 What is the *y*-coordinate of the solution to the following system?

$$\begin{cases} -2x + 3y = 12 \\ 3x - 3y = -15 \end{cases}$$

   A −3

   B 2

   C 3

   D 4

14 When Puff and Daddy got home from playing golf, they were so hungry that they ate all 32 chocolates left in the box of candy they had given Mom for Mother's Day. Because Puff was bigger than Daddy and was also a faster eater, he ate 5 more than twice as many chocolates as Daddy did. How many chocolates did Puff eat?

   F 19

   G 23

   H 25

   J 27

15 Which is an equation for the line that passes through both of the points graphed below?

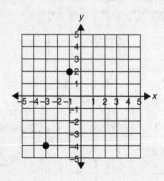

   A $y = 3x + 5$

   B $y = \dfrac{1}{3}x + 5$

   C $y = -3x + 5$

   D $y = 3x + 12$

16 Which equation is satisfied by $x = -3$?

   F $x^2 = 9$

   G $x^2 - 3x - 4 = 0$

   H $(x - 3)^2 = 0$

   J $-3x(x - 1) = 0$

17 Mom didn't want Daniel to find his birthday presents, so she hid them in a big box that was 2 feet tall. The volume was 48 cubic feet. If the bottom of the box was 2 feet longer than it was wide, what was the measure of the longest side of the box?

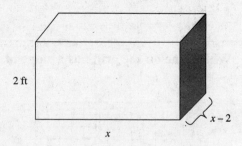

   A 4 ft

   B 6 ft

   C 8 ft

   D 12 ft

18 Which number solves the inequality $x > 6 + 2x$?

   F −8

   G −5

   H −2

   J 0

19 The formula for finding the area of a trapezoid is $A = \dfrac{1}{2}h(b_1 + b_2)$.

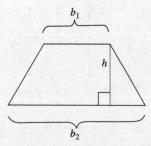

If the trapezoid shown has height $h = 5$ and bases $b_1 = 6$ and $b_2 = 10$, what is the area, in square units, of the trapezoid?

   A 20 in^2

   B 40 in^2

   C 75 in^2

   D 150 in^2

20 When Melissa took a new job as a computer salesperson, the company offered her a choice between two pay plans:

Option 1: 2% commission on sales plus $12,000 fixed salary
Option 2: 5% commission on sales

Which expression could represent the difference between the amount of money Melissa would earn under the two different pay plans?

Assume that x = total sales.

F $0.05x - (0.02x + 12{,}000)$
G $0.05x - (12{,}000 + 0.02)x$
H $12{,}000 - 0.03x$
J $(0.05 - 0.02)(x + 12{,}000)$

21 Which expression means "5 less than the product of x and y"?

A $5 - xy$
B $xy - 5$
C $xy < 5$
D $(5 - x)y$

22 Which expression is equivalent to $(3x^3y)^2$?

F $6x^6y^2$
G $9x^6y^2$
H $6x^5y^2$
J $9x^5y^2$

23 Consider the following models:

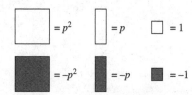

What polynomial is represented by this diagram?

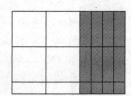

A $4p^2 - 6p - 4$
B $4p^2 + 10p + 4$
C $4p^2 + 6p - 4$
D $4p^2 - 4p - 4$

24 The family room of Veerpat's house has a beautiful stained-glass window shaped like the one shown below. The bottom of the window is a rectangle with dimensions $(x - 4)$ ft. and $(x + 2)$ ft. The top is a semicircle whose area is about 18 square feet. Which expression represents the area, in square feet, of the entire window?

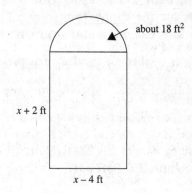

F $x^2 - 2x + 10$ ft^2
G $x^2 + 10$ ft^2
H $x^2 - 6x + 18$ ft^2
J $x^2 - 8x + 16$ ft^2

25 $\sqrt{3} + \sqrt{12}$ is equal to—

A $\sqrt{15}$
B 6
C $3\sqrt{3}$
D $2\sqrt{6}$

26 In scientific notation, the number 0.000467 would be written as $4.67 \cdot 10^k$, where k equals what value?

F -4
G -3
H 3
J 4

27 $\dfrac{10x^3y - 5xy}{5xy}$ simplifies to—

A $5x^2$
B $2x^2 - 1$
C $5x^2 - 1$
D $2x^2 - 5xy$

28 If one of the factors of $x^2 - 2x - 3$ is $(x - 3)$, what is the other factor?

F $(x - 2)$
G $(x + 1)$
H $(x^2 - 2)$
J $(x^2 - 3x)$

---

29 John built a kite using two wooden dowel rods for the supporting frame. The area of the kite can be found from the expression $\frac{1}{2}d_1 \cdot d_2$, where d_1 and d_2 are the lengths of the dowel rods. Suppose the area of John's kite is represented by $\frac{1}{2}(x^2 - 3x)$. Then the lengths of the dowel rods could be represented by—

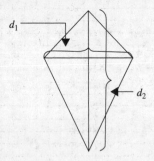

A x^2 and $3x$
B 3 and 9
C $x + 3$ and $x - 3$
D x and $x - 3$

---

30 $(x - 1)$ is a factor of all of the following polynomials except—

F $x^2 - 1$
G $x^2 - x$
H $x^2 - x - 1$
J $x^2 - 2x + 1$

---

31 Line L has slope $\frac{1}{2}$ and passes through the origin. Which point does *not* lie on line L?

A $(4, 2)$
B $(-3, -1.5)$
C $(200, 100)$
D $(1, 2)$

32

x	−4	−2	0	1	3	5
y	−16	−4	0	−1	−9	h

If the ordered pair **(5, h)** fits the pattern shown by the points in the table, what is the value of h?

F −27
G −25
H −21
J −16

33

t	20	35	50
C	90	112.5	135

The points in the table represent, in dollars, the amounts that Mr. Ed, the electrician, charges. These amounts are based on the length, in minutes, of his house call. If t represents the time Mr. Ed spends and C represents the charge to the customer, which equation best models the given data?

A $C = 3t + 30$
B $C = 1.5t + 60$
C $C = 1.5t + 90$
D $C = \frac{2}{3}(t + 90)$

34 What is the domain of the function shown in the graph?

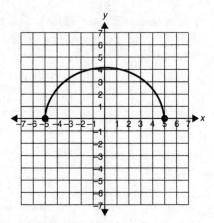

F All real numbers
G All real numbers between −5 and 5 (including ±5)
H All real numbers between 0 and 5 (including 0 and 5)
J All positive real numbers and 0

35 Alfred runs a rectangular fence around his garden to keep out Mr. Cottontail, who is eating Alfred's veggies. Alfred decides that the shorter side of the fence, x, should be between 8 and 10 feet. What would be the *range*, in feet, for the corresponding perimeter function, $P(x) = 2(x + 3) + 2x$?

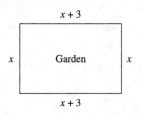

A $8 \le P \le 10$
B $88 \le P \le 130$
C $19 \le P \le 23$
D $38 \le P \le 46$

36 Which graph has the same *domain* as the function represented by the points in the table?

x	−2	2	4	6
y	−1	3	1	0

F
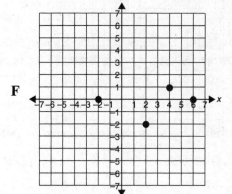

G
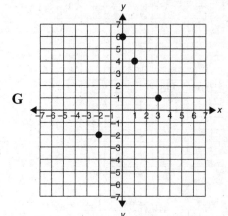

H
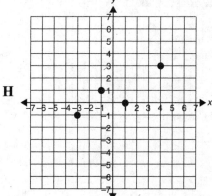

J
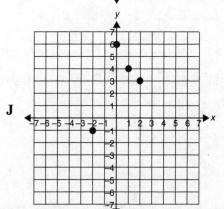

37 Which graph represents a direct variation between the variables x and y?

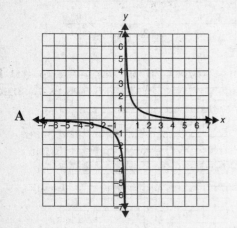

A

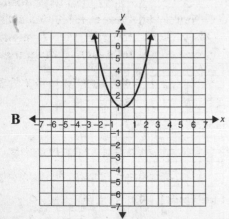

B

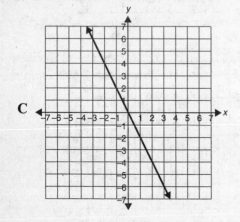

C

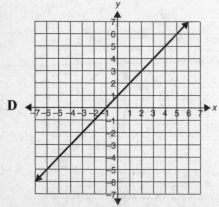

D

38 Which table of values does *not* represent y as a function of x?

F

x	y
−1	1
0	0
1	1
2	0
3	1

G

x	y
−2	4
−1	1
0	0
1	1
2	4

H

x	y
−2	−2
−1	−1
0	0
1	1
2	2

J

x	y
1	3
2	2
3	1
1	0
2	−1

39 Jerry was leaning out the viewing window of the Washington Monument when the Gobstopper he was eating fell out of his mouth. The function $h(t) = -16t^2 + 555$ gives the height, h, of the Gobstopper after t seconds had passed. How many seconds elapsed before the Gobstopper hit the ground?

A 34.7
B 11.3
C 5.9
D 3.2

40 Which function has exactly *one* zero?

F $y = x^2 + 1$
G $y = (x + 2)(x - 1)$
H $y = 3x - 1$
J $y = 0$

41 What is the value of $f(-2)$?

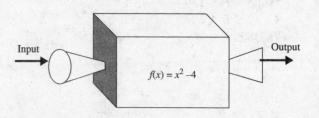

A −8
B −4
C 0
D $\sqrt{2}$

42 Which graph does *not* represent a function?

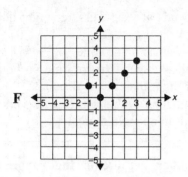

F

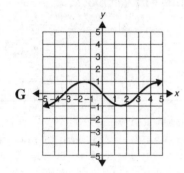

G

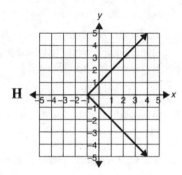

H

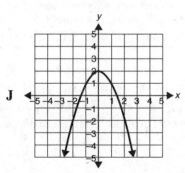

J

43 George was absent on the day that his class took a practice SOL test. Here are the scores of five of his friends:

33, 37, 50, 40, 35

George scored 38 on the make-up test he took. Relative to his friends' scores, George's score was—

A below the mean but above the median
B below both the mean and the median
C above both the mean and the median
D above the mean but below the median

44 Beauty, Beastie, and their lazy boys decided to start a family business making and selling dolls. They kept records for 2 months showing how many dolls each of them made.

	Beauty	Beastie	Lazy Boys
Goo Goo Dolls	15	5	2
Dolly Partons	23	8	0

Number of dolls made in November

	Beauty	Beastie	Lazy Boys
Goo Goo Dolls	42	10	4
Dolly Partons	28	12	0

Number of dolls made in December

Which matrix represents the *difference* in production from November to December?

F $\begin{bmatrix} 57 & 15 & 6 \\ 51 & 20 & 0 \end{bmatrix}$ G $\begin{bmatrix} 27 & 5 & 2 \\ 5 & 4 & 0 \end{bmatrix}$

H $\begin{bmatrix} 30 & 10 & 4 \\ 46 & 16 & 0 \end{bmatrix}$ J $\begin{bmatrix} 630 & 50 & 8 \\ 644 & 96 & 0 \end{bmatrix}$

45 If $[A] = \begin{bmatrix} 3 & -1 \\ 2 & 4 \end{bmatrix}$ and $[B] = \begin{bmatrix} -6 & 0 \\ 5 & -2 \end{bmatrix}$, then $2[B] + [A] = ?$

A $\begin{bmatrix} -6 & -2 \\ 14 & 4 \end{bmatrix}$

B $\begin{bmatrix} -9 & -1 \\ 12 & 0 \end{bmatrix}$

C $\begin{bmatrix} 0 & -2 \\ 9 & 6 \end{bmatrix}$

D $\begin{bmatrix} -36 & 0 \\ 20 & -16 \end{bmatrix}$

46 Which of the following represents a matrix operation that *cannot* be performed?

F $\begin{bmatrix} -3 \\ 0 \\ 3 \end{bmatrix} + \begin{bmatrix} 3^2 \\ 4^2 \\ 5^2 \end{bmatrix}$

G $\begin{bmatrix} 2.3 \times 10^3 \\ 3.4 \times 10^2 \end{bmatrix} - \begin{bmatrix} 6.2 \times 10^2 \\ 1.0 \times 10^3 \end{bmatrix}$

H $\dfrac{1}{3} \begin{bmatrix} 5 & 2 \\ -4 & 3 \end{bmatrix}$

J $\begin{bmatrix} 2 & 3 \\ 4 & 5 \\ 6 & 7 \end{bmatrix} + \begin{bmatrix} 3 & 4 & 5 \\ 9 & 10 & 11 \end{bmatrix}$

Use the following information for questions 47 and 48.

The students in Mr. Herring's math class had to keep track of the numbers of hours they spent on homework each night for 3 weeks. Here are the box-and-whisker plots that two of his students made to display their data:

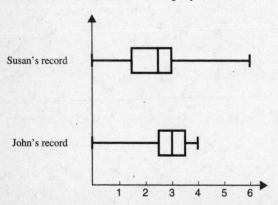

47 Which conclusion is most reasonable based on the data in the given plots?

A Susan spends at least 3 hrs per night doing homework.
B John always has homework.
C John typically spends more time on homework per night than Susan does.
D Susan and John both spent *exactly* 4 hrs on homework in a single night.

48 Which number represents the range for John's box-and-whisker plot?

F 2
G 2.5
H 3
J 4

49

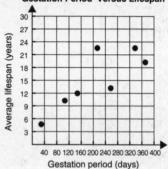

Gestation Period Versus Lifespan

The points on the scatterplot show the relationships between the gestation periods and the lifespans of various animals. Gestation period is the length of time from conception to birth.

On the basis of the scatterplot, which would seem to be the best estimate of lifespan for an animal having a gestation period of 300 days?

A 10 yr
B 14 yr
C 19 yr
D 25 yr

50 Older, industrialized cities in the Northeast and Midwest are losing residents. Norfolk, VA, has experienced one of the greatest declines.

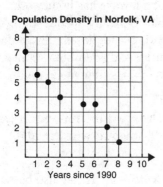

Which equation best represents a line of best fit for the data shown in the scatterplot?

F $y = -\dfrac{2}{3}x + 6.5$

G $y = -2x + 6.5$

H $y = x + 7$

J $y = -\dfrac{1}{2}x + 10$

Answer Key to Practice Test 3

1. A	11. A	21. B	31. D	41. C
2. H	12. H	22. G	32. G	42. H
3. B	13. B	23. A	33. B	43. A
4. J	14. G	24. F	34. G	44. G
5. D	15. A	25. C	35. D	45. B
6. J	16. F	26. F	36. F	46. J
7. B	17. B	27. B	37. C	47. C
8. G	18. F	28. G	38. J	48. J
9. C	19. B	29. D	39. C	49. C
10. F	20. F	30. H	40. H	50. F

Answer Explanations

1. **A** The distributive property states that $a(b + c) = ab + ac$. It can also be written in reversed form, $ab + ac = a(b + c)$. For the expression $x^2 + 3x$, x has been distributed to $(x + 3)$.

2. **H** Substitute 38 for A and 5.5 for l into the equation $A = \pi rl$, and solve for r:

$$38 = \pi \cdot r \cdot 5.5$$

$$\frac{38}{5.5\pi} = r$$

$$r = 2.19923 \ldots \text{ or approximately 2.2 in.}$$

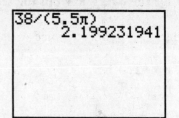

```
38/(5.5π)
          2.199231941
```

3. **B** When a linear function is shifted up 1 unit, the y-intercept increases by 1. Then $y = mx + 2$ becomes $y = mx + 3$.

4. **J** The statement $a - b = -1(b - a)$ is always true. This is the distributive property. You can distribute the -1 on the right side of the equation and obtain the left side:

$$a - b = (-1)b - (-1)a$$
$$a - b = -b + a$$
$$a - b = a - b$$

Alternative solution: You can also substitute numbers to verify. Substitute 3 for a and 4 for b:

$$3 - 4 = -1(4 - 3)$$
$$-1 = -1(1)$$
$$-1 = 1 \quad \checkmark$$

5. **D** The equation $3(1 - x) = x - 1$ is *not* satisfied by $x = -2$.
$$3(1 - (-2)) = (-2) - 1$$
$$3(1 + 2) = -3$$
$$3(3) = -3 \longrightarrow 9 \neq -3$$

6. **J** The boundary line has slope -1 and y-intercept 2. Its equation, using $y = mx + b$ form, is $y = -x + 2$. The boundary line is solid, so the inequality symbol must be $\geq$ or $\leq$. The point $(3, 0)$ lies in the shaded region, so substitute 3 for x and 0 for y into $y = -x + 2$:

$$0 = -(3) + 2$$
$$0 = -1$$

Since $0 \geq -1$, the symbol must be $\geq$. The inequality is $y \geq -x + 2$.

7. **B** Since slope $\frac{1}{3}$ is positive, the only possibilities are choices B and C. Choice C has a y-intercept of -1 instead of an x-intercept of -1. Therefore, choice B is correct.

8. **G** Use the slope formula for the points $(-2, 5)$ and $(1, -4)$:

$$m = \frac{y_2 - y_1}{x_2 - x_1} = \frac{-4 - 5}{1 - (-2)} = \frac{-9}{3} = -3$$

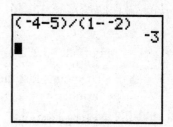

9. **C** You are looking for a line with a slope of -2. The slope of line D is positive, and the slope of line A is 0. The only negative-slope lines are B and C. Line B has a slope of $\frac{1}{2}$. Line C has a slope of -2.

10. **F** The equation of a vertical line always has the form $x =$ some number.

11. **A** Solve choice A, $2y = x$, for y; then put the equation into $y = mx + b$ form.

$$2y = x$$
$$\left(\frac{1}{2}\right)2y = \left(\frac{1}{2}\right)x \qquad \text{Multiply both sides by } \frac{1}{2}.$$
$$y = \frac{1}{2}x \qquad \text{Simplify.}$$

Now the slope of $\frac{1}{2}$ is easily obtained.

12. **H** The solution to a system of equations is a point of intersection. In choice H, the lines intersect at point $(-1, 1)$.

13. **B** The system is most easily solved by elimination. Add the two equations:

$$\begin{aligned} -2x + 3y &= 12 \\ +\quad 3x - 3y &= -15 \\ \hline x + 0 &= -3 \end{aligned} \qquad \longrightarrow \qquad x = -3$$

Substitute -3 for x into one of the original equations:

$$-2(-3) + 3y = 12$$
$$6 + 3y = 12$$
$$3y = 6 \qquad \longrightarrow \qquad y = 2$$

14. **G** Let x = the number of chocolates Daddy ate. The expression "5 more than twice as many" translates into $5 + 2x$, which represents what Puff ate. Together, they ate 32.

$$x + (5 + 2x) = 32$$
$$3x + 5 = 32$$
$$3x = 27 \quad \rightarrow \quad x = 9 \quad \text{(the number that Daddy ate)}$$

Puff ate $(5 + 2x) = 5 + 2(9) = 5 + 18 = 23$.

15. **A** The points that the line passes through are $(-3, -4)$ and $(-1, 2)$. Use the slope formula:

$$m = \frac{y_2 - y_1}{x_2 - x_1} = \frac{2 - (-4)}{-1 - (-3)} = \frac{6}{2} = 3$$

```
(2--4)/(-1--3)
                3
```

The slope can also be determined from the graph by taking the ratio of "rise" 6 to "run" 2: $\dfrac{\text{rise } 6}{\text{run } 2} = 3$.

Using the point $(-1, 2)$ on the graph and a slope of 3, you can determine the y-intercept to be 5. In $y = mx + b$ form, $y = 3x + 5$.

16. **F** Substitute -3 for x into $x^2 = 9$: $(-3)^2 = 9 \quad 9 = 9$ ✓

17. **B** Since volume = length · width · height:

$$48 = x(x - 2)(2)$$
$$48 = 2x(x - 2)$$
$$48 = 2x^2 - 4x$$
$$0 = 2x^2 - 4x - 48$$

Factor: $0 = 2(x - 6)(x + 4)$

$x - 6 = 0 \quad$ or $\quad x + 4 = 0$

$x = 6 \quad x = -4$ Length can't be negative.

The measure of the longest side of the box was 6 ft.

18. **F** Substitute -8 for x in the given inequality:

$$x > 6 + 2x$$
$$-8 > 6 + 2(-8)$$
$$-8 > 6 - 16$$
$$-8 > -10 \quad ✓$$

19. **B** In the formula $A = \dfrac{1}{2}h(b_1 + b_2)$, substitute 5 for h, 6 for b_1, and 10 for b_2:

$$A = \frac{1}{2}(5)(6 + 10) = \frac{1}{2}(5)(16) = 40$$

```
(1/2)(5)(6+10)
                40
■
```

20. **F** The difference, with x = total sales, is:

(commission of 5%) − (2% commission plus \$12,000 fixed salary)

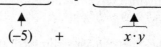

$$0.05x - (0.02x + 12,000)$$

21. **B** Translate the phrase "5 less than the product of x and y."

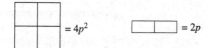

$$(-5) \qquad + \qquad x \cdot y$$

This becomes $xy - 5$. The expression "5 less than" means add −5.

22. **G** The power of 2 applies to all quantities in the parentheses. The expression $(3x^3y)^2$ can be simplified as follows:

$$3^2(x^3)^2y^2 = 9x^6y^2$$

23. **A**

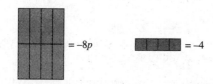

Sum all the tiles and simplify: $4p^2 + 2p - 8p - 4$

$$4p^2 - 6p - 4$$

24. **F** The area of the entire window equals:

the area of the semicircle + the area of the rectangle
18   + length × width
18   + $(x + 2)(x - 4)$

Multiply the binomials using FOIL: $18 + (x^2 - 4x + 2x - 8)$
$$18 + x^2 - 2x - 8$$
The area of the window is $x^2 - 2x + 10$.

25. **C** To add radicals, the numbers under the radicals must be the same. $\sqrt{12}$ can be reduced to $\sqrt{4 \cdot 3} = \sqrt{4} \cdot \sqrt{3} = 2\sqrt{3}$.

$$\sqrt{3} + \sqrt{12}$$
$$\sqrt{3} + 2\sqrt{3} \longrightarrow 3\sqrt{3}$$

26. **F** To write 0.000467 in scientific notation, you must move the decimal point to the right 4 spaces. The number becomes 4.67×10^{-4}. The exponent, k, is −4 because the decimal point moved to the right.

> To review how to use scientific notation mode on your calculator, refer to Section 1.8.

27. **B** The expression $\dfrac{10x^3y - 5xy}{5xy}$ can be split into two fractions:

$$\dfrac{10x^3y}{5xy} - \dfrac{5xy}{5xy} \longrightarrow 2x^2 - 1$$

28. **G** The expression $x^2 - 2x - 3$ factors to $(x - 3)(x + 1)$. This can be confirmed by multiplying with FOIL.

29. **D** The area of the kite can be expressed as $A = \dfrac{1}{2}d_1 \cdot d_2 = \dfrac{1}{2}(x^2 - 3x)$. Factor $(x^2 - 3x)$ by removing the GCF of x: $x(x - 3)$.

Therefore, $\dfrac{1}{2}d_1 \cdot d_2 = \dfrac{1}{2}x(x - 3)$.

This shows that $d_1 = x$ and $d_2 = x - 3$.

30. **H** The choices factor as follows:

F: $x^2 - 1 = (x + 1)(x - 1)$
G: $x^2 - x = x(x - 1)$
H: $x^2 - x - 1$ Not factorable
J: $x^2 - 2x + 1 = (x - 1)(x - 1)$

Therefore, $x^2 - x - 1$ does not have a factor of $(x - 1)$.

31. **D** Since line L passes through the origin, its y-intercept must be 0. With a slope of $\dfrac{1}{2}$, the equation in $y = mx + b$ form is $y = \dfrac{1}{2}x$.

Substitute 1 for x and 2 for y into $y = \dfrac{1}{2}x$:

$$2 = \dfrac{1}{2}(1) \longrightarrow 2 \neq \dfrac{1}{2}$$

Therefore, the point $(1, 2)$ does *not* lie on line L.

32. **G** The x-values in the table are all squared and then made negative. So, $5^2 \cdot (-1) = 25$.

33. **B** From the table you can identify the points (20, 90) and (35, 112.5). Use the slope formula:

$$m = \frac{y_2 - y_1}{x_2 - x_1} = \frac{112.5 - 90}{35 - 20} = \frac{22.5}{15} = 1.5$$

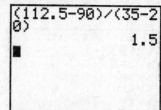

The correct answer must be either choice B or choice C. Since C has a y-intercept of 90, that choice cannot be correct because the table contains the point (20, 90). To be a y-intercept, the x-coordinate must be 0. Therefore, the answer must be B.

34. **G** The domain is a statement of possible inputs (the x-values). The graph begins at $x = -5$ and ends at $x = 5$. The domain, therefore, is all real numbers between -5 and 5 (including ± 5).

35. **D** The perimeter, $P(x) = 2(x + 3) + 2x$, has the restriction that x must lie between 8 and 10.

Substitute 8 for x: $P(8) = 2(8 + 3) + 2(8) = 38$
Substitute 10 for x: $P(10) = 2(10 + 3) + 2(10) = 46$

Therefore, the perimeter must lie between 38 and 46: $38 \le P \le 46$.

36. **F** Since you are comparing only domains, ignore the y-values in the table completely. Choice F has the x-coordinates $\{-2, 2, 4, 6\}$, which match the x-values in the table.

37. **C** Direct variation graphs must pass through the origin. Only choice C passes through the origin.

38. **J** To be a function, the x-values (inputs) cannot repeat. The table in choice J repeats the x-values 1 and 2. (NOTE: y-values (outputs) may repeat.)

39. **C** To find the zero of $h(t) = -16t^2 + 555$, set it equal to 0 and solve.

Algebraic solution:

$$0 = -16t^2 + 555$$
$$16t^2 = 555$$
$$t^2 = \frac{555}{16}$$
$$t = \pm\sqrt{\frac{555}{16}} = \pm 5.8896\ldots$$

The negative answer is not reasonable, so the answer is about 5.9 sec.

Graphical solution:

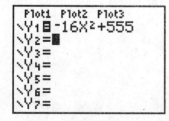 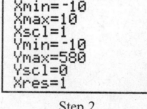 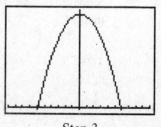

Step 1   Step 2   Step 3

The x-intercepts (or zeros) can be seen at about ± 6.

40. **H** Use your calculator to graph each answer choice. Only Choice H, $y = 3x - 1$, intersects the x-axis exactly once.

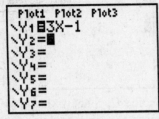

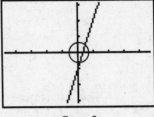

Step 1   Step 2   Step 3

41. **C** Since $f(x) = x^2 - 4$, you can find $f(-2)$ by substituting -2 for x:

$$f(-2) = (-2)^2 - 4 = 4 - 4 = 0$$

42. **H** To be a function, a graph must pass the vertical line test. If you pass a vertical line through the graph at any point, it may touch at most one point. Graph H does not pass this test and therefore does not represent a function.

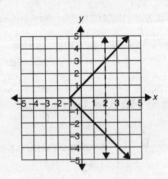

43. **A** The mean of $\{33, 37, 50, 40, 35\}$ is $\dfrac{33+37+50+40+35}{5} = 39$.

For the median, put the numbers in order from smallest to largest and find the middle value:

33, 35, 37, 40, 50

The median is 37.

Since George's score was 38, he was below the mean but above the median.

44. **G** Find the difference: December − November.

$$\begin{bmatrix} 42 & 10 & 4 \\ 28 & 12 & 0 \end{bmatrix} - \begin{bmatrix} 15 & 5 & 2 \\ 23 & 8 & 0 \end{bmatrix}$$

$$= \begin{bmatrix} 42-15 & 10-5 & 4-2 \\ 28-23 & 12-8 & 0-0 \end{bmatrix}$$

$$= \begin{bmatrix} 27 & 5 & 2 \\ 5 & 4 & 0 \end{bmatrix}$$

> For detailed instructions on using your calculator for matrices, refer to Section 4.2.

45. **B** To find $2[B] + [A]$:

$$2\begin{bmatrix} -6 & 0 \\ 5 & -2 \end{bmatrix} + \begin{bmatrix} 3 & -1 \\ 2 & 4 \end{bmatrix} = \begin{bmatrix} -12 & 0 \\ 10 & -4 \end{bmatrix} + \begin{bmatrix} 3 & -1 \\ 2 & 4 \end{bmatrix} = \begin{bmatrix} -9 & -1 \\ 12 & 0 \end{bmatrix}$$

46. **J** Matrices can be added only if their dimensions are exactly the same. In choice J, the two matrices are (2×3) and (3×2).

47. **C** Since the median in John's graph is 3 and the median in Susan's graph is 2.5, you can conclude that John "typically" spends more time on homework.

48. **J** To find the range, subtract the largest value from the smallest value on the plot. These values are located at the ends of the "whiskers."

$$4 - 0 = 4 \qquad \text{The range for the plot is 4.}$$

49. **C** Sketch the line of best fit. The value that corresponds most closely to a gestation period of 300 days is 19 yr.

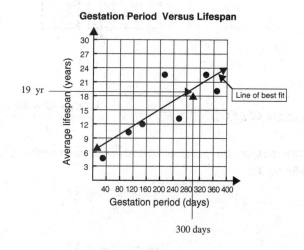

50. **F**   Draw a line of best fit on the graph, and then write the equation:

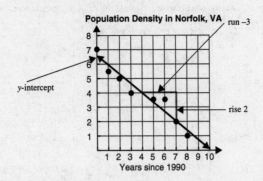

Slope is approximately $-\dfrac{2}{3}$. The y-intercept is approximately 6.5. Using

$y = mx + b$ form: $y = -\dfrac{2}{3}x + 6.5$

Index

Addition,
matrix, 193, 194
of polynomial expressions, 24
using algebra tiles, 15
Addition properties, 61
Algebra tiles, 15
Associative property, 13, 14
Average (*See* Mean)

Base (of an exponential expression), 17–19
Binomials,
definition, 7
operations on, 26
Boundary lines, 103
Box-and-whisker graphs (plots), 205–207

Calculator use,
ALPHA key, 6
changing decimals to fractions, 6
finding domain and range, 168, 169
getting a graph, 3, 97, 142, 143
intersections (points of), 5, 142, 143
lines of best fit, 212, 213
matrices, 195
scientific notation mode, 45, 46
solving equations, 67, 68, 142, 143
solving systems of linear equations, 133, 134
STO key, 6, 10, 19, 57
table, 4
trace, 3
values of a function, 5
window, 4
ZOOM, 3
zeros of a function, 5, 178
Central tendencies, measures of, 200–202
Closure property, 60
Coefficients, 17, 32, 34
Combining like terms, 14
Commutative properties, 13, 14
Complete graphs, 177
Constant of variation, 189
Cost problems, 39, 114
Counting numbers, 60

Difference of two squares, 32
Direct variation, 188–190
Distributive property, 13, 14, 31
Division of an expression, 19, 26
Domain, 153, 155, 166–169

Elimination method, 131, 132
Endpoints, 167

Equations (*See also* Linear Equations; Quadratic Equations),
definition of, 56
graphing, 95–97, 142, 143
literal, 77, 78
systems of (linear), 129–134
writing linear equations, 108–114
Exponents,
definition, 17
laws of, 19
negative and zero, 18
scientific notation, 44–46
Expressions,
cost, 39
definition, 7
equivalent, 19
evaluating, 6, 9, 10
linear, 65
simplifying, 8, 13, 14, 24–26

Factoring,
completely, 32
difference of two squares, 32
grouping, 33
perfect-square trinomials, 34
special products, 26, 32
to solve quadratic equations, 144, 145
trial and error, 34
trinomials, 32–34
Factors,
definition, 31
greatest common (GCF), 31
of a quadratic equation, 144, 145, 179
Factor theorem, 179
FOIL method, 26, 33, 34, 179
Formulas, 40, 77, 145
Function notation, 160–162, 169, 178
Function (*See also* Linear functions; Quadratic functions),
as a mapping, 154, 155
definition, 153
domain and range, 166–169
machines, 49, 153, 160, 161, 166, 176, 200, 201
notation, 160–162, 169, 178
parent ("granddaddy"), 121
transformations, 121–125
vertical line test, 153, 154
zeros, 176–179

Graphing calculators (*See* Calculator, use)
Graphs,
complete, 177

281